GLOBAL
SOUTH
ASIA

Padma Kaimal
K. Sivaramakrishnan
Anand A. Yang

SERIES EDITORS

The Afterlife of Sai Baba

COMPETING VISIONS OF A GLOBAL SAINT

Karline McLain

UNIVERSITY OF WASHINGTON PRESS

Seattle and London

Printed and bound in the United States of America
Composed in Warnock, a typeface designed by Robert Slimbach
20   19   18   17   16   5   4   3   2   1

University of Washington Press
www.washington.edu/uwpress

Library of Congress Cataloging-in-Publication Data
Names: McLain, Karline, author.
Title: The afterlife of Sai Baba : competing visions of a global saint /
    Karline McLain.
Description: Seattle and London : University of Washington Press, 2016. |
    Series: Global South Asia | Includes bibliographical references and index.
Identifiers: LCCN 2015037636 | ISBN 9780295995519 (hardcover : alk. paper)
Subjects: LCSH: Sri Sai Baba, 1836–1918—Cult.
Classification: LCC BL1175.S7 M38 2016 | DDC 294.5092—dc23
LC record available at http://lccn.loc.gov/2015037636

The paper used in this publication is acid-free and meets the minimum requirements of American National Standard for Information Sciences—Permanence of Paper for Printed Library Materials, ANSI Z39.48–1984. ∞

Contents

Acknowledgments

THIS book project has benefited from the generosity of many people and institutions over the past decade, and I am most grateful for this support. Grants from both private and federal institutions enabled me to undertake the multiple field research trips to India that were essential for this project, as well as to make repeat visits to Shirdi Sai Baba temples in Chicago and Austin in the United States. I owe sincere thanks to the American Academy of Religion, the American Council of Learned Societies, the American Institute of Indian Studies, the National Endowment for the Humanities (NEH), and the Wabash Center for Teaching and Learning in Theology and Religion for this material support. My home institution, Bucknell University, also supported my research with a yearlong sabbatical leave in 2012–13, which enabled me to devote one academic year to extensive reflection and writing, and with the award of an NEH endowed chair from 2012 to 2015 as well as an international summer research travel grant.

In my field research for this book, I have employed a multisited methodological approach, which means that I have many people to thank for support in several locations. In Shirdi, warmest thanks to Kishore More, Jitendra Shelke, Mohan Yadav, and Mita Diwan for opening doors and answering questions at the pilgrimage complex. In New Delhi and Gurgaon, I extend my gratitude to C. B. and Meera Satpathy, Kumkum Bhatia, Saurabh Vatsa, Sangeeta, and Azadram for patiently showing me around temples and answering questions. I extend heartfelt thanks to all those who opened their homes to me in India, including Madhu Malik and Gunmala Kapur and her family in New Delhi; Niru and Harshad Vasa in Mumbai; and Ganesh Shivaswamy and his family as well as Reena I. Puri and her family in Bengaluru. I must also thank S. A. Joshi and Geeta Ramana at the University of

Mumbai for their professional hospitality. I am also immensely grateful for the logistical support provided by the American Institute of Indian Studies on my multiple trips to India, especially to Elise Auerbach in the Chicago office, Purnima Mehta and staff in the New Delhi office, and Madhav Bhandare in the Pune office. I also thank Mukund Raj, who not only welcomed me into the Chicago temple but also opened many doors for me in Shirdi. In Austin, I am grateful to Craig Sastry Edwards and Jill Yogini Edwards and to the "sandwich seva" team. In all of these locations, I am grateful to the many devotees who agreed to speak with me about their faith in Shirdi Sai Baba.

Earlier versions of some chapters were presented at the invitation of the South Asia Institute at the University of Texas at Austin, the South Asian Studies Program at the University of Missouri, and the Religion Department at Bard College, as well as at multiple conferences, including that of the Association for Asian Studies, the Conference on the Study of Religions of India held at Drew University, the annual South Asia conference at the University of Wisconsin, and special themed conferences hosted at Denison University, the University of North Carolina at Chapel Hill, and Wabash College. I thank all of my colleagues in South Asian studies and religious studies who heard these presentations and responded with constructive criticism.

I am indebted to many scholars who read earlier drafts of one or more chapters and who offered advice, encouragement, and support along the way. In my department this includes my colleagues Maria Antonaccio, Brantley Gasaway, Rivka Ulmer, Carol Wayne White, and Stuart Young; I am also grateful to Kara van Buskirk for administrative support. Also at Bucknell I must thank Andrew Black, Isabel Cunado, John Enyeart, Michael Rabinder James, Susan Reed, and Amanda Wooden. Beyond Bucknell, I extend my heartfelt gratitude to Richard Davis, Corinne Dempsey, William Elison, Janice Leoshko, Philip Lutgendorf, Christian Novetzke, Patrick Olivelle, Karen Pechilis, Polly Roberts, Angela Rudert, Martha Ann Selby, and Joanne Punzo Waghorne for many conversations about Shirdi Sai Baba over the years and for helpful comments on my work in progress at different stages.

I have many folks to thank at the University of Washington Press, including my acquisitions editor, Ranjit Arab, for his enthusiasm for this project and his prompt professionalism; Jacqueline Volin and Nancy Cortelyou for seeing the book through all phases of production; and Julie Van Pelt, an excellent copy editor. I also thank the Global South Asia series editors for their support: Padma Kaimal, K. Sivaramakrishnan, and Anand Yang. I am extremely grateful to the two anonymous readers for their expertise and advice. I must also thank Diane Jakacki and Janine Glather in Bucknell University's Library and Information Technology Department, who produced the maps featured in this book. I also gratefully acknowledge the Arts and Sciences Dean's Office at Bucknell for providing material support at the indexing stage, and I thank Scott Smiley for compiling the index for this book. Jayita Prashant Sinha, then a graduate student at the University of Texas at Austin, worked as my research assistant in the summer of 2013, during which time she helpfully produced rough translations of several chapters of Athavale's Marathi biography of Das Ganu Maharaj.

Finally, my deepest thanks to my family and friends for their intellectual and emotional support in the years that I have worked on this book. Among these, I must mention my triple debt to my mom, who provided welcome companionship at some temple rituals and needed child care while I attended others; to Jonathan, who joined me for parts of my field research and who endured my absences at other times, who carefully read and commented on much of this manuscript, and who can be counted on for steadfast encouragement; and to Curran, who knew the face and name of Sai Baba by the time he was one year old and whose adventurous spirit rejuvenates me.

Note on Translation, Transliteration, and Orthography

THIS book draws upon sources in several Indian languages, including Hindi, Marathi, Sanskrit, and Urdu. The translations in this book are mine unless otherwise attributed. In the interest of readability and accessibility, I have transliterated words from Indian languages without diacritical marks, and I have used conventional romanized spellings of the names of people and places. I have also minimized the use of italics. Thus, terms from Indian languages that may not be familiar to all readers are italicized and defined at their first usage in each chapter but are not italicized for subsequent usages.

MAP I.1. Location of Shirdi in India

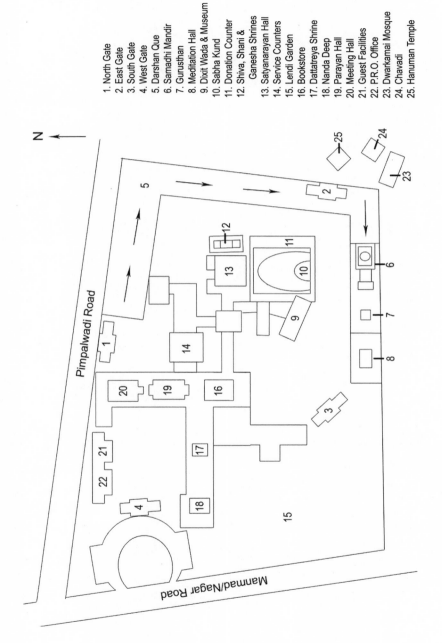

1. North Gate
2. East Gate
3. South Gate
4. West Gate
5. Darshan Que
6. Samadhi Mandir
7. Gurusthan
8. Meditation Hall
9. Dixit Wada & Museum
10. Sabha Kund
11. Donation Counter
12. Shiva, Shani & Ganesha Shrines
13. Satyanarayan Hall
14. Service Counters
15. Lendi Garden
16. Bookstore
17. Dattatreya Shrine
18. Nanda Deep
19. Parayan Hall
20. Meeting Hall
21. Guest Facilities
22. P.R.O. Office
23. Dwarkamai Mosque
24. Chavadi
25. Hanuman Temple

N

Pimpalwadi Road

Mammad/Nagar Road

MAP 1.2. Shirdi pilgrimage complex

THE AFTERLIFE OF SAI BABA

Introduction

1. Whoever puts their feet on the soil of Shirdi, their suffering will come to an end.
2. The wretched and miserable will rise into joy and happiness as soon as they climb the steps of my samadhi [tomb-temple].
3. I shall be ever active and vigorous, even after leaving this earthly body.
4. My tomb shall bless and speak to the needs of my devotees.
5. I shall be active and vigorous even from the tomb.
6. My mortal remains will speak from the tomb.
7. I am ever living to help and guide all who come to me, surrender to me, and seek refuge in me.
8. If you look to me, I look to you.
9. If you cast your burden on me, I shall surely bear it.
10. If you seek my advice and help, it shall be given to you at once.
11. There shall be no want in the house of my devotees.

ELEVEN SAYINGS OF SHIRDI SAI BABA

IN the mid-nineteenth century, an itinerant renouncer who would come to be known as Sai Baba—an appellation that loosely translates to "saintly father" or "swami father"—arrived in Shirdi. At that time, Shirdi was just a small farming village located in a rural part of western India (then a part of the colonial Bombay Presidency, now in the state of Maharashtra), containing approximately two hundred houses and no more than a thousand residents. Sai Baba chose to stop wandering and settle in Shirdi, and it is there

[3]

that he died many decades later in 1918, surrounded by a circle of close followers who lived in the village or visited it regularly from other parts of the region. Today, Shirdi has transformed into one of India's most popular pilgrimage destinations, drawing millions of pilgrims annually. Kishore More, an executive officer of the Shri Saibaba Sansthan Trust placed in charge of the day-to-day operations at Shirdi, claimed in my interview with him that Shirdi is now the second-largest pilgrimage destination in India in terms of the annual number of pilgrims, second only to the Tirumala Venkateswara Temple at Tirupati, receiving an estimated 35 million pilgrims annually.[1] The primary attraction at Shirdi is the tomb-turned-temple of Sai Baba, called the Samadhi Mandir. On an average day, approximately 25,000 pilgrims wait in line for entry into the Samadhi Mandir to be in the postmortem presence of Sai Baba and receive his blessing through his tomb; on holidays and festival days, more than 100,000 pilgrims descend upon this site. The pilgrims who flock here are primarily Hindu but also include Muslims, Sikhs, and Christians; they are men and women in roughly equal numbers; and they are predominantly middle- and upper-class urbanites who come from throughout India and, increasingly, from throughout the global South Asian diaspora.

Because Shirdi Sai Baba did not disclose the details of his upbringing, little is known with historical certainty of his early years: Was he born a Muslim or a Hindu? Where was he born and to whom? What was his birth name? With which spiritual masters did he study, and what were their religious backgrounds? Various hagiographies composed by his devotees provide different answers to some of these questions. What is known with some historical certainty is that Sai Baba was a young man of approximately twenty years when he arrived in Shirdi in the late 1850s.[2] Sai Baba wore a white robe and head scarf upon his arrival, not the saffron robes worn by many Hindu renouncers, and this garb caused the Hindu priest of the village temple to assume him to be a Muslim ascetic, or *fakir*. The priest therefore turned Sai Baba away, pointing him instead to the nearby mosque. Sai Baba eventually made that dilapidated mosque known as Dwarkamai his abode, and he went about his daily spiritual practices there. In time, Sai Baba began to acquire a number of followers in Shirdi and surrounding villages. They were drawn to his reputation for possessing miraculous powers, especially the ability to heal illnesses and grant offspring to childless couples. Other followers were drawn to Sai Baba for his ability to help them progress down their spiritual paths. As Sai Baba's reputation grew in the final decade of his

FIGURE I.1. Shirdi Sai Baba seated on a rock, prior to 1918. Photo: Anonymous.

life, so too did his following, which encompassed Hindus as well as non-Hindus living in western India. In the century since Sai Baba's death in 1918, his reputation has only continued to grow. Shirdi Sai Baba has now acquired a pan-Indian and increasingly global devotional following, and Shirdi has come to be recognized as the sacred ground where his afterlife presence is especially concentrated and potent.

The 11 Sayings attributed to Shirdi Sai Baba proclaim the power of his afterlife presence, asserting that he remains active and vigorous from his tomb in Shirdi. They stress his continued availability, reassuring devotees that he will provide guidance to all who look to him and who seek refuge in him. The 11 Sayings make his guidance contingent only upon the willing surrender of the devotee—not upon religious, caste, gender, or national identity. The language is inclusive, claiming that Sai Baba remains available to "whoever puts their feet on the soil of Shirdi" and to "all who come" or look to him. Nonetheless, Hindus make up the vast majority of those who make the pilgrimage to Shirdi and who look to Sai Baba for guidance both at Shirdi and in the temples dedicated to Sai Baba throughout India and around the world.

This book is not a study of the historical figure of Shirdi Sai Baba. Instead, it is conceived as an investigation of his growing devotional following during the one hundred years since his passing in 1918. During this period, many Indian gurus have risen to prominence in India and a number of them (sometimes called hypergurus) have established substantive transnational organizations and followings. Scholarship on such figures has tended to focus on charismatic living gurus, their teachings, and their interactions with their followers. Discussing these contemporary Indian "hypergurus" collectively, Amanda Lucia argues that they are "some of the most vibrant innovators who derive from the Hindu religious fold" (2014a, 253). Unlike these other gurus, Shirdi Sai Baba's popularity skyrocketed in the century after his physical death, due to the active proselytizing of a number of his Hindu devotees. Thus by decentering Shirdi Sai Baba and focusing on his afterlife interpretations, this book investigates how Hindu devotees have actively and variously interpreted Shirdi Sai Baba and in so doing have sought to reinterpret Hinduism as a modern and increasingly global religion through their faith in him. I argue that these Hindu devotees turned to Shirdi Sai Baba seeking not only spiritual succor but also freedom from aspects of traditional Hinduism that they found undesirable. In turning to the religiously ambiguous figure of Shirdi Sai Baba, then, these Hindu

FIGURE I.2. Shirdi Sai Baba street shrine with 11 Sayings, Mumbai.
Photo: Karline McLain.

devotees sought to reform Hinduism in varying ways. Paradoxically, however, these same devotees also utilized a range of ritual liturgies and technologies that have transformed this same religiously ambiguous figure into
a Hindu deity.

I first realized how popular Shirdi Sai Baba was in 2001–2 while I was
living in the bustling city of Mumbai on a research sabbatical for my first
book. At that time I would ride the bus daily between my research site in
central Mumbai and my rental apartment in the northern suburb of Vile
Parle. This was an air-conditioned bus, a slower but more comfortable commute than the notoriously packed commuter train cars of Mumbai, and the
white-collar passengers who could afford the bus ticket sat in comfort and
peacefully read the newspaper, catnapped, or chatted quietly with their
neighboring passengers as we made the one-and-a-half hour trek across the
congested city. At the stop in Irla, the bus stand was located next to a small
street shrine dedicated to Shirdi Sai Baba. From the bus, I could gaze
through the tinted windows directly into the shrine, taking in its small
statue, or *murti*, of Sai Baba and its various posters of him. The statue was
a small replica of the large marble murti that is at the center of the Samadhi
Mandir in Shirdi, a life-size carving of Sai Baba seated on a rock with his

right leg crossed over his left knee, wearing a head wrap, and gazing calmly at the viewer. The central poster in the shrine presented an image of that same murti. The subsidiary devotional posters featured Sai Baba alongside Dattatreya and Hanuman (also called Maruti), Hindu deities that are popular in western India.

Every day of my commute, I watched as residents of this northern suburb paused to express their devotion at the shrine, folding their hands in prayer while looking upon the images and making a small offering of cash, flowers, or fruit. I watched as the shrine's caretaker, a non-Brahmin Hindu, engaged in ritual worship, or *puja*, each morning: ringing the small bell, offering new flowers and a fresh coconut, and lighting incense. And I watched as my fellow commuters also expressed their devotion. As the bus stopped to allow passengers to enter and exit, several of the regular commuters would turn to face the shrine, staring intently at the posters and statue for the duration of the stop. Usually, these passengers would fold their hands together in a greeting of *namaste* as they gazed upon the images and softly muttered, "Om Sai Ram." During the morning commute each Thursday—Guruvar in Hindi, the day of the week most sacred to gurus, including Shirdi Sai Baba— one of the regular commuters would open his window and hold out a small cash offering of a few rupees, which the shrine's caretaker would quickly accept and stuff into the metal donation box.

The compounding effect of witnessing such devotional behavior twice a day, day after day, week after week, and then month after month, was that I began asking serious questions about Shirdi Sai Baba. Who was he, and why was he not mentioned in textbooks on South Asian religions? As my curiosity grew, I noticed just how ubiquitous his presence was. It seemed that everywhere I turned in Mumbai, Sai Baba was there: images of him hung on the walls in cafés and other places of business; stickers depicting his face were adhered to the backs of rickshaws, with catchy slogans like "Why Fear When I'm Here" and "If You Look to Me, I Look to You." I encountered small street shrines like the one in Irla in neighborhood after neighborhood, from the Fort business district to touristy Colaba, and from the upper-class neighborhood of Bandra to Dharavi, the largest illegal settlement (or "slum") in India. I noticed posters and small statues of him placed on the home altars of friends and colleagues I visited, and I heard devotional songs sung to him late into the evening every Thursday night by a group gathered in a neighbor's apartment. In the majority of these places, Sai Baba appeared in his guise as a Hindu holy man, wearing saffron-colored robes and frequently

FIGURE I.3. Shirdi Sai Baba street shrine, Mumbai. Photo: Karline McLain.

surrounded by Hindu ritual items; but in some places he appeared as a composite figure surrounded by symbols from multiple religious traditions, and in a handful of others he appeared as a Muslim holy man, robed in white and green. As my research took me to other cities that year—New Delhi, Kolkata, Bengaluru—I noticed that Shirdi Sai Baba had just as ubiquitous a presence in each of them.

One morning toward the end of my research sabbatical, as I sat sipping a coffee on the veranda of a popular café in Mumbai's Fort business district, I watched a stream of devotees making brief visits to an unpretentious little shrine to Shirdi Sai Baba on the other side of the street. Located just two blocks from Chhatrapati Shivaji Terminus, the frenetic downtown hub of the Central Railway suburban train line that carries millions of Mumbaikars each weekday, and a block from the shared taxi stand, this shrine is frequented by hundreds of devotees on a daily basis, each stopping for no more than a few minutes. Most of the visitors I watched were businessmen and women carrying briefcases and wearing cell phone headsets, who would pause a couple of feet in front of the shrine, slip off their shoes, fold their hands, and bow quickly in prayer before slipping their feet back into their shoes, resuming their calls, and walking briskly down the road. Watching this pattern of devotion to Sai Baba, and thinking about its implications for understanding popular religious practices and Hindu-Muslim relations in contemporary India, I resolved to undertake an in-depth study of the life and afterlife of Shirdi Sai Baba.

Several years later, after wrapping up my first book project, I began my study of Shirdi Sai Baba in earnest. My methodology for this book is two-fold. First, I draw upon extensive reading and translation of primary devotional "texts" (including written hagiographies and testimonial memoirs, as well as audiovisual sources such as hymns and films). I perform close readings of these sources to examine how Sai Baba has been understood by key interlocutors over the past century (including authors and filmmakers, pilgrimage site trustees, and temple founders), drawing out how their personal identities and religious quests, the historical context in which they lived, and their visions for the future of Indian religion and society have shaped their individualized interpretations of Sai Baba. Second, I rely on fieldwork conducted over multiple trips to India (in 2006, 2007, 2008–9, 2010, and 2011), during which I examined the diverse dynamics of contemporary Shirdi Sai Baba devotion. On these research trips I observed devotional rituals and conducted interviews with devotees at Shirdi Sai Baba temples in several Indian cities (including Mumbai, New Delhi, and Bengaluru); I conducted multiple interviews with founders of new Shirdi Sai Baba temples; and I took part in the pilgrimage to Shirdi and interviewed pilgrims, priests, and pilgrimage officials there. In addition, I did fieldwork at recently constructed temples to Shirdi Sai Baba in the United States, to better understand the global expansion of Shirdi Sai Baba devotion.

My interest in Shirdi Sai Baba arose out of professional intellectual curiosity, sparked by the desire to understand who this ever-present figure was and how it was that I, as a scholar of South Asian religions, knew relatively nothing about him from my prior textual studies. My interest was piqued when I realized that for many devotees, Sai Baba represented an alternative, more inclusive vision of Indian identity than that found in Hindu nationalist rhetoric. Given that my former work had explored Hindu nationalist influences in one facet of Indian popular culture (the popular *Amar Chitra Katha* comic book series), I was excited to explore the other side of the coin—someone often presented in Indian popular culture as a pluralistic and unifying figure. While I am not a devotee of Shirdi Sai Baba, this study would not have been possible without the generous faith of many devotees. Repeatedly in my conversations with devotees of Sai Baba, they stated that if I looked to Sai Baba, he would look back at me, and that this book was written under his oversight, whether I realized it or not. I certainly would not claim that this book has Sai Baba's blessing, but I am very aware that I benefitted from the belief of these devotees who attributed my research interest in Sai Baba to his will and guidance, and who therefore agreed to be interviewed.

This book seeks to accomplish three primary goals. The first is to provide an in-depth consideration of Shirdi Sai Baba's legacy and place within the broader Indian guru/saint/god-person phenomenon, by exploring some of the many different interpretations of Shirdi Sai Baba that have been put forth by his followers as his popularity has increased so noticeably during the century since his death. The first academic study of Shirdi Sai Baba was an article published in 1972 by Charles White. White begins by noting the dearth of scholarship on popular Indian saints, writing, "The time has long since passed when scholars of Indian religion should have begun to consider seriously the nature of Indian sainthood and more particularly the so-called 'living saints'" (1972, 863). Arguing that it is the scholar's task to try to understand how and why the popularity of a saint arises, he seeks with his article to make a contribution to the study of modern Hinduism and its saint leadership. He argues that the main contribution of Shirdi Sai Baba and other saints to Indian religious life is the sense of "relationship" they engender with and between their devotees. He notes that those devotees who are drawn to saints, including the large public that may not have ever met them in person, apprehend their "reality" in a very special way, feeling an "indissoluable [sic] bond between the Master and the disciple" as well as a bond of common devotion among the devotees (874–75). White further notes the unifying contribution of such saints, writing, "Whereas it is difficult for Hindus of unlike caste, social status or wealth to meet together and be at ease in most of the course of life, yet in homes, ashrams, and even in the context of the nation a socially unifying experience becomes possible in the presence of the saint" (875).

Since the publication of White's article in 1972, there have been a number of excellent academic studies of popular Indian saints and gurus, examining such modern figures as Sathya Sai Baba, Anandamayi Ma, and Mata Amritanandamayi, among others.[3] Together, these works explore the religious legacies of an array of Indian gurus, saints, and god-men and god-women, while also considering the reasons behind the surge of devotion to such figures in India and beyond. In this context, recent works by Tulasi

Srinivas (2010) and Smriti Srinivas (2008) discuss Shirdi Sai Baba as the prior incarnation of Sathya Sai Baba (1926–2011). However, while millions of devotees of Sathya Sai Baba do accept his declaration to be the incarnation of Shirdi Sai Baba, not all devotees of Shirdi Sai Baba accept this claim. Instead, for millions of devotees of Shirdi Sai Baba, he continues to be an active presence, even from beyond the grave. Thus, as one devotee politely told me in Shirdi, "When you have the original, what need is there of a Xerox?"[4] Other devotees of Shirdi Sai Baba, such as B. V. Narasimhaswami (the focus of chapter 3), have been even more explicit in their rejection of Sathya Sai Baba's claim to be an incarnation of Shirdi Sai Baba.[5]

A second goal of this book is to examine the afterlife appeal of Shirdi Sai Baba to his key Hindu interlocutors, who have been situated in different historical moments over the past century. Two book-length academic studies of Shirdi Sai Baba have been published to date: *The Life and Teachings of Sai Baba of Shirdi*, by Antonio Rigopoulos, and *Unravelling the Enigma: Shirdi Sai Baba in the Light of Sufism*, by Marianne Warren. Rigopoulos presents a biography of Shirdi Sai Baba in the first half of his book, drawing primarily upon the *Shri Sai Satcharita*, a hagiography composed in Marathi by Govind Rao Dabholkar (d. 1929), and upon the later English-language works of B. V. Narasimhaswami (1874–1956), both Hindu followers of Sai Baba. In the second half of his book Rigopoulos presents Shirdi Sai Baba's key teachings as he understands them, repeatedly comparing him with the medieval poet-saint Kabir. Rigopoulos seeks to reclaim Shirdi Sai Baba as a truly syncretic figure, one who was taught by both Hindu and Muslim gurus and whose lessons arise from both Hindu Vedanta and Islamic Sufi traditions. His concluding chapter is titled "Sai Baba's Universalism," in which he writes that Sai Baba's most important teaching was "his constant call to interreligious understanding and tolerance" between Hindus and Muslims (Rigopoulos 1993, 367). He views Sathya Sai Baba as inheriting the mantle of Shirdi Sai Baba and his universalism, writing: "It is significant that Satya Sai Baba [*sic*] has extended Shirdi Baba's universalism to comprehend the five main religions present on Indian soil (Hinduism, Islam, Buddhism, Christianity, and Zoroastrianism). In his *Sarvadharma* emblem (a lotus flower whose five petals contain the symbols of the faiths), all the religions are viewed as different paths leading to the same destination, symbolized by the center of the lotus, that is, the God-head or the Absolute" (372).

Warren's work, on the other hand, includes a translation of the diary kept by Abdul Baba (d. 1954), a Muslim follower of Sai Baba, which she uses to assert Shirdi Sai Baba's identity as a Sufi Muslim. She argues that Sai Baba traveled the Sufi path, and she identifies four phases in his spiritual evolution as a Muslim fakir: first as a child under the care of a Sufi fakir, followed by time spent with a Hindu or Muslim guru; second as a wandering and meditating Sufi aspirant; third as a resident in Shirdi's dilapidated mosque; and fourth from 1886 onward as a perfectly realized soul (Warren 2004, 125). Yet, she writes, given the ambivalent status of Sufism within Islamic circles, many orthodox Muslims have not sought to claim Sai Baba as part of their community: "Sai Baba was probably one of the last truly ascetic *Sufi* mystics who attained God-realization and became a great *Sufi* Master, although considered to be heterodox by many orthodox Muslims. He has not, therefore, been vigorously claimed as one of their own by the minority Muslim community in the Deccan, ever since his Muslim devotees were out-voted regarding the place and manner in which Sai Baba's body should be buried. On the other hand the Hindu majority soon recognized the greatness of Sai Baba and claimed him by honouring him in their own way. Without their ardent devotion, the name and message of Sai Baba may well have passed into obscurity" (336).

Both Rigopoulos and Warren agree on—and lament over—what they perceive as an increasing "Hinduization" of Shirdi Sai Baba over the past century, which has resulted in a lack of understanding about his "true" syncretic (Rigopoulos) or Muslim (Warren) nature. Rigopoulos (1993, 241–42) states that the "process of Sai Baba's Hinduization was thus completed" after his Hindu devotees took charge of his body for the funeral rites following his death in 1918. Warren (2004, 338–40), on the other hand, writes that the process of Hinduization is still ongoing at Shirdi and can also be seen in new temples and popular imagery. But rather than seeking to uncover the authentic identity of Shirdi Sai Baba or lamenting his "Hinduization," I find it more productive to ask why Hindus have turned to Sai Baba for their spiritual fulfillment and what this choice tells us about their relationship with modern Hinduism.

A third goal of this book is to use the growing devotional movement to Shirdi Sai Baba as a case study for reflecting upon religious ambiguity in modern South Asia. In India today, Shirdi Sai Baba is often viewed as a symbol of South Asian composite culture, the interpenetration of and interaction between two communities, Hindus and Muslims.[6] And yet, as Kathryn Hansen (2010, 296) importantly points out, composite culture can surreptitiously encode a Hindu majoritarian point of view and in some cases may acquire the feel of tokenism, gesturing inclusion of India's Muslim minority while taking for granted the unmarked status of the Hindu majority.[7] As I examine the various interpretations of Shirdi Sai Baba that have been set forth by his key Hindu interlocutors in the chapters that follow, I also ask what each interpretation of Shirdi Sai Baba implies about the interlocutor's vision for modern Hinduism and for religious pluralism: What elements of earlier Hindu traditions does each interpretation seek to reform or even break from? What elements of earlier Hindu traditions does each interpretation reaffirm? Where, on the wide spectrum of religious inclusivism, does each interpretation of Shirdi Sai Baba lie?

Any investigation into the life and teachings of Shirdi Sai Baba is complicated by the fact that Sai Baba wrote none of his teachings down (not even the 11 Sayings that are attributed to him), and thus they have only been preserved in hagiographies composed by his devotees. As a genre, hagiography serves as a source of "spiritual inspiration"; it is less concerned with providing a factual and critical biography of a historical person than it is with providing an inspirational account of a saint's life and deeds that enables followers to recall and relive the saint's presence (Rinehart 1999, 12, 46). Thus, hagiographers may each choose to highlight different facets of a saint, depending on how they have encountered and understood that figure as well as the type of religious practice they seek to inspire in their readers. This book is organized to examine Shirdi Sai Baba's portrayal in some of his most influential inspirational accounts, which have been composed in an array of devotional or hagiographic media, including written sacred biographies in multiple languages (Marathi, Urdu, Hindi, and English), performed hymns, mythological films, and temple sermons with their accompanying liturgical rituals. The principle of selection guiding the chapters that follow has been to choose those inspirational accounts that I believe have been the most influential in widening the circle of devotion to Shirdi Sai Baba, and to organize them chronologically.

Chapter 1, "Shirdi Is for Everyone: The Shri Saibaba Sansthan Trust's Plea to Pilgrims," provides an overview of Sai Baba's biography and identity as outlined by two of his closest followers in Shirdi: Govind Rao Dabholkar (d. 1929) and Abdul Baba (d. 1954). Dabholkar was a Hindu Brahmin from Bombay (now Mumbai) who first went to Shirdi in 1910 at the repeated behest of friends. There he felt immediately transformed, describing waves of joy surging within his heart as he had his first vision of Sai Baba. In 1916, Dabholkar asked Sai Baba for permission to write his biography. Sai Baba consented, announcing that Dabholkar was merely the instrument and that Sai Baba would write his own story through him. This Marathi-language work, called the *Shri Sai Satcharita*, has become the primary devotional text of the vast majority of devotees of Shirdi Sai Baba. Abdul Baba was a Sufi Muslim who arrived in Shirdi as a young fakir in the late nineteenth century (approximately 1889). He accepted Sai Baba as his Sufi master, and served him faithfully by tending to his daily needs (lighting candles, sweeping his residence, etc.) until Sai Baba's death in 1918. During these years, Abdul Baba recorded in his Urdu-language diary Sai Baba's expositions and lessons to him. Following Sai Baba's death, Abdul Baba served as caretaker for Sai Baba's tomb and used his diary to divine Sai Baba's wishes and prognosticate the future.

Govind Rao Dabholkar and Abdul Baba differed significantly in their understanding of Shirdi Sai Baba as an incarnate Hindu deity and as a Muslim Sufi saint, respectively, but overlapped in their shared contention that such sectarian distinctions were immaterial from a theological standpoint when Shirdi Sai Baba was properly understood as a sacred teacher who pointed all who turned to him to ultimate reality. Chapter 1 also investigates the role of the Shri Saibaba Sansthan Trust, the official governing body of the pilgrimage complex in Shirdi, in the divergent reception of these two works. Under the Trust's auspices, it is Dabholkar's hagiography of Shirdi Sai Baba as a Hindu deity that has been published, translated into multiple languages, and widely promoted; whereas Abdul Baba's hagiography languished in the archives at Shirdi after the author's death in 1954 and remains unknown to most devotees today.

Chapter 2, "Shirdi Is My Pandharpur: Das Ganu Maharaj's Plea to Brahmins and Non-Brahmins," focuses on the hagiography of Shirdi Sai Baba presented by Das Ganu Maharaj (1868–1962) in his Marathi work *Bhaktasaramrita* (1925). In the late nineteenth century and first decades of the twentieth century, a very active movement had arisen among the lower castes of western India seeking to protest Brahminical dominance in the public sphere and to challenge Brahminical religious values. As a Brahmin performer, Das Ganu was well aware of this movement, and his writings demonstrate that caste was a central concern in his interpretation of Shirdi Sai Baba. Whereas the radical critique of caste argued that caste itself must be abolished to ensure the equality of all, in the *Bhaktasaramrita* Das Ganu takes the reformist stance that caste divisions are inevitable but have been misinterpreted. Rather than ranking castes in a hierarchy, each caste should be valued for its unique contribution to society, just as each species of flower contributes to the garden's beauty. Das Ganu calls upon Brahmins and non-Brahmins to stop abusing one another, arguing at length that this will only end in mutual destruction and beseeching them to join together in mutual amity and devotion to Sai Baba. In his recasting of many of the same stories found in other hagiographies (particularly Dabholkar's *Shri Sai Satcharita*), he inserts a noticeable emphasis on Sai Baba's message about the urgent need for caste reform, and he repeatedly contrasts the "good" Brahmin (devout, generous, and inclusive) with the "bad" Brahmin (orthodox, greedy, and bigoted), suggesting that only when "bad" Brahmins transform into "good" Brahmins will harmony result in society.

Chapter 3, "Shirdi Is the Future of Religion in India: Narasimhaswami's Plea to Hindus," focuses on the hagiography of Shirdi Sai Baba presented by B. V. Narasimhaswami (1874–1956) in the English and Sanskrit works he composed between 1936 and 1956. Narasimhaswami believed that Sai Baba had two missions: the spiritual uplift of individuals and the temporal uplift of India. Scholars have focused on Narasimhaswami's discussion of the former mission, criticizing the Hindu ritual path that Narasimhaswami advocated to attain God-realization. Rigopoulos and Warren, in particular, allege that Narasimhaswami is a primary influence in the "Hinduization" of Shirdi Sai Baba. However, these scholars overlook Narasimhaswami's discussion of Sai Baba's second mission, the temporal uplift of India. This chapter argues that these two missions are inseparable in Narasimhaswami's writings. He conceived of God-realization as a transformative experience of loving union between the individual self and the All-Self. From this monistic standpoint, Narasimhaswami claimed that the essence of all religions is the same—love of God. It is over the "externals" that quarrels arise: temple versus mosque, this prayer versus that. Thus, in addition to the spiritual bliss that this monistic experience entails, it also has a worldly effect, for no longer can former quarrels stand as devotees experience an intimate, loving connection with one another. Narasimhaswami thus set out to share his experience of God-realization through worship of Sai Baba, so that other Hindus might experience it themselves and in so doing become not only better Hindus but also better Indians—and thereby save not only their own souls but the very soul of India, then divided by communal strife as India attained its independence from British colonial rule and was partitioned into two countries in 1947. Reaching out to an audience of fellow Hindus, he claimed that the future of religion in India entailed the fusion of Hinduism and Islam into one community, joined in common love of Sai Baba.

Chapter 4, "Shirdi Is for Unity in Diversity and Adversity: Bollywood's Plea to the Nation," turns to an examination of visual hagiographies of Shirdi Sai Baba presented in two Hindi (or "Bollywood") films that were released in 1977 and significantly raised popular awareness of Sai Baba. One was the entertaining blockbuster *Amar Akbar Anthony*, in which Sai Baba played a small but crucial part; the other was the niche-market mythological *Shirdi Ke Sai Baba*, which featured Sai Baba as the lead character. The 1970s were a decade that tested India's commitment to democracy: Prime Minister Indira Gandhi declared a state of emergency on June 26, 1975, during which civil liberties were suspended, the press was censored, elections were postponed, and opposition political parties were banned. Scholars of Hindi cinema have argued that the 1970s were a golden age in Indian cinema precisely because of the nation's political turmoil at this time, which inspired a new populist aesthetic of mobilization in the films of this period. This chapter examines how these two 1977 films set forth both a pluralist interpretation of Sai Baba as the patron saint of the nation, able to unite Hindus, Muslims, and adherents of other religious communities as members of a shared devotional community; and a populist interpretation of Sai Baba as the patron saint of the nonelite and dispossessed groups in Indian society, able to soothe the anger of these mobilizing classes and help them attain a happy ending. Chapter 4 also examines the different ways in which these two films affirm the centrality or normativeness of Hinduism in the Indian context even as they simultaneously promote pluralism.

Chapter 5, "Shirdi Is for Humanity: Many Gurus and Their Pleas to the World," examines the transnational afterlife of Shirdi Sai Baba in the context of two temples recently constructed in the United States: the Shirdi Sai Temple of Chicago and Suburbs, in Illinois (founded 2004), and the Sri Shirdi Sai Baba Temple of Austin, Texas (founded 2010). These temples were established by two different founders, each following a different guru lineage and thus articulating very different understandings of Shirdi Sai Baba's identity and teachings. In addition to exploring the founding history and guru lineage of these temples, this chapter also examines their liturgical programs. At both temples, the founders and the majority of devotees are Hindu, and Hindu rituals dominate in the worship of Sai Baba. However, in my interviews with them, these same Hindus repeatedly felt the need to include a disclaimer about ritual: "Faith is what matters, not ritual"; or, "There is no ritual for Sai Baba." This chapter argues that it is precisely the disclaimer that ritual does not matter that allows Hindu ritual practices such as image worship and fire sacrifice to become the primary mode of interacting with Sai Baba. This disclaimer works to redefine Hindu ritual, so that it is separated from its association with Brahminical orthodoxy and exclusivism and equated instead with meditative practice, science, and universal humanism. This paradox of ritual points to a larger ambivalence about what it means to be Hindu today, both in India and throughout the global Hindu diaspora.

Finally, the conclusion summarizes the differing inspirational accounts of Shirdi Sai Baba that have contributed to the growth of devotion to this figure throughout India and increasingly around the world during the past century. The conclusion further addresses wider issues about religious identity, ambiguity, and pluralism in an era of globalization. In his afterlife Shirdi Sai Baba is at once many things, often mixed together in startling ways: his tomb-turned-temple in Shirdi has become a place of cosmopolitan gathering even as Sai Baba's worship there is conducted by Hindu Brahmin priests in keeping with strict Hindu orthopraxy; he is upheld as a symbol of India's national and religious unity in diversity in a wide array of popular culture media and yet is simultaneously cast as a Hindu god incarnate in these same media; his leading hagiographers praise him in their written and oral works for embodying and teaching a synthetic blend of Hinduism and Islam and yet interpret him through a theological framework that is identifiably Hindu. It is precisely this ambivalent many-sidedness that is key to Shirdi Sai Baba's rising popularity. This book, then, provides both a history of the growing devotion to Shirdi Sai Baba through an examination of his many and shifting meanings to his devotees over time, and it offers an investigation into the ongoing politics surrounding religious inclusivism and pluralism in modern Hindu culture and society.

CHAPTER 1

Shirdi Is for Everyone

THE SHRI SAIBABA SANSTHAN TRUST'S PLEA TO PILGRIMS

> God is our Beloved and takes the name of Sai Baba.
> In the two worlds the name of Sai Baba resounds.
> Sai Baba embodies the Vedas, as also Allah.
>
> ABDUL BABA, *SHIRDI DIARY*

> If considered a Hindu, he looked like a Muslim;
> And if a Muslim, he exhibited all the qualities of a good Hindu.
> Who, even with all his proficiency and learning,
> Can describe such an extraordinary Avatar [incarnation]?
>
> GOVIND RAO DABHOLKAR, *SHRI SAI SATCHARITA*

ONE popular devotional poster of Shirdi Sai Baba presents him seated on a rock, his right leg crossed over his left knee and his right hand raised in blessing. As is common in Indian devotional prints, he is presented frontally and gazes directly at the viewer. Although this print is modeled on a historical photograph of Sai Baba (see figure I.1), several additions both enhance the devotional effect and present Sai Baba as a Hindu holy man.[1] In the print, his begging cup sits at his feet; he wears a simple robe and head wrap, both saffron, the color worn by Hindu holy men; and a halo encircles his head. A pastoral background has been inserted behind him: stars shine in the night sky, a calm river glides by forested plains, and a Hindu temple sits on the opposite riverbank. This image is intended to facilitate the reciprocal exchange of glances between the devotee and the divine persona, known as *darshan* in Hinduism, which serves as the central act of worship for most Hindus. Understanding the deity or divine persona to be present in the image, Hindu devotees seek to behold the image in order to convey their devotion to the deity and receive the deity's blessing in turn (Eck 1998).

This darshanic exchange of glances can and does take place in large Hindu temples, as it has since premodern times, where the central statue of the divine persona, or *murti*, has been ritually installed by a Brahmin priest who performs a formal eye-opening ceremony to bring to life the deity's presence in the image. But the rise of print technology and the reproduction of popular posters of Hindu deities and saints enables this auspicious darshanic exchange to take place in other, less formal venues as well. Today, these devotional posters (also commonly known as god posters, calendar art, bazaar art, and framing pictures) are omnipresent throughout India, where they can be seen not only in small street shrines and large temples but also in Hindu homes, in all manner of places of business, in taxis, buses, rickshaws, and other means of conveyance, and even in purses and billfolds. These images are significant for making the darshanic exchange available to devotees outside of the temple and the priest's purview. As such, they have helped make the Hindu gods more accessible to their devotees. However, it is only in the past several decades that scholars of Hinduism have begun to acknowledge the significance of such devotional posters. As Richard H. Davis pointed out in his study of god posters, such scholarship is important because it allows us to "begin to see these prints of the gods both as an evolving, changing genre of popular art and as an integral part of the history of modern Hinduism and modern India" (2012, 3). One of the changes within this genre is the insertion of a new divine figure into the pantheon during the twentieth century: Shirdi Sai Baba, who first began to appear in poster form in the late 1930s, when his devotee Narasimhaswami (discussed in chapter 3) first began printing them, and whose posters became increasingly widespread throughout India from the late 1970s onward.[2]

Yet Shirdi Sai Baba does not belong exclusively to the Hindu community. Another devotional poster—far less ubiquitous, but nonetheless visible in pockets of India's public culture today—presents Shirdi Sai Baba as a Muslim holy man. In this print he stands, his right hand raised with his index finger pointing toward the heavens. Again, he is presented frontally and gazes directly at the viewer. Here, too, he is dressed simply, but his robe, head wrap, and shawl are the green and white worn by Muslim holy men. Here, too, a halo encircles his head, and a pastoral scene unfolds behind him: the sky is clear blue and the trees are flowering, a lotus-filled river flows down from the mountains looming in the background, cattle graze upon the grass, and a mosque sits on the opposite riverbank. The Hindu idea that a deity is present in such images and can confer blessing upon devotees through an exchange of glances overlaps with the Sufi concept of *baraka*, the "blessing power," which is believed to emanate from a Sufi saint's tomb (*dargah*) or image.[3]

These posters point toward the possibility of two very different understandings of Shirdi Sai Baba, either as a Hindu holy man (*sadhu*) or god incarnate (*avatar*); or as a Muslim holy man (*fakir*) or Sufi embodiment of God (*Allah*). Yet, if paired side by side, these posters suggest yet another possible understanding of Shirdi Sai Baba—that he is Muslim by day and Hindu by night; Muslim when dressed in green and Hindu when dressed in saffron; Muslim when standing and Hindu when seated; Muslim when in the mountains and Hindu when on the plains; Muslim when at a mosque and Hindu when at a temple. Taken together, these posters signal the potential for a reconciliation of opposites in a syncretic understanding of Shirdi Sai Baba as neither exclusively Hindu nor Muslim, but both. Writing about Shirdi Sai Baba devotion in the Indian city of Mumbai, William Elison describes a site known as Sai Krupa, which presents just such a side-by-side scenario. Here, in Mumbai's Tardeo neighborhood, two middle-class families—one Hindu, one Muslim—have turned their adjacent ground-floor apartments into complementary Sai Baba shrines.

> The arrangements on either side of the building's entrance are similar, with each neighbor's foyer opening on a *puja* room dominated by a life-size, naturalistic sculpture of the saint, and the congregants' observances proceed along parallel tracks. At both stations, the exchange of glances enacted through *darshan* with the Baba is typically accompanied by a moment of communion through silent prayer and a complementary transaction enacted at a material level: worshipers deposit offerings of cash or flowers and realize blessings conducted through food (*prasad*) or sacred ash (*vibhuti*). It is the contrasting visual idioms that dominate

the two rooms—the one baroque, exuberant, decked with gilt and ornament; the other clean and spare, defined by stone surfaces and green accents—that provide the most striking indications that one shrine belongs to a Hindu household, the other to a Muslim one. (Elison 2014, 171)

At Sai Krupa, Shirdi Sai Baba is remembered as Hindu and as Muslim, and perhaps even as both simultaneously, depending on the visitor's interpretive inclination. As suggested by the chapter epigraphs from two of his early followers—the first a Muslim and the second a Hindu—Shirdi Sai Baba was accepted as a syncretic or composite figure by some of his devotees: a person who embodied the best of the teachings, qualities, and characteristics from both Hinduism and Islam. Reflecting this understanding of Sai Baba is a phrase regularly cited by devotees: "Sabka Malik Ek" (Everyone's Lord Is One). This phrase is also printed on numerous devotional posters. For instance, one such poster in my collection depicts Sai Baba seated, wearing a white robe, gazing out at the viewer. Above him are four religious symbols: the Muslim crescent moon, the Hindu Om, the Sikh Ik-Onkar, and the Christian cross. Behind Sai Baba's glowing halo is a large hand, with the index finger pointing upward to the heavens. Beneath Sai Baba, in bold Devanagari print, the Hindi-Urdu phrase "Sabka Malik Ek" brings the message home: "Everyone's Lord Is One." All paths lead to the One God.

Along these lines, Shirdi Sai Baba is also frequently presented as a symbol of India's national unity in diversity. An example can be found in another popular poster, wherein Sai Baba appears in a frontal position in the center of the image. His eyes make direct contact with viewers, blessing them with his gaze, while an auspicious ray of yellow light emanates from his hand raised toward viewers. Behind him, four buildings fill the background: in the upper-right corner is a Hindu temple, and beneath that is a Muslim mosque; a Sikh gurdwara is in the upper-left corner, and beneath that is a Christian church. Across the top of the poster, printed in the orange, white, and green of the Indian flag, reads the Hindi-Urdu slogan "Ek Bano, Nek Bano" (Be United, Be Virtuous). In its inclusive vision, this image provides an alternative to Hindu nationalist images by depicting multiple faith communities as equals under the national tricolor flag. It calls upon all Indians to look at it—not just Hindus, but also Muslims, Sikhs, and Christians—and in so doing to be transformed by this act of looking at Shirdi Sai Baba into unified, virtuous citizens of the nation.

Yet Patricia Uberoi has argued that in Indian poster art there is a tension

FIGURE 1.1.
"Be United, Be
Virtuous" Shirdi Sai
Baba poster in a
home shrine. Photo:
Karline McLain.

between a relatively egalitarian understanding of the principle of unity in diversity, in which all religious traditions are conceived as equivalent sources of truth, and a majoritarian understanding whereby other religions are appropriated to a Hindu order (represented by Mother India, the Mother Goddess, or the Mother Cow). Uberoi describes a poster featuring four cherubic young boys who are marked sartorially as Hindu, Muslim, Christian, and Sikh. The poster bears the Hindi-Urdu slogan "Ham Sab Ek Hain" (We Are All One). In the center of the poster is a medallion with the figure of Mother India inside. Calling our attention to this medallion, Uberoi writes that the manifestly egalitarian message of the slogan has been compromised, and "it is clear that the nation-state has been symbolically reinscribed here as a *Hindu* polity through the emblematic figure of Mother India/Durga" (2002, 195).

While the "Be United, Be Virtuous" poster in figure 1.1 does not compromise its egalitarian message, other images of Shirdi Sai Baba may. For

FIGURE 1.2. "Everyone's Lord Is One" Shirdi Sai Baba poster in a home shrine.
Photo: Karline McLain.

instance, in another poster Sai Baba gazes out at the viewer, with his right
hand raised in a gesture of blessing, the word *shanti* (peace) inscribed on it.
His image is set within a golden frame or medallion, and included beneath
it are three burning oil lamps. Written in the candle flame above the central
lamp is the "Everyone's Lord Is One" phrase, "Sabka Malik Ek." Yet in spite
of this egalitarian proclamation, Sai Baba is here visibly presented as a Hindu
god-man garbed in saffron robes. While oil lamps and candles are equally
used at Hindu temples and Sufi shrines in India, the inclusion of these elements in this poster before a saffron-clothed divine persona recollects other
Hindu posters that serve as images of and for Hindu ritual worship, known
as *puja*. As Richard Davis explains in his discussion of devotional posters of
Hindu goddesses, through the inclusion of ritual elements, such posters

become images of and for Hindu worship: "The introduction of elements of puja into the image, usually in the lower portion of the poster appearing closer to the viewer, provides a mirroring within the frame of the worship that a pious owner would offer to the goddess in the icon-poster outside its frame. The iconic image points to its own intended purpose" (2010).

As in these popular posters of Shirdi Sai Baba, in written hagiographies and other inspirational interpretations of this religiously ambiguous figure there is frequently a tension between the admiration of Sai Baba as a composite figure who can point the way toward a more inclusive society and the desire to preserve and protect some elements of a Hindu worldview or way of life. In the next sections I provide an overview of Shirdi Sai Baba's life and teachings as outlined in the hagiographies written by two of his closest followers in Shirdi: Abdul Baba and Govind Rao Dabholkar. In doing so, I seek to draw out the major similarities and differences in their interpretations of Shirdi Sai Baba. Following this, I examine the reception of these two hagiographies. I look at the role of the Shri Saibaba Sansthan Trust, the official governing body of the pilgrimage complex in Shirdi, in promoting the interpretation of Sai Baba set forth by Dabholkar, and I consider how this very tension between composite and cosmopolitan culture on the one hand and Hindu majoritarianism on the other hand is manifest in the pilgrimage experience in Shirdi today.

MUSLIM SAINT

Abdul Baba was born in 1871 in Nanded (in modern-day northern Maharashtra) to a Muslim man named Sultan. Aside from his birth date, birthplace, and his father's name, very little is known of Abdul's parentage or upbringing. However, Abdul was interviewed by B. V. Narasimhaswami in Shirdi on December 8, 1936, and in that interview he provided a brief biographical sketch. We learn from this record that at some time during his childhood, Abdul's parents placed him into the care of a Sufi master called Amiruddin, who then eventually directed him to Sai Baba in Shirdi: "I came to Shirdi 45 years ago (1889) from Nanded on the banks of Tapti. I was under the care of Fakir Amiruddin of Nanded. Sai Baba appeared in the dream of that Fakir and delivering two mangoes to him directed him to give those fruits to me and to send me to Shirdi. Accordingly the Fakir told me of his dream, gave me the fruits and bade me go to Sai Baba at Shirdi. I came here in my twentieth year" (Narasimhaswami 2008, 152).[4]

When Abdul arrived in Shirdi, Sai Baba had few loyal followers in the village, perhaps none. He lived as an obscure ascetic, begging for his food and supplies but otherwise keeping to himself. Indeed, it was one or more years after Abdul's arrival that Sai Baba garnered a following among the villagers of Shirdi. This reportedly happened around 1892, when Sai Baba performed the alleged miracle of lighting oil lamps that were filled with water. According to the *Shri Sai Satcharita*, Sai Baba used to visit the village grocers daily to beg for the oil with which he lit candles at night. One day, the grocers decided that they were tired of giving handouts to Sai Baba, so they all refused when he came begging. Sai Baba returned to the mosque, calmly mixed the little bit of oil he had remaining with water, and then used this solution to light his candles, which miraculously burned all night long (Dabholkar 2007, 82). In Narasimhaswami's (1980, 21–24) discussion of this incident, he explains that it was this miracle that first caused many of the villagers to begin worshiping Sai Baba as a divine saint or god incarnate. Abdul was thus one of Sai Baba's earliest devotees, perhaps even the earliest, coming to him before his reputation as a miracle performer began to spread throughout the village.

Upon Abdul's arrival in Shirdi, Sai Baba greeted him with the phrase "My crow has come," suggesting that he was expecting him.[5] Abdul reports in his interview with Narasimhaswami that he devoted himself entirely to serving Sai Baba by lighting candles, fetching water, washing Sai Baba's clothes, and sweeping the floor and removing the night soil (Narasimhaswami 2008, 152–55). In another interview with Narasimhaswami, on March 10, 1938, Abdul reports that after performing such service for Sai Baba, he would then study the Quran, often late into the night, and he describes the ascetic practices that Sai Baba encouraged him to undertake: "Baba's practical advice to me was that I should not go to sleep over my Koran reading. He said, 'Eat very little. Do not go in for variety of eatables. A single sort, i.e., dish, will suffice. Do not sleep much.' I followed the advice. I ate very little. I kept awake all night and in a kneeling posture was going on repeating the Koran etc., near Baba and meditating. Baba told me to have Dhyan [meditation] on what I read. 'Think of who I am' he said to me" (Narasimhaswami 2008, 154).

Marianne Warren notes that such acts of renunciation—limiting one's diet, spending extended periods of time in meditation, and so on—are all preliminaries for initiates on the Sufi path, the mystical tradition of Islam.[6] Based on this report, she therefore concludes that Abdul had accepted Sai

Baba as his *murshid*, or Sufi guide, and that Sai Baba had accepted responsibility for Abdul's spiritual development (Warren 2004, 263). She finds further evidence that Sai Baba accepted Abdul as his disciple in this same interview with Narasimhaswami, when Abdul notes that the guru who had first directed him to serve Sai Baba—presumably the Sufi master Amiruddin—came to Shirdi at some point and asked Abdul to go away with him. Abdul states that he told his guru he could do so only with Sai Baba's permission. But such permission was not granted, so Abdul states, "I stayed on with Baba and my former Guru went away from Shirdi" (Narasimhaswami 2008, 155).

While studying with Sai Baba, Abdul would often take notes: "I read Koran near him at the mosque. Baba occasionally opened the Koran and made me read the passages on the page at which he opened the book. He occasionally quoted passages from the Koran. I went on writing down what Baba was uttering. This is the book (in Mahratti and Modi script) which contains the gracious utterances of Baba. Everything which fell from his lips is sacred" (Narasimhaswami 2008, 152). In all, Abdul's diary contains 112 pages of notes written in Deccani Urdu and another 25 pages in Marathi in the Modi script, though Narasimhaswami seems to have only been familiar with the Marathi portion of the diary. Abdul said that this diary recorded Sai Baba's words, which were all noted down by "Baba's order or permission" (Narasimhaswami 2008, 153). Following Sai Baba's death in 1918, Abdul remained in Shirdi, where he continued to offer daily service to Sai Baba by acting as the caretaker for his tomb until his own death in 1954 (except for a brief time beginning in 1922 when he was legally barred from performing this service, as discussed below).

During these decades, Abdul used his diary not only to continue his study of the Quran but also to divine Sai Baba's afterlife wishes and prognosticate the future: "I make use of this record in the following way. By Baba's blessings, I have full faith in what he has said, guiding me and every one aright. When any one wished to know about the future or other unseen and unknown matter, he comes to me and states the problem. Then I reverently consult this book of Baba's utterances and the answer that comes out of the page opened comes out correct. This has been tried and proved many times. This gift of prophecy is due to Baba's grace" (Narasimhaswami 2008, 152). In his 1936 and 1938 interviews with Narasimhaswami, Abdul provides several examples of such prophesies, noting that he consulted his diary to successfully predict how deep the well should be dug at the Samadhi Man dir, whether barrister Gedgil's son would return from England, and whether various women would get married or have children (153–57).

Marianne Warren obtained a copy of Abdul Baba's diary from V. B. Kher, a trustee of the Shri Saibaba Sansthan Trust, and translated it into English in her book *Unravelling the Enigma: Shirdi Sai Baba in the Light of Sufism*. In describing the 137–page diary, she writes: "The whole manuscript looks like a typical student's note-book, with bits of scribble and half-finished sentences interspersed with pages of serious notation. On the whole the manuscript largely pertains to Muslim and *Sufi* material in Deccani Urdu. There are a number of quotations in Arabic included from the *Qur'an* and *hadith*" (Warren 2004, 267). The diary is not a cohesive narrative. Rather, it contains numerous short discourses on a range of spiritual teachings: understanding the true form of God; the centrality of the ascetic path in pursuit of a higher stage of spirituality; virtues and vices; the need to protect oneself from false teachers and fakirs; the greater value of constantly remembering God over the lesser value of prayer (*namaz*) or other external rituals; the stages on the Sufi path; and the creation of the cosmos and of humankind. It also contains various lists: the names of the ten companions of the Prophet Muhammad; names of the Sunni caliphs and the Shia imams; lists of different Sufi orders, along with the names of their founders and subsequent teachers (i.e., Sufi lineages, or *silsilas*); the family tree of the Sufi Master Khwaja Muinuddin Chishti; names of Hindu sages and deities; names of Hindu avatars or gods incarnate; and genealogical lists of Hindu kings. Interspersed throughout the pages of the diary are passages from and paraphrasings of the Quran, verses from Rumi and other Sufi poets, mystical words, and numerous doodlings.

Although there is no cohesive, linear narrative in the diary, there is nonetheless a consistent theme about the spiritual path to God-realization. According to Abdul's recording of Sai Baba's lessons, the means to realizing God entailed renouncing worldly pleasures and objects. Thus, page 14 of the diary states that *tapas*—austerities—are required of those walking the path of righteousness. Furthermore, such tapas will be rewarded with divine insight. On pages 32–40, the importance of cultivating virtues and shunning vices is discussed. Page 40 declares that good habits allow one to find the true self within, while bad habits "are like the smoke or darkness which obscures the heart" (Warren 2004, 284). Pages 99 and 103 declare the need for severe renunciation and celibacy in order to reach a higher stage of spirituality, and they mention practices in keeping with those undertaken by

Abdul Baba himself under Sai Baba's guidance: "That means that he should be awake at day and night, stay away from women, abjure from delicious food and reside in jungles and mountains" (Warren 2004, 299). Page 110 declares that the Beloved—God in the Sufi understanding—is enthroned within the heart, and thus the best way to find God is to turn within to meditate upon and pray to Allah throughout the day and night. When one realizes that God is within, there is no need for such external rituals as prayer in the mosque or pilgrimage to Mecca. Summarizing the diary as a whole, Warren states that Sai Baba's message as recorded by Abdul Baba entailed "a constant urging, cajoling, and insistence that the only thing in this world worth striving for is divine insight leading to God-realization. This alone, he insisted, would dispel the veils of ignorance" (2004, 315).

Warren (2004, 277) concludes that the significance of Abdul Baba's man-uscript "is that it establishes beyond doubt that Sai Baba was totally familiar with both the Islamic and *Sufi* traditions, and that as a *Sufi* master he taught this tradition to Abdul, who was his *murid* [disciple]." Sufism teaches a doctrine of Divine Oneness or Unity, *tawhid*. According to this doctrine, God is the One and the Absolute and is also the heart of our inner selves, the Self of all selves. The goal of the Sufi path is to awaken to the reality of tawhid by remembering God fully and constantly (Nasr 2007, 117). In Sufism, the path to fully understanding and experiencing tawhid has many steps or stages through which a disciple must progress. Ideally, the disciple's experi-ential quest on this path should be guided by a spiritual master, who may be called a *pir* (elder), a murshid (guide), or even a *wali* (saint). The master will instruct the disciple in methods of remembering God, such as repetition of the ninety-nine names of Allah, and serve as spiritual guide as the disciple progresses from one stage to the next along the path.

Many Sufi orders, or *tariqas*, came into existence in the medieval period, each tracing its lineage (silsila) back through a long chain of Sufi masters to its original founder, and each teaching a distinct means for progressing along the path and experiencing the ultimate reality of tawhid. In India, one of the most prominent Sufi orders is the Chishti Order, founded by the Sufi Master Khwaja Muinuddin Chishti (d. 1236). Warren (2004, 328) states that the contents of Abdul's diary, along with Sai Baba's practice of singing and dancing, suggest that Sai Baba may have been affiliated with the Chishti Order, though this cannot be definitively confirmed. The Chishti Order was known for several practices that distinguished it from other Sufi orders: it emphasized poverty and withdrawal from political authorities among its initiated disciples; it utilized music (*sama*), particularly in the form of *qaw-wali* devotional songs, to remember God; and its adherents frequently min-gled with Hindus, and the order brought many Hindus to Islam (Nasr 2007, 197–98; Ernst and Lawrence 2002, 27–46).

Abdul's diary does not provide a biographical account of Sai Baba's life. However, with regard to the identity of Sai Baba, Abdul mentions him in two very different contexts. First, on page 49, following several pages that list various Hindu kings, sages, and divine incarnations or avatars, Abdul records: "There are thousands of *avatars* in the Kaliyuga. The methods of worship for everyone are different. The present Kaliyuga *avatar* is Sai Baba. In this world there are always 10–20 *avatars* of similar kind living at the same time" (Warren 2004, 287). Following this are several pages that list various Muslim holy figures, including Sufi saints, Shia imams, and Sunni caliphs. Second, on pages 54–56, Abdul records a qawwali in praise of Sai Baba. Composed by Abdul Baba himself (as evidenced by the inclusion of his "signature," or *takhallus*, in the final verse of the poem), this poem praises Sai Baba's ability to grant petitioners this-worldly miracles, such as the birth of sons, and his ability to grant insight into the spiritual path and nature of God. In the verses praising the latter ability, Abdul proclaims:

> Who can sing the praises of our Sai Baba?
> Every man is a slave of Sai Baba.
> Spirits as well as men are captivated by Sai Baba.
> God is our Beloved and takes the name of Sai Baba.
> In the two worlds the name of Sai Baba resounds.
> Sai Baba embodies the Vedas, as also Allah.
> We give Sai Baba all honours respectfully saluting and bowing before him.
> Sai Baba operates on two planes, in Shirdi and all over the world.
> Sai Baba is Supreme in both the present world and the next.
> The whole universe is vibrant with Sai Baba. (Warren 2004, 288)

For Abdul Baba, then, Sai Baba was first and foremost a Sufi master and saint, whose guidance helped Abdul progress on the Sufi path toward expe-riencing the ultimate reality of tawhid, Divine Unity. Sai Baba provided this guidance to Abdul in person for nearly three decades. After Sai Baba's death in 1918, Abdul believed that he continued to provide personal guidance through the medium of Abdul's diary. Although Abdul Baba conceived of Sai Baba primarily through concepts originating in Sufi Islam, he also acknowledged Sai Baba as a composite figure, held sacred by both Hindus and Muslims, and simultaneously as an avatar and a wali, the embodiment of Hindu and Muslim concepts of divine or near-divine beings. For when properly seen from the monistic standpoint of tawhid, such differences between lover and Beloved, self and God, collapse; so also do the differences between sacred scriptures such as the Rig Veda and Quran and concepts of God in the form of Bhagwan and Allah.

HINDU GOD-MAN

Govind Rao Dabholkar was born in 1859 in Thane District, Bombay Presidency, to an impoverished Hindu Brahmin family. He received a limited education but managed to pass the Public Service Examination, enabling his appointment to government service. He was appointed to various posts, working as a village officer, then as a clerk and head clerk, and finally as a special officer on famine relief works (Narasimhaswami 1983, 212–13). In 1903 he was appointed resident magistrate in Bandra (now a suburb of Mumbai). It was in this post that Dabholkar came into contact with Nana Saheb Chandorkar and Hari Sitaram Dikshit (also known as Kaka Saheb), who both became committed devotees of Sai Baba after hearing about him and then making a pilgrimage to Shirdi in 1909. Narasimhaswami (1983, 213) notes that in spite of the urging by Chandorkar and Dikshit to visit Shirdi, Dabholkar was skeptical, for he had come under the influence of the Prarthana Samaj in Bombay, a socioreligious reform group that encouraged belief in one God and discouraged devotion to saints and holy men. Nonetheless, Dabholkar was finally persuaded to visit Shirdi in 1910, though he did so with skepticism.

Dabholkar records in his hagiography, the *Shri Sai Satcharita*, his mindset upon his first visit to Shirdi. He confesses that the recent death of a dear friend's only son had him pondering dejectedly the uselessness of holy men in the face of karmic destiny, asking, "Why go to Shirdi at all?" and "What can a guru do before destiny?" (Dabholkar 2007, 26). However, upon arriving in Shirdi, Dabholkar immediately felt transformed: "As I alighted from the *tonga* [carriage], my heart was so full of eagerness for Baba's *darshan*, that I could hardly wait to fall at his feet! Waves of joy surged up in my heart!" (27). Dabholkar describes in detail the impact of his first vision of Sai Baba, writing of it as the highlight of his life: "Never before had I heard of or seen Baba's comely figure. Seeing it now, my eyes were calmed; hunger, thirst, everything was forgotten; all senses stood still. . . . Sai's kindly glance destroyed the sins accumulated over past births and gave rise to the hope that his holy feet will bring me eternal joy" (28).

From 1910 to 1916, Dabholkar returned to Shirdi regularly on holidays from work. As a converted skeptic, he was very interested in the miracles performed by Sai Baba, and he began to gather stories from Chandorkar, Dikshit, and others in their growing circle of devotees. In 1916, Dabholkar retired from government service and asked Sai Baba for permission to write his biography. He records that Sai Baba consented to this request, announcing to Dabholkar and others present: "Make a collection of all the authentic stories, experiences, conversations and talks, etc. It is better to keep a record. He has my full support. He is but the instrument; I myself will write my own story. . . . Listening to my stories, narrating them to others in a *kirtan*, contemplating on them will propagate love and devotion for me, which will destroy ignorance, instantly. Wherever there is faith and devotion together, I remain enslaved forever" (Dabholkar 2007, 23). Written in Marathi verse and comprising fifty-three chapters, the *Shri Sai Satcharita* contains within it Dabholkar's account of his own interactions with Sai Baba in Shirdi; a biographical account of Sai Baba's lifetime, focusing on his time in Shirdi; philosophical discussions of the nature of Sai Baba, his mission on earth, and the greatness of the guru; ritual discussions of the importance of darshan and *udi* (sacred ash); spontaneous expositions given by Sai Baba on scriptures such as the Bhagavad Gita and the Isha Upanishad; stories of Sai Baba's many *lilas* (miraculous acts), including healing various ailments; and stories of the conversion experiences of many fellow devotees in Dabholkar's circle.

Dabholkar relates more of his own story in chapters 18 and 19 as he recounts a lila that he personally experienced. In 1917, in spite of being devoted to Sai Baba for the past seven years, he still felt a spiritual restlessness. He longed for Sai Baba to grant him a vision, as he had to others, so that he could make greater progress toward experiencing God-realization. Sai Baba sent him to a villager named Shama, telling him to chat with him, presumably to add his story to Dabholkar's growing collection of devotees' miraculous encounters with Sai Baba. Shama recounted to Dabholkar the story of an elderly woman who approached Sai Baba and asked to be formally initiated by him as his disciple and to be given a mantra. When Sai Baba did not comply, she undertook a hunger strike. Sai Baba then recounted his own story to her, stating that in the twelve years that he had served his own guru with faith and forbearance, the guru had never whispered a mantra in his ear. Thus, he asked her, how could he whisper a mantra in her ear? Instead of a mantra, simply have steadfast faith in the guru and spiritual progress will follow: "You look up to me with single-minded devotion. And I will look after you, similarly. My guru never taught me anything else" (Dabholkar 2007, 305).

As he listened to Shama tell this story, Dabholkar realized that Sai Baba was speaking directly to him. He returned to Sai Baba and, once seated before him, he felt his spiritual restlessness dissipate, making way for single-minded devotion. Sai Baba then explained: "Sai Baba is himself a storehouse of perfect, complete Knowledge, based on experience. And to know his nature truly and completely is in itself the act to propitiate and meditate upon him. This is his true *darshan*. To obtain a total release from the bondage of ignorance, desire and *karma*, there is absolutely no other device. Have this firmly fixed in your mind. Sai is not merely yours or ours, he really dwells in all the beings. As the sun belongs to the whole world, so also does he" (Dabholkar 2007, 311). This lesson about Sai Baba's all-pervasiveness and accessibility through darshan recurs again and again in the stories throughout the *Shri Sai Satcharita*. This auspicious exchange of glances with Sai Baba enables the devotee to not only express devotion to Sai Baba but also receive Sai Baba's blessings. These blessings are often material, particularly in the stories of devotees who are healed of physical illnesses and ailments by Sai Baba, but they may also help a devotee to make spiritual progress toward enlightenment, as Dabholkar did himself. And because Sai Baba dwells in all beings, his darshan can easily be obtained by those who have faith and know how to look properly.

Another example of the lesson of Sai Baba's all-pervasiveness and accessibility through darshan is found in the story of Balaram Mankar, told in chapter 31. Mankar was a widower from Bandra who went to Shirdi and became one of Sai Baba's followers. One day, Sai Baba commanded Mankar to leave Shirdi and travel to Machchindergad to undertake meditative austerities. Mankar despaired of leaving Sai Baba and asked him, "What will I do there—where I cannot even have your *darshan*?" But he was a devout follower, so he bowed at Sai Baba's feet and then left. Upon reaching Machchindergad, he promptly sat down to meditate. Suddenly, he experienced darshan with Sai Baba. Dabholkar writes that this experience of meditative darshan was so strong that Mankar was able not only to see and be seen by Sai Baba but also to communicate with him. Mankar asked why Sai Baba had sent him there, to which Sai Baba replied: "While in Shirdi, many notions, many doubts assailed your mind. . . . For you I did not exist outside Shirdi and apart from this abode [i.e., body], three-and-a-half cubits in length, which is made up of layer upon layer of a mixture of the five elements, like the earth, water, etc. But I, whom you see here and now, am the same as the one there" (Dabholkar 2007, 508). The lesson to be learned from this story is that Shirdi Sai Baba is not limited to a single place or time; he is all-pervasive, and with the proper devotional mind-set he is accessible to his followers anywhere and anytime, even after the death of his physical body. Throughout the *Shri Sai Satcharita*, Dabholkar therefore encourages his readers to engage in darshan with Sai Baba, writing in another chapter before recounting yet another miracle, "Let us then, concentrate the mind thus, and gaze at Baba's form, from the toes right up to his face and prostrating before him with loving devotion, let us continue with our narrative" (325).

With regard to the identity of Sai Baba, Dabholkar tackles this topic most explicitly in chapter 7 of the *Shri Sai Satcharita*.

> If considered a Hindu, he looked like a Muslim; and if a Muslim, he exhibited all the qualities of a good Hindu. Who, even with all his proficiency and learning, can describe such an extraordinary *Avatar* [incarnation]? No one could trace in the least, whether he was a Hindu or Muslim, for his conduct towards both these was always the same. . . . If a Muslim, his ears were pierced; but if a Hindu, his circumcision proved it to be otherwise. Neither a Hindu nor a Muslim—such was this Sai, the very incarnation of sanctity. If he is called a Hindu, he always lived in the mosque, and if he is called a Muslim, the fire burns day and night in the mosque. (Dabholkar 2007, 104–5)

In this chapter, Dabholkar goes on to describe how Sai Baba celebrated both Hindu and Muslim religious festivals, how he treated members of all castes equally, how he showed no favor for the wealthy over the poor or for men over women, how he showed kindness to lepers and other social outcastes, and how he distributed on a daily basis all of the monetary donations made to him, known as *dakshina*. He states that people wondered why a Hindu would live in a mosque or why a Muslim would be worshiped by Brahmins. Out of curiosity, they would come to visit Shirdi, and then after taking Sai Baba's darshan, they would suddenly fall silent in understanding, for "he who seeks refuge in *Hari* (God/Vishnu), forever, how can he be called a Hindu or a Muslim?" (Dabholkar 2007, 106).

For Dabholkar, then, Sai Baba was first and foremost a Hindu guru and god-man, whose guidance helped him to progress on the Hindu path toward liberation, or *moksha*, and the experience of God-realization. Sai Baba provided this guidance to Dabholkar through darshan, the single-minded devotional focus on Sai Baba, either in his physical form or an inward vision of it. After Sai Baba's death in 1918, Dabholkar believed that he continued to provide this personal guidance, remaining accessible through meditative darshan. Although Dabholkar conceived of Sai Baba primarily through concepts originating in Hinduism, he also acknowledged Sai Baba as a composite figure, revered by both Hindus and Muslims, and simultaneously Hindu and Muslim in his own physical being, teachings, and habits. For when properly seen from the monistic standpoint of Hindu Vedanta philosophy, such differences between self and God, *atman* and *Brahman*, collapse. So also do the differences between Hindus and Muslims, Hari and Allah.

THE SHRI SAIBABA SANSTHAN TRUST

Govind Rao Dabholkar and Abdul Baba differed significantly in their understandings of Sai Baba as a Hindu guru and god-man, on the one hand, and as a Muslim Sufi master and saint, on the other. However, they overlapped in their shared contention that such sectarian distinctions were immaterial from a theological standpoint, with Shirdi Sai Baba properly understood as a divine figure who pointed all who looked to him with sincere faith to ultimate reality. They also overlapped in their shared belief that Sai Baba was all-pervasive and remained accessible to devotees even from beyond the grave. Finally, they overlapped in their shared assertion that they were recording the words of Sai Baba in their respective hagiographies, with Sai Baba's express consent.

In spite of these similarities, the reception of these two hagiographies could not be more different. Today, Dabholkar's *Shri Sai Satcharita* is viewed as *the* authoritative scripture by the vast majority of Shirdi Sai Baba's devotees, who understand this text as containing the words of Sai Baba, written by Sai Baba himself after his death in 1918 through the medium of a chosen devotee. In reading or listening to the stories told within it, these devotees believe that they continue to interact with Sai Baba, who remains accessible— even "enslaved"—to them despite the fact that he is no longer embodied in human form (Dabholkar 2007, 23). Furthermore, for most devotees, the *Shri*

Sai Satcharita does not simply contain sacred words and stories; it is itself a sacred object of worship. Abdul Baba's diary, on the other hand, is unknown to the vast majority of Sai Baba's devotees. The story of how this came to be is intertwined with the early history of Shirdi as a developing pilgrimage center, in the years leading up to and following Sai Baba's death, and with the founding history of the Shri Saibaba Sansthan Trust.

In the mid-nineteenth century when Sai Baba first arrived in Shirdi as a wandering renouncer, it was a rural farming village. Located in Ahmednagar District of the Bombay Presidency, it was 296 kilometers from the city of Bombay and 83 kilometers from the city of Ahmednagar. The nearest railway station was in Kopargaon, 15 kilometers to the north, and the nearest permanent market was in the village of Rahata, 5 kilometers away. Shirdi contained approximately two hundred houses and not more than a thousand inhabitants. Just a few shops provided day-to-day needs, such as grains, salt, oil, sugar, soap, tea, and tobacco. One well served the whole village. A *chavadi* (public building) served as the village school, tax office, and resting place for official visitors. The majority of the village population was Hindu, and three Hindu temples could be found in Shirdi: one dedicated to the god Hanuman (Maruti); one dedicated to the god Vithoba; and one dedicated to the god Khandoba, which was just outside the village. Muslims comprised approximately 10 percent of the village population, and a small mosque stood near the Hanuman temple, though it was dilapidated. The majority of the village population was engaged in farming and agricultural activities. Life was not easy for these rural farmers, for Ahmednagar District was then known as the Famine Belt. Throughout the nineteenth century, the region was stricken by frequent droughts, leading to famine, as well as by outbreaks of cholera and the plague (Rigopoulos 1993, 59–60). Part of Sai Baba's growing appeal to the villagers in Shirdi was his purported ability to provide material relief and comfort in such times, and the *Shri Sai Satcharita* is replete with stories of his ability to miraculously provide food in periods of famine and to keep the village free from cholera and other illnesses.

At the time of Sai Baba's death in 1918, Ahmednagar District had transformed from the Famine Belt into the prosperous Sugar Belt through the government's construction of the Godavari and Pravara irrigation canals and the active promotion of sugarcane cultivation. By this time, Sai Baba's following entailed not just the Maratha-Kunbi farming villagers of Shirdi and surrounding villages but also a cadre of more elite devotees employed as civil servants in the colonial government, who visited regularly from

Bombay and other administrative centers of the Bombay Presidency. One of these wealthy devotees was Bapu Saheb Buty of Nagpur, who relocated to Shirdi in 1910 to remain in Sai Baba's presence. According to the history provided by Narasimhaswami, who interviewed many of Sai Baba's follow-ers and recorded their statements in the 1930s, several years prior to Sai Baba's death Bapu Saheb Buty dreamed that Sai Baba wanted him to build a *wada*, a visitors' resting place, that would also function as a Hindu temple. He asked for and received Sai Baba's permission to go forward with the construction. However, when he was ready to install a murti of Krishna, Sai Baba stopped him, saying, "After the temple is built, we will reside there." At the time of its proclamation, Sai Baba's followers were uncertain what this enigmatic statement meant. As Sai Baba's death neared, he stated: "I am going. Place me in the (Buty) Wada. Brahmins will reside near me." Imme-diately upon Sai Baba's death, many of his Hindu followers proclaimed that these statements meant that Sai Baba would himself be the murti that would reside in the temple and that Hindu Brahmin priests should attend to him. Thus they chose the Buty Wada in Shirdi, as it had come to be known, as Sai Baba's final resting place. Narasimhaswami writes: "The Hindus, by a large majority voted that Baba's remains should be placed in Buty wada and that was done. Baba's Samadhi [tomb] is now there" (1954, 138).

While Narasimhaswami (1954, 138) notes that Hindus and Muslims had a "hot contest" in determining whether Sai Baba should be entombed in the Buty Wada, other sources elaborate on the friction that existed between the village's majority Hindu and minority Muslim communities in the immedi-ate aftermath of Sai Bab's death. Govind Rao Dabholkar (2007, 718–19) notes in the *Shri Sai Satcharita* that following Sai Baba's death, Hindus and Mus-lims "debated the whole night as to what would be proper and what not," with Hindus seeking to entomb his remains in Buty Wada and Muslims seek-ing to bury them in the Muslim cemetery. While cremation is the standard practice for handling a deceased person's remains in Hinduism, ascetics and renouncers are not cremated, as they are understood to have already passed through a symbolic cremation of their former selves at the time of their initiation into asceticism. Therefore, they are typically buried or immersed in rivers. In Islam, burial is the standard practice for handling a deceased person's remains. Thus, both the Hindus and the Muslims agreed to bury Shirdi Sai Baba. However, according to these reports, they did not agree on *how* or *where* the burial should be conducted, nor *who* should be in charge of this rite of passage.

Antonio Rigopoulos cites an interview he recorded with one elderly devotee of Sai Baba named Bappu Baba, who witnessed the events. According to Bappu Baba, each group claimed Sai Baba's body, saying that he had really been one of them. For several days, the body remained on a plank inside the chavadi, until the district collector ultimately decided to give the body to the Hindu majority to perform the funeral rites according to their tradition. They did so, burying Sai Baba as a Hindu renouncer. Rigopoulos concludes that with this burial under Hindu oversight, "the process of Sai Baba's Hinduization was thus completed" (1993, 242).

Buty Wada, now known as the Samadhi Mandir, is the primary focus of pilgrims' activity at Shirdi, for it is here that Sai Baba's body was interred. For the first several years following Sai Baba's death, from 1918 to 1922, Abdul Baba served as the caretaker for the shrine. He kept it clean, placed daily offerings of flowers on the tomb, and lived on the offerings of food and cash (dakshina) made by devotees. In 1922, however, a Hindu devotee and a lawyer by trade, named Hari Sitaram Dikshit, also known as Kaka Saheb or Uncle, decided to establish a public trust through the Ahmednagar District Court for the administration of the shrine. Ramalingaswamy (1984, 176) reports that this provoked a legal countersuit by Abdul Baba: "Shri Abdul Baba was then the only local leading devotee of Baba. He was then having about four or five thousand rupees of Baba's dakshina amount with him offered by Baba's devotees. Some well wishers of him induced him that he was the legal heir to Baba and that the formation of the Trust was against justice. Thereby Abdul Baba filed a suit stating that he was the legal heir to Baba, against the Trust Body in the District Court, Ahmednagar." Abdul Baba lost his case and as a result was forbidden from acting as caretaker of the shrine and from receiving devotees' offerings of food and cash. Marianne Warren notes that after a few years these severe restrictions were relaxed and Abdul Baba was allowed to play a role in the maintenance of the shrine until his death in 1954. However, she writes, "the overall result was that, starting in 1922, any Muslim claim to Sai Baba's shrine was effectively silenced by the Hindus" (Warren 2004, 269). One must note, however, that it was the court (under imperial rule) that actually did the silencing in this case.

The public trust founded by Kaka Saheb Dikshit's legal action in 1922 was the Shri Saibaba Sansthan Trust. From 1922 until today, the Trust has served as the authorized body to control and manage the day-to-day activities at the Samadhi Mandir complex. For the first several decades following the death of Sai Baba, the focus of devotion within the Samadhi Mandir was the tomb, although historical photographs in the museum at Shirdi show that at some point between 1922 and 1954 a large print of the photograph of Sai Baba seated on a rock was also placed behind the tomb for devotees to gaze upon. On October 7, 1954—the year in which Abdul Baba passed away—the Shri Saibaba Sansthan Trust ritually installed the life-size murti of Shirdi Sai Baba that is the primary focus of pilgrims' devotion today. Sculptor Balaji Vasantrao Talim of Bombay carved it from white Italian marble, using as a guide the photograph of Sai Baba seated on a rock with his right leg crossed over his left knee (see figure I.1). The murti was formally installed by Swami Sai Sharan Anand (1889–1982), a Hindu renouncer who had first met Shirdi Sai Baba in 1911 and who maintained that Sai Baba was a Hindu Brahmin by birth (Anand 1991). Marianne Warren (2004, 269–70) reports that the installation of this murti in 1954 caused some controversy among Sai Baba's Muslim followers, some of whom chose to stop visiting the Samadhi Mandir at that time.

Today, the murti is worshiped in keeping with orthodox Brahminical Hindu ritual tradition. The temple is open from 4:00 A.M. until 11:15 P.M. and holds four primary *aaratis*, or prayer sessions, each day: the morning prayer at 4:30 A.M., before the sun rises; the midday prayer at noon; the afternoon prayer at sunset; and the evening prayer at 10:30 P.M. During each of these sessions, devotional songs praising Sai Baba are sung, devotees take darshan with Sai Baba and present their offerings to him (flowers, sweets, cash donations, etc.), and the priests wave their lit candles before the murti of Sai Baba.[7] In my 2010 interview with Kishore More, an executive officer of the Shri Saibaba Sansthan Trust placed in charge of day-to-day operations at Shirdi, he stated that the temple then employed nineteen priests in all, twelve main priests plus seven assistants. During the daily aaratis, four priests were always on duty, while at less busy times only two priests may be on duty. When I asked about the priests' training, More told me: "They are all Brahmin and have studied in Vedic school, in Varanasi or in Trimbakeshwar, so they are well trained. Vedic school means they have learned the Vedas, the holy books, they know all the chants."[8]

As Shirdi has grown more and more popular as a pilgrimage destination over the past century, and as the Samadhi Mandir has brought in increasingly more wealth in the form of pilgrims' donations, the state government's oversight of this pilgrimage complex and its governing trust has increased.[9] The Shree Sai Baba Sansthan Trust (Shirdi) Act of 2004 specifies that the Shri Saibaba Sansthan Trust must have a management committee composed of no more than seventeen members, appointed by the Maharashtra state government to serve three-year terms. To qualify for appointment, one must be a permanent resident in the state of Maharashtra and a declared devotee of Shirdi Sai Baba. Committee members receive an annual honorarium paid from the Trust's management fund. It is the duty of the Trust officers to work together to "manage the properties and affairs of the Sansthan Trust, efficiently, to make proper arrangement for the conduct and performance of rituals, worship ceremonies and festivals in the Temple according to the custom and usages, to provide necessary facilities and amenities to the devotees and to apply the income of the Trust to the objects and purposes for which the Trust is to be administered" (Government of Maharashtra 2004, 11). Beyond everyday management, officers of the Trust are also charged with propagating "knowledge about the life, activities, *leelas* [miracles] and teachings of Shri Sai Baba"; undertaking activities "aimed at promoting the feelings of brotherhood, unity, faith and equality among the devotees of Shri Sai Baba"; promoting "secular education of all types" in Shirdi; and promoting "any other noble cause aimed at achieving human well being or, to help human beings in calamities" (12). The Trust Act of 2004 also specifies how the abundant donations made by pilgrims in Shirdi can be utilized. Among the approved expenditures of the Trust fund are the maintenance and administration of the temple and related properties; the performance of rituals and festivals in the temple; the provision of facilities for devotees, including accommodations; the provision of meals to devotees; and propagating the teachings of Sai Baba (15).

In this 2004 legislation, the Shri Saibaba Sansthan Trust's mission is worded in intentionally inclusive language. One must be a devotee of Sai Baba to be a member, but one need not be Hindu; and the type of rituals and festivals to be undertaken within the temple are to be done according to "custom and usages" but are not explicitly equated with Brahminical Hinduism. In practice, however, it is rare in the history of the Trust for a non-Hindu to serve as a trustee, and the rituals practiced within the Samadhi Mandir are performed by Brahmin priests who have been thoroughly trained in orthodox liturgy. This tension between inclusive pluralism and adherence to Hindu tradition has shaped the Trust's response to the works by Abdul Baba and Dabholkar, strongly affecting the reception of these works among devotees of Sai Baba and their resultant understandings of who Shirdi Sai Baba was and what he taught.

As noted above, Govind Rao Dabholkar received permission from Sai

Baba to write his hagiography in 1916 but had only completed two or three chapters at the time of Sai Baba's death in 1918. The bulk of the *Shri Sai Satcharita* was written between 1918 and 1929, the year that Dabholkar passed away. The chapters were initially published in the monthly Marathi magazine *Sai Leela*, which was founded by Dikshit and Dabholkar in 1923 and published by the Shri Saibaba Sansthan Trust. In 1929, after Dabholkar passed away, members of the Trust gathered all of the chapters together, added a table of contents as the final chapter (written by trustee Balkrishna Viswanath Dev), and published the whole as a book. Today, the *Shri Sai Satcharita* is readily available in the two official bookstores maintained by the Trust at Shirdi, and it is widely disseminated beyond Shirdi. Most temples and organizations dedicated to Shirdi Sai Baba in India and around the world stock multiple copies of the *Shri Sai Satcharita*, offering them for free or a minimal donation to anyone who expresses interest in learning more about Sai Baba. The Shri Saibaba Sansthan Trust has also made the *Shri Sai Satcharita* available in English and in eleven Indian vernacular languages, to cater to an increasingly pan-Indian and global following of devotees.[10]

Abdul Baba's diary, on the other hand, was respectfully wrapped in a silk cloth after his death in 1954 and preserved in the archives in Shirdi by the Shri Saibaba Sansthan Trust. The Trust undertook no efforts to publish or translate the diary, though it did eventually give Marianne Warren a copy of the manuscript, which enabled her to translate and publish it in her book *Unravelling the Enigma*. Warren (2004, 267) suggests that Abdul Baba's diary has remained neglected by the Trust because of its Islamic content: "The fact that the manuscript's Islamic nature does not fit in with the accepted Hindu interpretation and presentation of Sai Baba may explain why it has remained unpublished by the *Sansthan*." Whatever the Trust's motivations, the result is that the *Shri Sai Satcharita* serves as the primary devotional text for the vast majority of Shirdi Sai Baba devotees, whereas most are not even aware that Abdul Baba's diary exists.

SHIRDI AS A PILGRIMAGE DESTINATION

In several important ways, the pilgrimage experience in Shirdi today reflects the tension between inclusive pluralism and adherence to orthodox Hindu tradition that has informed the historical development of the site under the auspices of the Shri Saibaba Sansthan Trust. As noted above, the 2004 Trust Act explicitly charges trustees with providing necessary facilities and amenities to pilgrims. In my interview with trustee Kishore More, he stated that his greatest challenges as an administrator of the pilgrimage site are handling the constantly increasing influx of pilgrims and providing the necessary services for them. The rise in pilgrims to Shirdi, More told me, is not only due to Sai Baba's steadily growing more popular throughout India and around the world during the past century but also due to recent advancements in modes of transportation that have made it easier to reach Shirdi, including the opening of a railway station there in 2009: "In addition [to the train station], during the past ten to fifteen years the roads have improved. So now buses come with the poor, the middle class comes in SUVs, even the wealthy now can come by helicopter."[11] In light of the ever-increasing numbers of pilgrims, More said that his top three priorities in managing Shirdi were darshan, food, and accommodations.

With regard to the first priority, darshan, More stated that at peak times between 8,000 and 9,000 people stand in line waiting their turn to take darshan with Sai Baba within the temple, and a maximum of 114,200 devotees can go through the queue each day. "For darshan we have organized the queue to improve the wait time—now it is maximum two hours—and to prevent accidents, stampedes. But we are now using part of the road; there is no other way. And the crowd will continue to grow. So this must be addressed in future."[12] My first experience in the darshan queue took place on a Thursday morning. Because I knew the temple would be packed on the day most sacred to Sai Baba, I arrived at 8:00 A.M., hoping to avoid the aarati rush hour. The line was nonetheless very long, and it took me two hours to move through from start to finish. I found myself sandwiched between the members of an extended Hindu family from Hyderabad. They were quite friendly, and they helped shelter me from the occasionally surging crowd. The parents introduced their children to me in formal English greetings but could not speak more English than that. Happily, they did speak Hindi, so we were able to converse. I learned that they try to come to Shirdi at least once a year, during the children's summer school holiday, and then make additional trips as circumstances demand—for instance, they have come after the birth of each new child to have him or her blessed by Sai Baba.

The darshan line starts on the ground level, with pilgrims feeding into it from four different gates. Then it snakes back and forth, with metal lane dividers set up to control and direct the crowd. Then the line moves up onto a second level, again snaking back and forth, before moving up some stairs and into the Samadhi Mandir itself, where one enters a waiting area. There the crowd splits in two directions, half moving to the right side of the murti, half to the left. Depending on whether one is routed into the inner or outer lanes on each side, one finds oneself directed for the darshan experience either to the open space directly in front of the tomb and murti, for a frontal view of Sai Baba, or to the side of the tomb and murti, for a profile view of Sai Baba.

Despite the long wait and the overwhelming heat, the crowd was remarkably happy and friendly. People were smiling, eagerly anticipating darshan with Sai Baba. At various intervals, one person or another would call out a verse from a popular devotional song to Sai Baba, and others would join in the singing. Many whom I spoke with that day said they were there simply for darshan with Sai Baba; others had come seeking Sai Baba's help with a particular problem, such as the healing of a sick family member; and still others explained that they were fulfilling a promise made on a prior visit, having vowed to return and make a donation if Sai Baba granted their request. Small donation boxes were placed strategically throughout the line, and as we got closer to the tomb and murti I witnessed more and more people making offerings: many people made offerings of cash; a man in front of me took a fancy silver pen from his shirt pocket and dropped it into the box; a woman in the line next to me dropped in one of her gold bangles.[13] After darshan, as I exited the Samadhi Mandir in the midst of a great outpouring of pilgrims, I was repeatedly asked, "Are you happy?" And indeed I was, quite happy to have begun my research tour of the Shirdi pilgrimage complex. In spite of the long, congested wait for darshan, everyone emerged from the experience smiling, hopeful that Sai Baba had actually been present and heard their prayers.

The majority of the pilgrims I met that day were Hindus, though I did speak with several Sikh families and one Muslim one as the line twisted and turned. Unlike some orthodox Hindu temples in India that do not allow non-Hindus inside the innermost areas, the Samadhi Mandir is open to visitors of all faiths, castes, and national backgrounds, in keeping with the Trust's inclusive mission. Nonetheless, the emphasis on darshan and ritual worship performed by Brahmin priests does limit the range of non-Hindu visitors interested in visiting or entering the site. Kishore More, however, maintained that in spite of the centrality of Hindu ritual, Muslims in particular do have a place. "The same rituals started during Baba's lifetime," More told me. "Whatever he accepted is what we do. But it is not just Hindu—every day at 9:45 A.M. Muslims come, they line up with roses. And

Abdul Baba's samadhi is here. But this is why we are now working on a standard operating manual for the temple. So that modifications don't take place, so that new rituals aren't added according to one person's whims. The book will apply for all Shirdi Sai Baba temples around the world. It will help to minimize the fighting over small issues."[14] As I discuss in detail in chapter 5, Shirdi Sai Baba engaged in composite religious practices during his daily routine, such as offering lights and incense in the Hindu manner and saying namaz in the Muslim manner. He also offered his blessings to people from a variety of religious backgrounds (Hindus, Muslims, Christians, Zoroastrians) who approached him in various ways, in keeping with the customs of their respective traditions. For his Hindu followers, he acquiesced during the last decade of his life to being worshiped in the manner of a Hindu deity (this is discussed in greater detail in chapter 5). It is this form of worship that the Trust has lent its sanction to and that it seeks to enforce as the authorized liturgical program for all temples dedicated to Sai Baba. In my field observations I witnessed a few local Muslims bringing roses to Sai Baba, but they left these offerings at the outer gate rather than entering the temple.[15]

With regard to the Shri Saibaba Sansthan Trust's two other priorities—food and accommodations—according to Kishore More the Trust has built facilities to provide both for pilgrims at a price well below market rate. The Prasadalay is a large cafeteria—indeed, the Trust claims that it is Asia's largest dining hall. It was constructed in 2009, with a seating capacity of 5,500 people and the ability to serve 100,000 meals a day to devotees. It is an impressive facility, with seventy solar panels on the roof that power the cooking through steam heat for most of the year (oil fuel must be used to power the kitchen during the cloudy monsoon season); a spotless kitchen with top-of-the-line cooking, refrigeration, and dishwashing machinery; and a water purification system. The meal provided is an all-you-can-eat Maharashtrian *thali*, including rice, dal, two vegetable curries, chapatti, and a sweet. The fee is ten rupees in the main dining hall, and there is a smaller, separate Annadaan dining hall (seating 1,000 at a time) within the Prasadalay that serves free meals to those who cannot afford the charge. More explained that the pilgrimage complex has no set income, because it runs on donations made by pilgrims, but it does have fixed expenses—salaries for workers, maintenance costs, taxes, and the like. Thus, the complex charges a nominal fee for the meal in order to encourage donations: "We charge ten rupees per person at the Prasadalay. If we gave the food free of charge, then

FIGURE 1.3. Shirdi Sai Baba statue at the Prasadalay cafeteria in Shirdi. Photo: Karline McLain.

the whole system would collapse, no one would donate anymore. The actual cost per person for the food is seventeen rupees. So it is still charity. In this way the financial administration is very important. It is the crucial work of the Trust for the long run."[16]

At the entrance to the Prasadalay, elevated so that it is the first thing pilgrims see as they enter the facility, is a large three-dimensional statue of Shirdi Sai Baba standing in front of a *handi*, a large earthen cooking pot. His right arm is thrust deep into the pot, stirring its hot contents. At night, the flames under the pot light up in a neon glow. This is a narrative image that depicts one of Sai Baba's most popular lilas. Chapter 38 of the *Shri Sai Satcharita*, titled "The Description of the Handi," puts forth an argument for *annadaan*, feeding others, as the best form of charity and the best means for attaining moksha. Sai Baba reportedly prepared food for all who came to see him in his earthen pot. The text emphasizes that Sai Baba fed both Hindus and Muslims, creating both vegetarian and meat-based dishes depending on the preferences of his visitors, and that he simultaneously received the blessings of the local Hindu priest and the Muslim mullah over the food. Miraculously, there was always more than enough food in the pot, no matter how many people arrived. Furthermore, Sai Baba used his own hand to stir the hot food, not a utensil, and was never burned:

> When the steam rose out of the boiling handi, scorching hot, Baba would pull up his sleeves and, thrusting his hand inside, would stir up the contents up and down. Seeing that the vessel was boiling and ready to be stirred, Baba would show his marvelous leela at that moment. Oh! Where the hand of flesh and blood, and where the vessel scorching hot! But neither any sign of the burns nor a frightened face could be seen! And how could the fire hurt a hand which removed the threefold afflictions of the devotees, the moment it fell on their heads! Did it not know its greatness? (Dabholkar 2007, 633)

As pilgrims wait in line to enter the cafeteria, they pause to take photos of family members standing before the statue, re-creating for their own albums a personalized version of this miracle. I have found this story especially popular among the working-poor devotees of Shirdi Sai Baba, who struggle to earn enough to feed themselves and their families on a day-to-day basis. For these devotees, this image reflects Sai Baba's promise, the eleventh of his 11 Sayings, "There shall be no want in the house of my devotees." However, this story is also popular with upper-class devotees of Sai Baba who have taken to heart his teaching that annadaan is the best form of charity in this age. Many Shirdi Sai Baba temples in India have annadaan programs every Thursday, when those in need of a meal can line up to receive one for free. In the United States, many Shirdi Sai Baba devotees carry out weekly "sandwich *seva*" (sandwich service) programs, making peanut butter and jelly sandwiches to donate to local soup kitchens or homeless shelters to carry on this tradition.

Within the main dining hall of the Prasadalay, one encounters row upon row of stainless-steel cafeteria tables and seats. Each person is given a tray, and staff in chef's aprons come around to serve the various items on that day's menu. On my first visit to the Prasadalay, a special sweet was being served, *semiya*, which is vermicelli cooked in sugar milk. I learned that a devotee in New Jersey had given a donation to the temple, specifying that every pilgrim be given this special desert for two months. The pilgrims I ate with at lunch that day found the meal delicious, as did I. Like at the Samadhi Mandir itself, all visitors to Shirdi are welcomed to the Prasadalay for a

FIGURE 1.4. Pilgrims at the Prasadalay cafeteria in Shirdi. Photo: Karline McLain.

meal, no matter their religious, caste, or national identity. However, all of the food prepared and served is described as *prasad*, that is, sanctified food that has first been offered to Shirdi Sai Baba and thus carries his blessing, in keeping with Brahminical ritual tradition. Indeed, it is on behalf of this Hindu ritual tradition that the Prasadalay received its name, which means "abode of prasad." Furthermore, although Sai Baba could miraculously produce vegetarian or nonvegetarian food, depending on his Hindu and Muslim visitors' needs, the Prasadalay is strictly vegetarian, in keeping with Hindu orthodoxy.[17]

With regard to the Shri Saibaba Sansthan Trust's third priority, accommodation, the Trust maintains multiple buildings to provide overnight lodging for pilgrims. On my tour of the facilities in 2010, with a guide supplied by the Trust, I visited two of these buildings, the Sai Bhakta Niwas and the Dwaravati Bhakta Niwas. The Sai Bhakta Niwas was the largest pilgrim hostel run by the Trust at the time, with 525 rooms in a total of four buildings. The buildings are arranged in a square pattern, with a large grassy space in the center between them, where children were running about and playing. The rooms are basic but clean and are available to pilgrims on a first-come, first-served basis (no advance reservations). On my visit, the large lobby was filled with families of pilgrims camping out and waiting their turn for a room, each holding a number. I spoke with one man who had number 43—the waiting-list board showed 35—and he was looking forward to getting a room for his family soon. They had come via train from Uttar Pradesh and had been waiting for just one day, he said with a smile. The room fare was one hundred rupees for up to six people. My guide told me that a hundred rooms used to have air conditioning, and these rooms had cost five hundred rupees per night. However, because many families could not afford that, these rooms were often empty, even when people were camping out in the lobby overnight waiting for a room to open up. Thus, all of the rooms in this facility were changed to non–air conditioned, in order to accommodate the pilgrims' budgets.

The other hostel I toured, Dwaravati Bhakta Niwas, was built in 2008. It is a four-story building with 320 rooms, each a bit more upscale than the rooms in the Sai Bhakta Niwas (e.g., with beds instead of cots). Rooms in this second hostel cost five hundred rupees per night, or one thousand for the air-conditioned rooms on the fourth floor, and all of the rooms in this hostel can be booked in advance. Catering to more middle-class pilgrims, this hostel has parking spaces available, a twenty-four-hour water supply, and guaranteed electricity with a backup generator. Together, these two buildings demonstrated the class diversity of the pilgrims and the Trust's awareness of the need to cater to both working-class and middle-class devotees.[18] In 2012, construction of Sai Ashram (phases 1 and 2) was completed, an accommodation that now provides more than fifteen hundred rooms for overnight pilgrims, with a variety of amenities and charges.[19] At all of these lodgings, small canteens are available, which serve the same sanctified food (all-you-can-eat Maharashtrian vegetarian thali) provided in the Prasadalay, for the same nominal fee of ten rupees. Furthermore, all of these lodgings insist that overnight residents refrain from imbibing nonvegetarian food or liquor on the premises, in keeping with Brahminical orthopraxy.

Beyond providing necessary facilities and amenities to the pilgrims, the Shri Saibaba Sansthan Trust is also charged with undertaking activities "aimed at promoting the feelings of brotherhood, unity, faith and equality among the devotees of Shri Sai Baba," promoting "secular education of all types" in Shirdi, and promoting "any other noble cause aimed at achieving human well being or, to help human beings in calamities" (Government of Maharashtra 2004, 12). Kishore More stressed the Trust's work in the fields of health care and education as the two primary ways that it has sought to fulfill this mandate in recent years. With regard to health care, the Trust has established two charitable hospitals in Shirdi for the benefit of both the local residents and visiting pilgrims. The Shri Saibaba Hospital was built in 2006 as a specialty hospital focused on cardiology. It has a catheterization lab, five cardiac operating rooms, and an eighteen-bed intensive care unit. The Shri Sainath Hospital is a general hospital with two hundred beds that provides more routine medical services. The administrator I spoke with at the latter hospital said that the services most in demand were diagnosis of eye problems, cataract operations, family planning, and emergency snakebite care for rural farmers. Both hospitals provide free or reduced-cost services for those patients who are officially classified as "Below Poverty Line" according to the government of India's poverty threshold. On my tour of these facilities, several doctors and administrators told me that Sai Baba's teaching was that God was within each of us, and therefore the best service one could render to God was to serve humanity. The Trust also recently approved plans for a larger hospital that will hold six hundred beds.

Within the specialty hospital, I noticed many images of Shirdi Sai Baba lining the walls of the main intake hall. These images re-created scenes from the *Shri Sai Satcharita*, many of which are healing miracles performed by Sai Baba. For the devotees who come to the hospital seeking cures for their maladies, such images reflect Sai Baba's promise in the first of his 11 Sayings: "Whoever puts their feet on Shirdi soil, their suffering will come to an end." When I asked about this, the administrator giving me the tour stated: "Yes, Sai Baba performed many healing miracles here in Shirdi. So, many of the patients who come here think that they will be cured here, even if they have not been cured elsewhere. But of course it is science that heals them, when they are healed." One of the cardiac surgeons I interviewed was more open to the possibility of Sai Baba's continuing presence in Shirdi and his healing potential. He proudly stated that the hospital performs more surgical procedures than other hospitals with similar facilities, and the mortality rate is far lower than those other places. He then pointed to the framed picture of Sai Baba hanging in the operating room and told me about a patient who had asked Sai Baba to show him a sign that he was present just before his surgery began. "Just then," the doctor said, "a metal stool that had been stacked up fell onto the floor, making a loud clanging noise. I had done hundreds of other procedures in this same room, and this hadn't happened before. So why this time? Perhaps it is just coincidence. Or perhaps it is because Baba is here, perhaps that is why we have a better success rate than other hospitals. Perhaps this is why we can fix some of the lost causes that come to us, people who have seen other doctors but given up hope for a cure."[20]

With regard to education, the Trust has established several schools within Shirdi for residents of the region. The Shri Saibaba Adhauyogik Pra-shikshan Kendra is an industrial training school established in 1984. In my tour of the classrooms, I saw male students studying tractor and auto mechanics, refrigeration and air conditioning, and welding. These were either one-year programs of study with two-year internships, or two-year programs with one-year internships. The school also offered a course in basic computer skills, which enrolled both male and female students. The co-ed Shri Saibaba English Medium School was established in 1990 for children from the first to tenth standard (equivalent to through the tenth grade). A third school founded by the Trust is the Shri Saibaba Kanya Vidya Mandir, a Marathi-medium school for girls that charges only five rupees for admission and whose mission is to provide basic education in the Marathi vernacular to girls in the region. The vice principal of the English-medium school told me that when the school opened, it had fifty-four students; as of 2010, it had over fifteen hundred.[21] She said the tremendous growth is due to two factors: First, Shirdi has itself grown significantly over the past twenty years.[22] Second, the fees charged are nominal compared to other English-medium schools, and the school has a higher student pass rate, sug-gesting that it provides a better education. Most of the students come from a farming background and are first-generation students. Therefore, the school runs extra classes and tutoring sessions, without charge, recognizing that the parents often cannot help the students study. Like many of the doc-tors and hospital administrators, the vice principal also told me—while pointing to the large framed print of Sai Baba hanging in her office—that Sai Baba taught that the best service one could render to God was to serve humanity. This she does by educating the next generation, teaching them in turn to educate the generation that follows.

In addition to the Samadhi Mandir, the Prasadalay cafeteria, the hostels, hospitals, and schools, the Shri Saibaba Sansthan Trust also oversees many other places in Shirdi that are historically associated with Sai Baba. Most prominent is Dwarkamai, the mosque where Sai Baba lived, located just outside of the eastern gate of the pilgrimage complex. Here one can view Sai Baba's personal cooking stove; the constantly burning fire that provided the sacred ash, called udi or *vibhuti*, that he gave to devotees; the large stone that Sai Baba sat on in the iconic photograph of him; and the place where he breathed his last breath. Also near Dwarkamai are the chavadi, the Hanu-man Temple, and Abdul Baba's cottage. Additional highlights within the pilgrimage complex are the Lendi Garden, now a small shaded pasture;

Gurusthan, the site of the neem tree that Sai Baba took shelter under upon his first arrival in Shirdi; and the Dixit Wada Museum, which contains photographs of Sai Baba and his relics, including the white robe he wore, his pipe, his bedroll, and the tumbler he drank from. Also on official pilgrimage grounds are multiple administrative offices, including a bookstore; donation counters; a meditation room; and the Public Relations Office (PRO), where one can apply for VIP passes for darshan and aarati within the Samadhi Mandir (these passes are regularly granted to the disabled who are unable to wait in the long queue for darshan, as well as to nonresident Indians from abroad and to Indian officials).

Beyond the walls of the official complex, and also beyond the official oversight of the Trust, are still other sites, including the Khandoba Temple and the houses of some of Sai Baba's earliest devotees. Touts roam outside of the complex walls, trying to entice pilgrims to visit nearby sacred sites, such as the Sakori Ashram of Upasni Maharaj just five kilometers south of Shirdi, or the Shani Temple in Shingnapur, sixty kilometers away. Other touts encourage pilgrims to combine their religious tourism with a fun-filled family vacation, offering to transport them to and from the water parks and other entertainment centers that have recently cropped up just outside of Shirdi. Stalls have also appeared outside of the pilgrimage complex walls, selling a range of souvenirs for pilgrims to take home: framed posters of Sai Baba for one's home altar, pamphlets in various vernacular languages about Sai Baba's miracles and teachings, and DVDs of the popular films and TV serials that have been made about Sai Baba.

SHIRDI AS A COSMOPOLITAN/HINDU PILGRIMAGE CENTER

Shirdi has become a cosmopolitan sacred space, a place where Indians from many regions and differing class and caste backgrounds engage one another; where Hindus of various sectarian persuasions interact; and where Indians, nonresident Indians, and non-Indians may encounter one another. The tremendous amount of pilgrimage traffic to Shirdi, and the increasingly global sway of Shirdi Sai Baba, was brought home to me one morning as I witnessed the biweekly process of counting the pilgrims' donations. In the basement of the Samadhi Mandir, thirty employees were seated counting money, while several guards were posted outside. One table had several men examining the gold jewelry that had been left in donation boxes: bangles, earrings, rings, and necklaces. Another table had several men examining the plated gold and silver ornaments that had been donated for the murti to wear. Several men were engaged in pouring coins into coin-counting machines. The bulk of the men were at two long tables, each sorting Indian currency into stacks of same-denomination bills and counting them out. However, one man was sorting all of the foreign currency into stacks, and I was informed that they regularly receive donations in twenty different types of foreign money, tangible testimony to the expansion of Shirdi Sai Baba devotion beyond the borders of India.

Trustee Kishore More stated that Shirdi has now become the second-largest pilgrimage destination in terms of the number of annual pilgrims, and it is also the second-richest temple in India in terms of annual donations received—second on both counts only to the Tirumala Venkateswara Temple at Tirupati in the state of Andhra Pradesh. Both More and my official tour guide that the Trust provided expressed confidence that it was just a matter of time before Shirdi would overtake the Tirumala Venkateswara Temple to become both the number-one pilgrimage destination and the wealthiest temple in India. When asked why, my guide replied simply: "Because Baba is for all, not just Hindus, like Tirupati. He is the incarnation of the age." More agreed: "Yes, Baba is for everyone. Tirupati is for the Hindus only. Baba is for Hindus and Muslims. He is for all Indians. He is also for you."[23]

The managing trust of the Tirumala Temple in Tirupati has intentionally defined that temple as Hindu, and the customary practice has long been to bar entry to those who are visibly non-Hindu. Technically, non-Hindus are not forbidden from entering the temple for darshan with the presiding deity within, Lord Venkateswara; however, it is mandatory for those belonging to faiths other than Hinduism to sign a declaration form before entering the temple, wherein they officially swear that they have faith in Lord Venkateswara (Shukla 2012). At Shirdi, by contrast, pilgrims of all faiths and nationalities are welcomed into the temple for darshan, as I have personally experienced and witnessed, and there is no requirement to sign a legal declaration of faith in Sai Baba before entering. In this way, the trustees and officials of Shirdi envision it as a cosmopolitan pilgrimage center. They also see it as a composite pilgrimage center, given that the Samadhi Mandir can be construed as both a Muslim dargah and a Hindu *tirtha*. A dargah is a Sufi shrine, a place where a Sufi saint has been buried and where pilgrim-devotees can come into contact with the saint's baraka, the saint's blessing power.[24] A tirtha is a Hindu site of sacred crossing, a place where pilgrim-devotees can come into contact with the Hindu gods and goddesses, most often in the form of murtis, and seek their blessings.[25] Finally, the Trust envisions itself as promoting such values as unity, pluralism, and secularism in Shirdi and beyond through its significant humanitarian and charitable work in the fields of health care and education.

In these important ways, Shirdi does stand apart from Tirupati as a sacred site and pilgrimage destination. And yet, in other equally important ways, Shirdi overlaps with Tirupati. Both adhere to a strict liturgical schedule performed by Brahmin priests in keeping with Hindu orthopraxy. Both follow a strict vegetarian policy for the pilgrimage site, also in keeping with Brahminical orthopraxy. And—despite the much more welcoming attitude of the Trust in Shirdi toward non-Hindus—both attract a predominantly Hindu following. As Kiran Shinde and Andrea Pinkney write, based on their fieldwork in Shirdi: "From a doctrinal perspective, Shirdi Sai Baba is universal in his message and appeal. Yet, from the perspective of lived religious practices, the saint's appeal appears to be particularly attractive to Hindus—Maharashtrian and Andhra devotees in particular" (2013, 570).

Two of Sai Baba's closest followers, Govind Rao Dabholkar and Abdul Baba, understood Sai Baba quite differently: the former saw him as a Hindu guru and god-man; the latter, as a Muslim Sufi master and saint. However, they shared the belief that such sectarian distinctions were theologically irrelevant; rather, Shirdi Sai Baba was properly understood as a divine figure pointing all who looked to him with sincere faith to ultimate reality. Nonetheless, in the century since Sai Baba's passing, Dabholkar's interpretation of Sai Baba as a Hindu god-man has eclipsed Abdul's interpretation of Sai Baba as a Muslim saint, and Dabholkar's *Shri Sai Satcharita* has become the primary scripture for devotees of Sai Baba. Similarly, though Shirdi is a destination that since Sai Baba's time has welcomed Hindus, Muslims, and others, from high castes and low, both wealthy and poor, in the century since Sai Baba's passing Shirdi has grown increasingly attractive to Hindus as a pilgrimage destination. The following chapters turn to some of Shirdi Sai Baba's key Hindu interlocutors, asking why they turned to Sai Baba for their spiritual fulfillment, why they encouraged others to do so as well, and what we can learn from this about contemporary Hinduism in practice.

CHAPTER 2

Shirdi Is My Pandharpur

DAS GANU'S PLEA TO BRAHMINS AND NON-BRAHMINS

Shirdi is my Pandharpur, and Sai Baba is its God.

Pure devotion is the Chandrabhaga River,

And intense concentration is the seat of Vithoba.

Come along, everyone, come and pray to Baba,

Ganu says, O Sai Baba, my Mother, hurry and lift me in your arms.

DAS GANU MAHARAJ, *SAMAGRA VANMAYA*

D AS Ganu Maharaj (1868–1962) was a *kirtankar*, a devotional poet and performer, who can be credited with spreading the name of Shirdi Sai Baba throughout the area of modern-day Maharashtra in the first half of the twentieth century as he traveled from city to city, singing his devotional hymns before audiences in Hindu temples, in the homes of patrons, and at public festivals. Three of Das Ganu's *kirtans*, or hymns, have become especially important in Shirdi Sai Baba devotional circles, for they have been incorporated into the daily *puja*, or worship service, at the Samadhi Mandir in Shirdi.[1] The majority of Shirdi Sai Baba temples throughout India and around the world model their worship services on that of the Shirdi temple, and thus these songs are now known by heart by a great many Sai Baba devotees, who often sing along during the performance of the puja.[2]

In all three hymns, Das Ganu appeals to Sai Baba as a parental figure.[3] In Hymn no. 1 (composed in Hindi), he asks Sai Baba to show mercy on his children, who are blinded by worldly illusion, by giving them a vision of God:

> Oh Sai, show us mercy,
> And take care of your children.
> You know this expansive universe,
> It is a world of illusion.
> Oh Sai, show us mercy,
> And take care of your children.
> I am blind, bound to you,
> Give me a vision of God.
> Oh Sai, show us mercy,
> And take care of your children.
> Das Ganu says, What more can I say?
> My tongue has grown tired.[4]

In Hymn no. 2 (also composed in Hindi), he continues the theme of pleading for mercy and release from worldly illusion, proclaiming Sai Baba to be the one true companion in life, the loving Master (Malik) that Das Ganu is bound to serve:

> Show me mercy now, my Sai,
> Aside from you I have no one—no mother, father, or brother.
> I am blind, bound to you,
> I know nothing of God.
> Show me mercy now, my Sai,
> Aside from you I have no one—no mother, father, or brother.
> I have fallen to this empty world,
> In the end I have no true companion.
> Show me mercy now, my Sai,
> Aside from you I have no one—no mother, father, or brother.
> Ganu is the broomstick of your mosque,
> Sai Baba, you are my Master.

The most popular hymn in devotional circles is Hymn no. 3 (composed in Marathi), which is translated in this chapter's epigraph. In this hymn, Das Ganu makes reference to the traditional Maharashtrian pilgrimage center of Pandharpur, located on the Bhima River (which is also called the Chandrabhaga River at Pandharpur). Pandharpur is the home of the Vitthal Rukmini Temple, which houses the deity known as Vithoba (also commonly called Vitthal and Pandurang, sometimes referred to as Krishna or Vishnu, or even as Shiva or Mother by some devotees), to whom Varkari pilgrims throughout the region travel regularly to offer devotion. As R. C. Dhere and Anne Feldhaus have discussed in detail, Vitthal was originally a pastoralist folk deity from the southern Deccan who has long been worshiped by Marathas, but over time he became Vaishnavized and embraced by Brahmins as well. For Dhere, Vitthal is a "convergence, synthesis, or confluence" of many different streams of Indian religious traditions, including nonelite and elite, Shaiva and Vaishnava, Hindu and non-Hindu (Dhere and Feldhaus 2011, xiv). In the first line of Hymn no. 3, Das Ganu proclaims that Shirdi is his Pandharpur, and Sai Baba is his Vithoba (Vitthal). In equating Sai Baba with Vithoba, Das Ganu was certainly referencing the confluence described by Dhere, calling on everyone in western India to come and pray to Baba now, just as they have to Vithoba for centuries past.

Of Das Ganu's many poems, it is Hymn no. 3 that has received the most scholarly attention, where it has been criticized as an example of Das Ganu's Brahminical Hindu bias toward Shirdi Sai Baba. B. V. Narasimhaswami (who is discussed in greater detail in chapter 3) interprets this hymn as a hollow statement, a wishful declaration of Sai Baba's identity as God that is empty of true faith. In explanation, he recounts in his work *Sri Sai Baba's Charters and Sayings* an incident in which Das Ganu wanted to visit Pandharpur and requested permission from Sai Baba as his guru to allow him to leave Shirdi in order to attain an inner personal vision, or *sakshatkara*, of Vithoba.[5] Sai Baba replied: "Vittal [Vithoba] will appear. But there must be intense devotion" (Narasimhaswami 1954, 37). But when Das Ganu made the trip and took *darshan* (auspicious gazing) of Vithoba in the temple, he did not experience sakshatkara. He then returned to Shirdi and asked Sai Baba when he would have sakshatkara. Sai Baba replied: "You see *me*. That is sakshatkara. I am God" (38). But Narasimhaswami tells us that Das Ganu was not satisfied with this response, and he determined that it was not his destiny to experience sakshatkara in this lifetime (37–38).

Narasimhaswami deduces that the root problem was Das Ganu's bias as an orthodox Brahmin, which made it impossible for him to fully accept a non-Brahmin—indeed, a non-Hindu—as his God. In volume 2 of *Life of Sai Baba*, Narasimhaswami writes, "Das Ganu's inability to think of Baba as pure Vittal [Vithoba] or God is an instance where a person gets very great benefits from Baba but something or other hinders his deriving the fullest benefits as prejudices die hard and old habits cannot be easily erased" (1983, 144). In volume 4, Narasimhaswami is even more explicit in his criticism of Das Ganu: "A particular bhakta [devotee], who was favoured highly by Baba, still believes that Baba was a Muslim, and he wonders how anybody could take him to be a Brahmin; and his association of Muhammadanism [Islam] with Baba is greatly detrimental to his bhakti [devotion]. This sort of clas-sification of Baba as belonging to one caste or another is the result of one's own Dehabhimana i.e. the idea that one is one's body, and that one is of superior Brahmin Caste Hindu religion" (1982, 102).[6]

Though he praises Das Ganu for making great strides in his personal spiritual pursuits during his time in Shirdi with Sai Baba, and for spreading devotion to Shirdi Sai Baba through his hymns and song-sermons, Narasim-haswami concludes that ultimately Das Ganu was unable to have full faith in Sai Baba as God incarnate because of his caste bias—as a Brahmin Hindu, he looked down upon Sai Baba as an impure Muslim and could not see his cho-sen god, Vithoba, in him, despite his proclamations to the contrary. Other scholars have followed Narasimhaswami's lead. For instance, in her intro-duction to Das Ganu's *Shri Sainath Stavanamanjari*, Zarine Taraporevala similarly praises Das Ganu for his poetic work and criticizes him for lacking full faith in Shirdi Sai Baba as a result of his caste bias. She concludes that for Das Ganu, only Vithoba was God; "he wanted a vision of God in that form alone and not the Sai form he saw at Shirdi" (Das Ganu 1987, ix). Likewise, in his book *The Life and Teachings of Sai Baba of Shirdi*, Antonio Rigopoulos criticizes Das Ganu for his desire to go to Pandharpur, writing: "This episode demonstrates how Das Ganu, though highly revering Baba, could not iden-tify him *tout court* with his *istadevata* [personal deity]. This, however, was precisely the realization that Baba wanted to impart to Das Ganu, that is, that Sai and all deities are verily 'one and the same'" (1993, 223).

In this chapter I take a different approach than these scholars. Rather than asking how genuine Das Ganu's faith in Shirdi Sai Baba was, I instead ask what is at stake in Das Ganu's proclamation that Shirdi is his Pand-harpur and Sai Baba its God, Vithoba? What might such a claim have been intended to signal to its audience, those Brahmin and non-Brahmin Hindus attending Das Ganu's kirtan performances throughout Maharashtra? And what does this claim suggest about his unique interpretation of Shirdi Sai Baba's life and teachings? To answer these questions, I look into Das Ganu's oeuvre beyond Hymn no. 3. Doing so, I argue, complicates the conclusions drawn by Narasimhaswami and those following him. For instance, a closer investigation of Hymn nos. 1 and 2 reveals that in these poems Das Ganu draws on not only the Hindu *bhajan* (hymn) tradition but also the Islamic *qawwali* tradition as he begs God for mercy. He refers to God using the Arabic term *Allah* as opposed to the Sanskrit term *Bhagwan* in Hymn no. 2, and he uses the Urdu word for "mercy," *raham*, in Hymn nos. 1 and 2, hearkening to God as Ar-Rahim, the Merciful. Such careful pairing of Hindu and Islamic phrasing for the divine might suggest that Das Ganu did seek to assert to his audience that all deities—Allah and Vithoba—are "one and the same" after all.

Das Ganu has an extensive body of devotional work composed primarily in Marathi (but also incorporating Hindi poems) that has not been translated into English or studied by scholars and that as a result also remains unknown to most devotees of Sai Baba.[7] Looking beyond the three hymns used in temple liturgy, I examine Das Ganu's compositions about Sai Baba that have been compiled in his *Samagra Vanmaya* (Collected works), focusing especially on the hagiography of Sai Baba included in his *Bhaktasaramrita* (composed in 1925). My examination reveals that Das Ganu's discussion of Sai Baba is rife with didactic messages about the need to overcome caste and communal prejudice. When seen in this light, Das Ganu's proclamation that Shirdi is his Pandharpur suggests another meaning entirely. He addresses an audience of Hindus, singling out his fellow Brahmins as well as non-Brahmins, and urges them all to visit Shirdi. There, he claims, is a living god incarnate, Vithoba for the modern age, in the form of Sai Baba. Here Das Ganu references the annual Varkari pilgrimage tradition, familiar to all who live in western India, wherein Hindus from various sects (Vaishnavas and Shaivas) come together to trek to Pandharpur, singing along the way the poems praising Vithoba that were composed by medieval saints from across the caste spectrum: Brahmins such as Jnaneshwar and Eknath; Shudras such as Namdev and Tukaram; "Untouchables" such as Chokhamela and his wife, Soyarabai. For Das Ganu, this pilgrimage—in which Hindus of all sects, castes, and genders participate together—represented the ideal community that Sai Baba was enacting in Shirdi.[8]

During Das Ganu's lifetime, substantial discussion of caste was ongoing in the public sphere, and as a Brahmin Das Ganu was undoubtedly aware of the criticisms then being raised about Brahminical culture. Yet as a kirtan-kar, he regularly performed before mixed audiences of Brahmins and non-Brahmins, and frequently Brahmins were in the minority of such audiences. How, then, was he to navigate such troubled caste waters as a performer? He did so by relying on a strategy used by numerous Brahmin *bhakti* (devotional) performers in Maharashtra before him to separate Brahminism and Brahmins discursively, one that Christian Novetzke has termed "the Brahmin double." Novetzke defines the Brahmin double as "the character of a 'bad Brahmin,' who is portrayed as foolish, greedy, pedantic or casteist, and who serves as a 'double' for a 'good' Brahmin. This 'bad Brahmin' is thus a 'body double,' receiving abuse and deflecting polemical attack from the performer, giving legitimacy to a Brahmin performer standing before a largely non-Brahmin audience" (2011, 235). By utilizing this strategy of the Brahmin double, these Brahmin performers were able to separate being born a Brahmin from being Brahminical and therefore to "speak both outside and inside their fold, to criticize their caste superiority while suggesting a way to maintain status within public discursive networks, especially those of *bhakti* performance" (236).

This chapter argues that Das Ganu was one of the Brahmin bhakti performers in late-colonial Maharashtra who used the Brahmin double to offer a reformist critique of caste. In his utopian vision of Shirdi, the Pandharpur of western India for this modern age, Brahmins and non-Brahmins, Vaishnavas and Shaivas, Hindus and Muslims could all get along, united as loving siblings under the protective gaze of Sai Baba. For this to come about, differences such as caste and creed need not be eliminated; rather, "bad" Brahmins must be led to Sai Baba, so that through him they can be transformed into "good" Brahmins, enabling all castes to be equally valued as societal differences flourished harmoniously.

BECOMING DAS GANU

The most extensive biography of Das Ganu Maharaj was written by his disciple Anant Damodar Athavale, who composed his Marathi hagiography, *Santakavi Shridasaganumaharaja: Vyakti ani Vanmaya* (1955), during the final decade of Das Ganu's life, with his consent. Athavale also compiled Das Ganu's extensive Marathi poems and writings into the multi-volume *Samagra Vanmaya* and was therefore well acquainted with Das

Ganu's literary output and life. Athavale regarded Das Ganu as his guru, and thus the goal of his "biography" was not simply to retell the major incidents in Das Ganu's life but to present him as a religious exemplar—the ideal guru who traversed from the secular to the spiritual realm, who expressed his faith through his poetry, and who called others into the faith through his poetic performances. For Athavale, writing the hagiography of Das Ganu and editing his collected works was an act of embodied devotion, or bhakti, toward his guru.[9]

A second and much briefer biography of Das Ganu was written by B. V. Narasimhaswami, who first met Das Ganu upon his own arrival in Shirdi in 1936. Over the next few years, Das Ganu and Narasimhaswami spent significant time together touring throughout Maharashtra to spread the name of Shirdi Sai Baba. They kept in touch after Narasimhaswami returned to Madras (now Chennai) in 1939 and founded the All India Sai Samaj, and at Narasimhaswami's invitation Das Ganu served as president of the All India Sai Devotees' Conference held at Coimbatore in 1948. In volume 2 of Narasimhaswami's four-volume *Life of Sai Baba*, he discusses the first disciples of Shirdi Sai Baba, focusing on Das Ganu in the third chapter. Narasimhaswami viewed Das Ganu as a friend and co-devotee of Sai Baba but did not accept him as his personal guru. Thus, unlike Athavale, Narasimhaswami did not set out to present Das Ganu as a religious exemplar by charting out his entire life and examining in depth his spiritual transformation and accomplishments. Instead, Narasimhaswami focused on Das Ganu's encounter with Sai Baba, seeking to relate the impact that Sai Baba had on his first devotees and to critically examine what it means to have faith in Sai Baba. Here I draw upon both sources to compile a brief biographical overview of Das Ganu, keeping in mind the differing intentions of both authors and how this affects their evaluation of Das Ganu.

Das Ganu was born Narayan Dattatreya Sahasrabuddhe on January 6, 1868, though during his youth he commonly went by the name Ganapati, given to him by his grandfather. He was born into a Chitpavan Brahmin Hindu family that traced its origins to the Ratnagiri District of the Konkan region of modern-day Maharashtra. Athavale tells us that the Sahasrabuddhe family was learned in the Rig Veda scripture and had served the esteemed Patwardhan family during the height of the *peshwa* era, a time beginning in 1714 when a series of Brahmin ministers (peshwas) ruled over parts of the Maratha Empire, while the king Shahu Bhonsle and his successors served as mere figureheads.[10] When the British East India Company formally annexed the Maratha Empire in 1818, Das Ganu's great-grandfather, Appaji Narayan Sahasrabuddhe, left his native village of Karkamb and moved to Ahmednagar District, where he attained the post of mamlatdar (the officer in charge of a *taluka*, or subdistrict in the colonial government). Athavale (1955, 3) notes that Appaji Narayan was able to successfully navigate such changing times because he did not have a "frog-in-the-well" sort of mentality. Though the onset of colonial rule officially put an end to Brahmin rule in the form of the peshwa administration, Brahmin power did not necessarily diminish in western India. Indeed, Prachi Deshpande argues that Brahmin power actually increased: "By the mid-nineteenth century, Brahmans, especially Chitpavans, outnumbered all other groups in schools and government offices not just in the Bombay Presidency but also in the Marathi districts of the Central Provinces and the administrations of the princely states of Gwalior, Baroda, Indore, and Dhar. Far from being merely a continuation of Pewshwai dominance, Brahman power was consolidated in the nineteenth century within the new institutional structures of colonialism" (2007, 82). Athavale's writing suggests that the Sahasrabuddhe family was one of the Chitpavan Brahmin families that benefited from this consolidation of Brahmin power under the auspices of the colonial government.

Appaji Narayan's fourth son, Eknath, carried on his father's position as mamlatdar after the former retired from the post to became a renouncer. Eknath excelled in this work and prospered, eventually passing the post of mamlatdar on to his second son, Janardan. Eknath's eldest son, Dattatreya, did not share his father's and brother's head for business, however; Athavale (1955, 5–6) characterizes him as being generous, honest, and pleasure loving in temperament, with a great love of music and song. Dattatreya's eldest son, Narayan/Ganapati—who would later come to be known as Das Ganu—seemingly inherited these traits from his father. Athavale describes the young Das Ganu as delighting in play with other children and pranks on family and friends. Das Ganu's formal education lagged, beginning when he was nine years old and ending when he was approximately sixteen and only in the fourth standard in an English-medium school. Athavale (1955, 15–16) writes that though Das Ganu was exceptionally intelligent, his ways remained uncultured, and he turned his innate poetic powers toward *tamasha* performance. Asha Kasbekar defines *tamasha* as a secular form of folk theater that arose during the Maratha Empire and grew increasingly vulgar in the colonial period. It incorporates many themes, including "military chiefs and kings, a merchant and his mistress, a warrior meeting a young maiden in a foreign land, two brothers quarreling over a piece of land, a henpecked husband with two wives. Mythological and historical romances abound. Like all folk plays, the *vag* [main play] concludes with the moral that truth will shine and falsehood will perish. The hilarious jokes, erotic songs or *lavanis*, provocative dances, and powerful singing and drumming constitute the main body of the play" (Kasbekar 2006, 46). Narasimhaswami characterizes Das Ganu as being "very clever in composing Lavani metre songs in Mahratti impromptu and in taking a female's part in lewd village dramas. He would put on female dress and dance about in the village and take great pleasure in that achievement" (1983, 123).

Das Ganu's marriage to his wife, Saraswati, was arranged by his family when he was twenty-three years old; yet even this did not encourage him to settle down. Das Ganu refused to hold a steady job, and he continued to delight in tamasha. Athavale records that this led to a series of quarrels between Das Ganu and his uncle Janardan, who was then the patriarch of the joint family household. Ultimately, Das Ganu left the family home and accepted employment as a constable in Shrigonda village, Ahmednagar District, under Police Superintendent Kennedy. This appointment angered Janardan, who reportedly expressed his shame that a member of the Sahasrabuddhe family, which had produced three generations of mamlatdars, would accept the low-ranking job of a constable. However, the position gave Das Ganu the independence that he seemingly desired (Athavale 1955, 18–19).

As Das Ganu worked in various villages in Ahmednagar District, he continued to take part in tamashas, and his reputation as a poet and stage performer grew. He composed poems covering a wide range of subjects, from historical events (*povadas*) to erotic stories (lavanis), and from satirical caricatures of village officials to extolling the virtues of saints. During this phase of his life, Das Ganu came into contact with Vamanshastri Islampurkar, a government official posted in Madras whom Das Ganu was assigned to aid during his official visit to Shrigonda. Das Ganu was so impressed by Islampurkar's knowledge of Sanskrit texts and his devotional mind-set that he asked to become his disciple. Islampurkar was a Brahmin who originally hailed from Osmanabad District in modern-day Maharashtra; as a Varkari who had made the pilgrimage to Pandharpur on many occasions, he was familiar with the devotional landscape of western India. Upon initiating Das Ganu as his disciple, Islampurkar reportedly gave him a Shiva mantra in acknowledgment of his family's Shaiva tradition, but he also ordered Das Ganu to make the pilgrimage to Pandharpur to pay homage to Vithoba. Athavale writes that it was after his initiation that Das Ganu first began to use the name "Das Ganu" (or alternately, Ganudas) in his poems, calling himself Ganu (short for Ganapati, his nickname), the servant (*das*) of his guru and of God. Athavale also reports that it was due to this command from his guru that Das Ganu began to undertake the annual pilgrimage to Pandharpur—reluctantly, at first, given that Vithoba was not his chosen deity, but ultimately becoming a sincere Varkari (Athavale 1955, 23–31). Das Ganu wrote in one verse in his *Bhaktasaramrita* (1925) that it was Islampurkar's grace that destroyed his "narrow bhakti," allowing him to recognize that there is no distinction between Shiva and Vishnu (Vithoba), no difference between Hari and Har (Athavale 1955, 31).

One year, not long after his initiation, Das Ganu and Islampurkar made the pilgrimage to Pandharpur together. The elderly Islampurkar then bid farewell to Das Ganu, telling him that the older man's time had come to depart for Kashi (Varanasi) to live out the remainder of his days. Das Ganu began to despair, but Islampurkar told him not to, saying: "Didn't you visit Shirdi a few times? Shri Sai Baba is a glorious being. Accept him as my form. The two of us are one. Henceforth he will guide you from time to time" (Athavale 1955, 31–32). Das Ganu had first visited Shirdi in approximately 1896 in his official capacity as constable, under the deputy collector Nana Saheb Chandorkar.[11] Chandorkar was very fond of tamasha and as such came to befriend Das Ganu. Chandorkar was also a disciple of Sai Baba and therefore visited Shirdi two or three times each month as he made his official rounds from village to village. Athavale (1955, 54–55) reports that Das Ganu had little respect for Sai Baba initially, but with repeat visits at the behest of Chandorkar his faith grew, to the extent that he famously proclaimed (as in Hymn no. 3), "Shirdi is my Pandharpur, and Sai Baba is Vithoba." Narasimhaswami includes a similar account: "When first he came to Shirdi, he came as the 'orderly' of (i.e. constable attending on) Nana Saheb Chandorkar, and whenever Chandorkar visited Shirdi, Ganpat Rao followed him as his Constable, not at all out of faith in, or love for, Sai, but because the master compelled him to. . . . For a very long time, Das Ganu could not appreciate Baba" (1983, 122).

Sai Baba apparently recognized Das Ganu's poetic sensibilities and encouraged him to focus on composing devotional poems. On one early visit, Sai Baba said to Chandorkar: "Invite all the saints to a meal. Make sure the arrangements are perfect and give our Ganu the task of calling all the guests. He will bring all of them. Do this, Ganu, it will benefit you." Athavale explains that the deeper meaning of this cryptic statement was that Das Ganu should compose the lives of the saints in the Marathi *ovi* metre, just as the eighteenth century poet-saint Mahipati had done. So, under the auspices of Sai Baba, Das Ganu began composing poems about the prominent saints of Maharashtra, including Sai Baba among their ranks. Athavale comments approvingly, "Thus, the stream of Shri Das Ganu's poetry gave up its turbulent flow in the seas and ravines of erotic lavani poetry, and moved to the still plains of bhakti" (1955, 55).

Sai Baba also encouraged Das Ganu to give up his profession in order to focus on his religious quest. Narasimhaswami (1983, 123–27; 1954, 180–81) writes that Das Ganu was weaned from tamasha theater with great difficulty; however, weaning him from his career in the police service proved even more challenging. Das Ganu pleaded with Sai Baba to allow him to be promoted to the level of subinspector before retiring from service, as he had already passed the departmental examination. Sai Baba reportedly replied that he would personally see to it that Das Ganu did not receive the promotion and that he would present him with innumerable difficulties to pressure him to resign. Some of these difficulties included facing the scheming of his jealous fellow constables, a near-death experience with a bandit, and a professional accounting entanglement. In 1903, after receiving repeat urgings each time he was in Shirdi, Das Ganu resigned from the police service.

Narasimhaswami (1983, 123) explains that Sai Baba insisted that Das Ganu resign because the police service was a corrupt colonial institution and would therefore hinder his spiritual progress: "For one who was ambitious to rise in it [the colonial police force], one's regard for truth, righteousness, fair dealing, etc. would practically be nil, and scruples, conscience, and character were unwanted hindrances to efficiency." Athavale sheds further light on this negative assessment of Das Ganu's profession, writing that even though Das Ganu worked as a police constable for the colonial government, he was an exception in that he remained a patriot and a public servant. During the devastating Bombay bubonic plague of 1896–97, for instance, the colonial police force brutally evacuated residents, pulled down shanty housing, and burned piles of contaminated clothing and possessions as part of their anti-plague measures. Athavale writes: "The government's measures against the plague were a thousand times more troublesome to the people than the scourge itself, but there was no way to utter a squeak against them.

It was as though the ember of anger that burned day and night in the hearts of the people took the form of the Chapekar brothers, and they seized Rand as a sacrificial offering.[12] During this tumult, Shri Das Ganu received accounts of the plague administration. Risking the anger of his superior officers, he tried to ease the situation for as many people under his jurisdiction as he could. . . . Although Shri Das Ganu belonged to the police cadre, the constitution of his mind was entirely different" (1955, 59–61).

Both biographers also emphasize Das Ganu's patriotism in his early poetry as well as his profession, noting that prior to 1903, Das Ganu had composed not only erotic poems for the tamashas that he took part in but also anticolonial, pronationalist songs of the *rashtriya kirtan* genre.[13] Most notable on the nationalist front were his verses praising the seventeenth-century Maratha king Shivaji, which he sang at the annual Ganapati festival in Maharashtra in 1898. The nationalist politician "Lokamanya" Bal Gangadhar Tilak (1856–1920) had first used the annual Ganapati Chaturthi Hindu festival as a setting for nationalist agitation in 1893. Tilak recognized that while the British often suppressed political meetings, they were more hesitant about interfering with religious meetings and festivals, and he therefore sought to use the festival to call upon Hindus of all castes and classes in western India to unite under the god Ganapati in the quest for self-rule. In 1895, Tilak began a similar process with the historical king Shivaji, organizing a Shivaji festival and seeking to promote the king as another figure that all the castes and classes of western India could unite behind in the cause for Indian independence.[14] Narasimhaswami describes the sticky situation Das Ganu found himself in—as a police officer employed in the colonial British service—for participating in the Ganapati festival and singing nationalist verses about Shivaji:

> As verses on Sivaji rouse up patriotism and the National spirit, which the
> foreign rulers then in power dreaded, he [Das Ganu] was called on by his
> Inspector to explain how he, a Government servant, took this prominent part
> in helping on a national movement. His answer was that he was an *Asukavi*
> [one who versifies impromptu], that verses in Lavani metre flowed out of him
> at the barest request of anybody and that the request of some one made him
> sing impromptu the song or verses on Sivaji. As a proof he offered to compose
> impromptu verses on the officer himself at once. The officer wished to test the
> truth of the statement and asked him for verses on himself (the officer). Ganu's
> *Asukavitva* or poetic genius was equal to the occasion. At once, he sang up the

high qualities (real or fancied) of the officer, in lavani metre and in a few
minutes there were numerous verses on the excellences of the officer who
was greatly pleased and dropped the charge against Ganu then known merely
by his police No (e.g. 808). (Narasimhaswami 1983, 147)[15]

After resigning from the police force in 1903, Das Ganu spent the next
couple of years in Shirdi. Athavale (1955, 74) characterizes this period as Das
Ganu's transition into full-fledged bhakti, the sort not pursued for common,
worldly ends: "While living in Shirdi, the company of Shri Sainath [Sai Baba]
had a profound impact on Shri Das Ganu's inner being. His various past
experiences had caused his inherently pure self to turn toward God, but he
was now single-minded in his pursuit." At the advice of Sai Baba, Das Ganu
then moved to Nanded with his wife, where he put his faith in Sai Baba to
provide for their daily provisions, since he would no longer be earning a
steady professional income. Sai Baba also encouraged Das Ganu to pursue
the spiritual path from within his own religious tradition, prescribing the
study of sacred Hindu scripture. Thus, from 1903 to 1918, Das Ganu routinely traveled between Shirdi and Nanded while pursuing the study of
Marathi and Sanskrit scripture, including the *Amritanubhava*, by the
Marathi poet-saint Jnaneshwar, and the Isha Upanishad, which he translated into Marathi from Sanskrit.

In the years after Shirdi Sai Baba's death in 1918, until his own death in
1962, Das Ganu lived as an itinerant kirtankar, visiting cities throughout the
Bombay Presidency as he performed kirtans. Das Ganu followed a regular
pattern from year to year, returning to Shirdi annually to organize the Ram
Navami festival held during the month of Chaitra (March/April), after
which he would stay for a couple of months. Next he would go to Pune,
arriving in time to see the palanquin of Saint Jnaneshwar as it came through
town from Alandi on its way to Pandharpur for the Varkari pilgrimage
(June). By the start of Shravan (mid-July), he would move on to Nanded,
spending several months there. Finally, he would travel to Pandharpur for
Dasara (early to mid-October), staying there for approximately four months,
until Makarasankranti (mid-January). Das Ganu would perform his kirtans
at temples and in homes in each of these places, always surrounded by a
crowd (Athavale 1955, 204–8). He would also make excursions to stay with
acquaintances in other cities, such as Bombay, when invited to perform.

Both Athavale and Narasimhaswami credit Das Ganu's kirtans with
spreading the name of Shirdi Sai Baba throughout the Bombay Presidency,

for Das Ganu always included kirtans about Sai Baba in his mix of song-sermons about Hindu gods and Maharashtrian saints. Athavale writes: "Shri Sai Baba's popularity as an extraordinary being in the province of Bombay and indeed, in all of India, can be traced to Shri Das Ganu Maharaj. His melodious kirtans made the masses aware of Shri Sai Baba's saintliness" (1955, 116). Narasimhaswami goes into much greater detail about Das Ganu's role in spreading devotion to Sai Baba. When he interviewed devotees in the 1930s for his three-volume work *Devotees' Experiences of Sri Sai Baba*, Narasimhaswami learned that a great many of them were initially drawn to Sai Baba after hearing one of Das Ganu's kirtans. For instance, the renouncer Narayan Asram recalled that he first learned of Shirdi Sai Baba in 1910, when he was working in Bombay in the Customs Department and heard Das Ganu singing a moving kirtan about Sai Baba: "I asked him 'Is Sai Baba living?' He said 'Yes, at Shirdi.' In five days of that I went to Shirdi and saw Sai Baba. In six months thereafter, I paid Baba nine visits. I often went to him in later years also" (Narasimhaswami 2008, 63). Similarly, W. Pradhan and his family learned of Sai Baba in 1910 through Nana Saheb Chandorkar, but questioned whether he was a genuine saint. After Pradhan's brother made the pilgrimage to Shirdi, he returned with a picture of Sai Baba and a pamphlet describing Sai Baba's miracles composed by Das Ganu (chapter 31 of his *Bhaktalilamrita*). The power of this poetic composition dispelled Pradhan's doubt as he read the verses aloud to his wife: "The effect was deep and electric. All the doubt that I had expressed to my mother vanished. I was converted. From that moment I got a firm belief that Baba was a true and great saint if ever there was one. My wife's faith was even greater" (Narasimhaswami 2008, 98).

Narasimhaswami (1983, 122) believed that Sai Baba had pulled Das Ganu to Shirdi for two purposes: "Baba drew him to himself for the double purpose of improving his (Ganu's) own spiritual condition and thereafter rendering signal service to the public for the spread of Sai faith." Narasimhaswami credits Das Ganu's kirtans with contributing substantially to the rising tide of pilgrims arriving in Shirdi during the final fifteen years of Sai Baba's life and continuing in the first decades after his passing. Narasimhaswami had also witnessed Das Ganu's impact firsthand when he toured with Das Ganu throughout Maharashtra in the late 1930s, holding lectures (led by Narasimhaswami) and kirtan sessions (led by Das Ganu) to spread devotion to Sai Baba. He describes how people reacted to Das Ganu's performances:

Das Ganu was specially good at kirtans. He had a fine metallic voice, and he was a very able performer of kirtans. He would hold an audience of 2,000 people spell-bound in rapt attention listening to him for six or eight hours, and as he never asked for even one pie [cent] and made no collections, his kirtans were popular, and in all his kirtans, he would place Baba's picture next to him and even though his katha [story] was about Tukaram or Namdev or Jnanadev, yet he would always refer to Sai Baba as the living Sant [Saint] or Satpurusha, i.e. as the present Great Saint, whom it would be a great blessing for people to have darsan [darshan] of, as the very darsan would purify and benefit the visitor. As soon as his kirtans ended, people started in numbers to go to Shirdi and see Sai Baba. These numbers included high officials of good and great position, as also the poor. Thus he has been the means of sending some tens of thousands of people to Baba. (Narasimhaswami 1983, 128)[16]

Despite their differing intentions and overall evaluations of Das Ganu, both of his biographers agree that Das Ganu deserves credit for spreading devotion to Shirdi Sai Baba throughout western India and that his public kirtan performances were the means by which he accomplished this.

SINGING FOR GOD, REGION, AND NATION

The circa thirteenth-century Varkari poet-saints Jnaneshwar and Namdev are the first documented kirtankars of Maharashtra. Anna Schultz (2013, 25–26) describes these medieval kirtan performances as "venues for spiritual teaching and generating collective, ecstatic devotional experiences," emphasizing that such performances were understood not as entertainment, nor even as a vehicle for preaching about bhakti, but as bhakti itself. Arising out of this *varkari kirtan* tradition in the eighteenth century, under the peshwa regime, came a new genre of kirtan performance known as *naradiya kirtan*. As opposed to its parent, naradiya kirtan is more oriented toward solo performance, entails a more eclectic mix of songs and themes (incorporating songs about pan-Hindu gods and goddesses and about historical figures like Shivaji, in addition to the more traditional songs about Marathi gods and saints), and includes a narrative philosophical discourse as well as the telling of entertaining stories about the deeds of saints and deities (Schultz 2013, 24–25). Such performances are typically theatrical and interactive, often combining singing and storytelling with music, dance, theatrical flourishes, and call and response with the audience (Novetzke

2008, 81). Schultz (2013) describes in detail how Marathi kirtans became more politicized in the late nineteenth and early twentieth centuries as some naradiya kirtankars turned toward nationalist figures and topics, resulting in the creation of a new subtype of naradiya kirtan known as rashtriya kirtan.

It is in this context that Das Ganu arose as a kirtankar, and his oeuvre incorporates devotional kirtans of the more traditional naradiya kirtan genre, focused on Vithoba and the Varkari saints as well as on pan-Hindu gods and goddesses, but also includes rashtriya kirtans about regional and national historical heroes. In his discussion of Marathi kirtans, Christian Novetzke notes that the "aesthetic of presentation, and the musical mastery of a performer, are of central importance to the success of a *kirtan*" (2008, 82). Given Das Ganu's earlier passion for the theater, one can imagine that he was well suited to becoming a kirtankar, following his growing interest in bhakti devotion, as he was already used to interacting with and entertaining an audience through his composition of lavani and povada poems in combination with his stage acting. As Das Ganu roamed from one city to the next, performing his kirtans, his reputation grew, as did his repertoire of poems, stories, and songs about the many saints of Maharashtra.

In addition to hundreds of kirtans, Das Ganu's multivolume *Samagra Vanmaya* includes his lengthier Marathi prose writings about an array of saints, gods, and historical figures of regional and national significance. Das Ganu's biographers highlight that he was not well educated, and they proclaim that his ability to compose such a vast corpus of devotional literature, and especially to render a complex Sanskrit text into Marathi, are miracles wrought by the grace of Sai Baba. Narasimhaswami (1983, 129), for instance, notes that Sai Baba guided Das Ganu in his studies, writing that although Das Ganu was not a formally educated scholar of Hindu scripture, "Baba gave him a special capacity to understand things which others could not ordinarily understand."

An example of such inspired guidance is related in chapter 20 of the *Shri Sai Satcharita*, composed by Govind Rao Dabholkar (discussed in chapter 1). When Das Ganu was working on his Marathi translation of and commentary on the Isha Upanishad, it seems that he doubted whether he had truly grasped the full meaning of this brief but profound scripture. Dabholkar notes that Das Ganu's knowledge of Sanskrit was "inadequate" to the task at hand (Dabholkar 2007, 326). According to Athavale (1955, 125), the phrase "enjoy by renouncing" especially vexed him. Recognizing his inadequacy,

Das Ganu bowed before Sai Baba and shared his concerns. Sai Baba blessed him, saying: "And pray, what is so difficult in all this? As you return to the place from where you came, that maid-servant of Kaka's will most surely resolve your doubt!" (Dabholkar 2007, 328). Hari Sitaram Dikshit, also known as Kaka Saheb or Uncle, was a devotee who lived in the Vile Parle suburb of Bombay. Das Ganu and the others present were puzzled by the suggestion that a maidservant could explain the meaning of the Isha Upanishad, for how could a woman, and a low-caste one at that, have such wisdom? But Das Ganu did return to Bombay shortly after this proclamation, and he stayed at Kaka Saheb Dikshit's house. In the morning, Das Ganu heard the somber but melodious singsong of the maidservant. She was just eight years old, a scrawny girl dressed in a torn rag of a sari, and sang verse after verse about desiring a splendid golden-bordered silk sari. Out of compassion, Das Ganu purchased a new sari and gave it to the girl. She received it with joy and wore it the next day. But the day after that, she reappeared in her former torn sari, having stowed away the new one. Das Ganu noted that though she appeared as impoverished as before, there was no longer any sorrow in her singsong, for she no longer wore torn rags out of poverty and helplessness, but by choice (Dabholkar 2007, 329–32).

This incident sparked a revelation for Das Ganu about the meaning of the Isha Upanishad: bliss lies in finding God within, not in the externals. Narasimhaswami elaborates: "The girl's happiness lay not in the external sari . . . but in herself. And Isavasya [Isha] Upanishad says the same thing. 'All this world,' says the first verse, is covered by the Maya [illusion] of Iswara [God]. So enjoy bliss, not by having the externals, but by rejecting the externals" (1983, 130–31). Athavale explains it in these words: "When Shri Das Ganu saw this scene, the deep meaning of the phrase 'enjoy by renunciation' flashed upon his inborn poetic talent and he was filled with indescribable joy. God is all-pervading and none can live separate from him, so all objects in the universe are mine. I am their owner. When this feeling becomes awakened, the presence of the object is not necessary. Because of the experience of all-pervasiveness, one can enjoy objects without possessing them" (1955, 126–27). According to Dabholkar (2007, 333), this incident also sparked a revelation for Das Ganu about the significance of Shirdi Sai Baba, for the sudden realization that "God dwelt even in that poor little maid-servant" helped him to understand on an intimate and experiential level the abstract monistic philosophical doctrine not only propounded in the Isha Upanishad but also taught by Sai Baba.

It is important to note in response to these biographical depictions of Das Ganu that although his formal education ended when he was approximately sixteen years old, and he only completed the fourth standard in an English-medium school, Das Ganu did receive the instruction in Sanskrit language and literature that was standard for Brahmin boys in his time, and he was well educated in the Marathi vernacular. Thus, while Das Ganu had no advanced training in English language and literature (unlike many high-caste members of the Indian nationalist elite at this time), he was far from the "illiterate" that these sources suggest. Like Jnaneshwar and other medieval Marathi kirtankars before him, Das Ganu had exactly the sort of "literacy" that mattered to become an acclaimed kirtankar: knowledge of the lives of the saints, the skill to compose poems about them in Marathi, and the ability to perform those poems before an audience.[17]

In the first decades of the twentieth century, Marathi kirtan was patronized by Bal Gangadhar Tilak, who sought to bring this genre of performance to "modern, educated" Indians seeking national sovereignty, and he encouraged kirtankars to turn toward nationalist topics. In tandem with this promotion of kirtans, some kirtankars began to utilize printing-press technology to publish Marathi *kirtan akhyans*, or song collections, and Marathi books containing both song texts and prose narratives (Schultz 2013, 34–35). Das Ganu initially kept a *bada*, a simple notebook to record songs and make notes on his performances. Later, his disciple and eventual biographer, Damodar Athavale, wrote down Das Ganu's poems and prose compositions for him, acting as his devoted secretary. Significantly, some of Das Ganu's songs and prose narratives were published in pamphlet form—including three chapters about Shirdi Sai Baba from his *Bhaktalilamrita* (chapters 31–33). These were published in 1906 as pamphlets and sold in Shirdi even before the *Shri Sai Satcharita*, which Dabholkar began writing in Marathi in 1916 but which was not published until 1929. Ultimately, Athavale collected all of Das Ganu's notebooks and used them to compile the multivolume *Samagra Vanmaya*.

Naradiya kirtan (including rashtriya kirtan) in Das Ganu's time was not only influenced by the nationalist anticolonial movement but also by interrelated debates about religious reform and revival that began taking place in the late nineteenth century. Generally speaking, kirtankars were Brahmin men who were well versed in Sanskrit literature and Hindu tradition. Anna Schultz notes that taken as a whole, rashtriya kirtankars generally promoted conservative values in that they "supported and politicized socioreligious issues like cow protection, the caste system, and Brahmanism. By detailing the scriptural basis for these customs, rashtriya kirtankars positioned themselves at the zenith of a caste and religious hierarchy, and they argued that the British, as outsiders, were unable to protect these systems" (2013, 43). She cites as an example the resolutions passed by the 1918 and 1919 meetings of the All-India Kirtan Sammelan (Conference), noting that the third of five resolutions passed in both years advocated a stance on caste: "As might be expected from a community of conservative Brahmans, they proposed that kirtankars should act according to *varnashramadharma*, that is, upholding one's caste duties and maintaining the caste system" (47).

By the late nineteenth century, a very active movement had arisen among the lower castes of western India, protesting Brahminical dominance and challenging Brahminical religious values. Perhaps the most influential leader of the non-Brahmin movement during the nineteenth century was "Mahatma" Jotirao Govindrao Phule (1827–90), a Shudra born into the Mali (gardening) caste who fought oppression of the Shudras and Adi-Shudras (Dalits) by the upper castes. He authored numerous Marathi works—most notably *A Ballad of the Raja Chatrapati Shivaji Bhosale* (1869), *Priestcraft Exposed* (1869), and *Gulamgiri* (Slavery) (1873)—in which he set forth an alternative history that portrayed Shudras and Dalits as the displaced and deprived descendants of the Kshatriya warriors of pre-Aryan India, and Brahmins as the descendants of invading Aryan conquerors who used religious trickery to enslave the indigenous majority. Infused in all of these works was a call to non-Brahmins to unite and rise up in the quest for emancipation from "Brahminical slavery." In 1873, Phule formed the Satyashodhak Samaj, or Truth-Seeking Society, in an attempt to persuade both non-Brahmins and colonial British officers of the evils of orthodox Brahminical religion.[18] By the turn of the twentieth century, anti-Brahminism surged in western India even as a distinctively Dalit identity arose that questioned the unity of Shudras and Adi-Shudras. As Dalit politicization increased in the early twentieth century, Mahars and other Dalits sought access to temples, schools, and water tanks, all places typically under Brahminical oversight and from which Dalits alone (not Shudras) were excluded.[19] In the 1920s–1930s, Dr. Bhimrao Ramji Ambedkar (1891–1956) ascended as a Mahar spokesperson and politician who argued that Dalits were not Hindus but had long suffered under Brahminical Hindu socioreligious discrimination and therefore deserved enfranchisement in India as a minority group with protected democratic rights.[20]

Das Ganu was keenly aware of both the active movement against Brahminical dominance and religious values and the conservative Brahmin defense of their caste position and hierarchy. It was in this context of heated public debate about caste that he performed his kirtans before audiences composed of Brahmins and non-Brahmins alike, encouraging all present to direct their devotion to Shirdi Sai Baba. Das Ganu articulated a position of reform—neither a radical rejection of the caste system outright, nor a conservative defense of the caste status quo. To do so, he relied on the strategy of "the Brahmin double," pitting "bad Brahmins" against "good Brahmins" in his performances and writings in order to criticize Brahminical practices surrounding caste superiority without going so far as to denounce all Brahmins or the caste system in its entirety. Focusing on the literary-performative field of bhakti devotionalism, Christian Novetzke provides several examples of this strategy in the precolonial period from the thirteenth, sixteenth, seventeenth, and late eighteenth centuries. He argues that the Brahmin double was utilized during these times because they were eras of "vernacularization," when Brahmins employed this dual mode of critique and protection in order to reorganize caste status to align with the political power exercised by a dominant non-Brahmin caste conglomeration (Novetzke 2011, 247). He suggests that this legacy of caste critique enunciated by Brahmin intellectuals and public figures in precolonial Maharashtra was then magnified in the colonial context.

Das Ganu's poetic and prose compositions—and his interpretation of Shirdi Sai Baba found therein—must be considered in this colonial context. In addition to his hundreds of kirtan song-poems and his Marathi translation of the Isha Upanishad, Das Ganu also composed three lengthier devotional works in Marathi, which have been compiled in his *Samagra Vanmaya*: the *Santakathamrita*, the *Bhaktalilamrita*, and the *Bhaktasaramrita*.[21] In the *Santakathamrita*, Das Ganu relates stories of and teachings given by a wide array of saints. The vast majority are Marathi saints, including medieval Maharashtrian saints such as Namdev, Janabai, Eknath, and Gunda Maharaj; as well as many contemporary Maharashtrian saints, including Tukaram Maharaj of Yehalegaon, Ramachandra Maharaj of Shevand, Chinmayanand of Umarkhed, and Vasudevanand Saraswati. Also included are a handful of cross-sectarian saints from the medieval and modern eras, such as Guru Gobind Singh and Ramakrishna Paramahansa. Das Ganu dedicates chapter 57 of this work to Shirdi Sai Baba, and in this chapter he recounts a lecture given by Sai Baba on the nondual nature of ultimate reality.

In the *Bhaktalilamrita*, Das Ganu was inspired by the biography of saints from thirteenth- to seventeenth-century Maharashtra, written by the Marathi poet Mahipati. Envisioning himself as continuing this work, Das Ganu recounts the major miracles, or *lilas*, associated with several dozen saints, all of whom lived in eighteenth- and nineteenth-century Maharashtra. Here, in chapters 31–33, Das Ganu includes several of the miracles associated with Shirdi Sai Baba and provides a discourse on the proper path to attaining salvation. Das Ganu continues his collection of stories of the Maharashtrian saints in the *Bhaktasaramrita*. In this work, he incorporates some additional Marathi saints and expands on his stories of those saints featured in his earlier works. He focuses on Shirdi Sai Baba in three chapters, discussing his parentage and religious training in chapter 26, his arrival in Shirdi in chapter 52, and the lessons he gave in Shirdi to several of his devotees in chapter 53.

While caste concerns play a role in all three of these devotional works, it is in the *Bhaktasaramrita* that Das Ganu features his most detailed interpretation of Shirdi Sai Baba's life and message, as well as his most extensive discussion of caste. The next section examines the *Bhaktasaramrita* in detail. Because many of the stories that Das Ganu tells about Sai Baba's life and teachings are related in other sources composed by other devotees, we can usefully compare Das Ganu's tellings with these others to draw out his unique interpretation of Shirdi Sai Baba and his plea to Brahmins and non-Brahmins regarding caste reform.

LIKE MANY SPECIES OF FLOWERS IN A GARDEN

In chapter 26 of the *Bhaktasaramrita*, Das Ganu maintains that Shirdi Sai Baba was born in the village of Manwath to Muslim parents.[22] His father was a *fakir* (Muslim holy man) who passed away when Sai Baba was just a young boy. On his deathbed, the fakir told his wife to take the boy to Selu village. She did, appearing dressed in rags to seek refuge at the feet of Gopalrao Deshmukh. Gopalrao was a Brahmin landowner who had gained some fame in the region for his generosity and single-minded devotion to God. Das Ganu writes that when Gopalrao first settled in Selu, the villagers asked him for refuge and he promised to protect the Brahmins, weavers, blacksmiths, goldsmiths, carpenters, and all the eighteen castes there (verse 44). Das Ganu characterizes most *zamindars*, or landlords, of the day as high-handed and unprincipled brigands who indulged in lavish expenditure, had many wives and concubines in their harems, and were arrogant monsters of vice and sin (verses 49–51). Gopalrao, however, was kind and merciful to all. To demonstrate just how different Gopalrao was from other landlords, Das Ganu relates the following story: Once, Gopalrao was overtaken by lust at the sight of a beautiful young Shudra woman. Aghast at this sin of lusting after another's wife (and a low-caste woman, at that), he immediately went into his puja room. There, seated before an image of the god Venkatesha, he took a needle and blinded himself in both eyes, begging God to help him focus his senses upon God in his quest for salvation from the cycle of rebirth and redeath.

When Sai Baba arrived in Selu with his mother, Gopalrao offered them shelter in his home, saying that he had been waiting for Kabir's mother to bring Kabir (verse 161). Das Ganu states that Gopalrao was the fifteenth-century saint Ramananda of Kashi reborn, and Sai Baba was his disciple Kabir reborn, both with the purpose of uplifting humanity in a dark time (verses 15, 133–35, 176, 205). Gopalrao then raised Sai Baba, spending long hours with him in meditation in the forest. Gopalrao's relatives were dismayed by this, and their displeasure is phrased in terms of caste and community. They exclaim that Gopalrao is a Brahmin, whereas Sai Baba is a "Yavana" (a Sanskrit term that in this context means Muslim); Gopalrao is like the holy Godavari River, while Sai Baba is but a shallow pond (verse 173). They cannot understand why Gopalrao casts favor upon this Muslim urchin instead of one of their own Brahmin sons. So, in a jealous rage, they decide to kill the boy. They follow them into the forest and throw stones at Sai Baba when he is seated in meditation. Gopalrao saves the boy by taking the blows upon his own head. Before dying, he gives instructions for his *samadhi* (burial) site and gives Sai Baba some final advice. Handing over his head cloth, he tells the boy that he is passing on his entire wealth to him. He instructs him to leave Selu, to remember that he is Kabir incarnate, to remain celibate, and to always remember that the world and God are one. He makes milk flow from a barren cow and then tells the boy to drink it.[23] Sai Baba does so, after bowing at Gopalrao's feet, and then he attains God-realization: wherever he looked, everything appeared as God (verse 204). At the conclusion of this chapter, Das Ganu states that this boy—who was heretofore unnamed—was Sai Baba of Shirdi (verse 232).

In this chapter, Das Ganu makes several unique moves in recounting the early biography of Shirdi Sai Baba. First is his claim that Sai Baba was born to Muslim parents, which is contrary to B. V. Narasimhaswami, who insisted that Sai Baba was born to Hindu Brahmin parents—though he similarly viewed Sai Baba as a composite figure for his study with both a Muslim fakir and a Hindu guru (see chapter 3).[24] Second, Das Ganu claims that Sai Baba is the reincarnation of Kabir, the medieval northern Indian bhakti poet-saint who is often remembered as a spokesperson for Hindu-Muslim unity in India today; but who is more accurately described as rejecting both orthodox Hinduism and Islam in his poetry in favor of an inward-focused devotion on the one, unnamed God (Hawley and Juergens-meyer 1988, 40–41). Third, in addition to the more common discussion of the influence of Hinduism and Islam on Sai Baba, Das Ganu brings caste issues to the forefront by depicting Sai Baba's guru, Gopalrao, as a good Brahmin. In this narrative, Gopalrao is praised as a merciful landlord, the kind who gives refuge to the destitute, no matter their caste, creed, or gender. Gopalrao is characterized as the opposite of other Brahmin landowners, who are condemned as greedy, lustful, and lacking in true faith. He is also characterized as the opposite of other Brahmins in the form of Gopalrao's own family members, who are condemned as murderous bigots. Though Gopalrao dies at the hands of such bad Brahmins, he is nonetheless successful in transmitting his teachings to his chosen disciple, Sai Baba. Here, Das Ganu sets the stage for a repeated theme of good Brahmins being pitted against bad Brahmins in his discussion of Sai Baba's life and teachings.

In chapter 52, Das Ganu picks up his biography of Sai Baba with his arrival in Shirdi. Wandering from Selu at his guru's order, Sai Baba went to a forest near Daulatabad to meditate. There, a Muslim named Chandbhai, who was frantically looking for his runaway horse, happened upon him. Sai Baba helped him find his horse, while also offering a short lesson on the insignificance of such mundane concerns in the overall scheme of things. Grateful, if a bit overwhelmed, Chandbhai invited Sai Baba to his house. On Sai Baba's arrival the next day, both Hindus and Muslims came for his darshan. Das Ganu tells us that the Muslims called him a great Awliya (Sufi saint), and the Hindus called him Sainath (Lord Sai); both had faith in Sai Baba (verses 58–59). Chandbhai happened to be leaving for Shirdi to attend the wedding of his wife's sister, so Sai Baba came along with the wedding procession. Once in Shirdi, Sai Baba attempted to enter the Hindu temple to the god Khandoba, but its resident Brahmin priest, named Marthand Mhalsapathy, forbade him entry and told him to go to the mosque.

This is an oft-retold story, with most versions claiming that the priest Mhalsapathy forbade Sai Baba entry, saying that Muslims must go to the mosque; but soon thereafter he became one of Sai Baba's first devotees, after realizing him to be a genuine holy man.[25] In his telling, Das Ganu retains this conversion narrative but also inserts a short sermon about the ultimate immateriality of caste and communal differences. Sai Baba tells Mhalsapathy that there is only one God, who is the same for both Hindus and Muslims. While each community should attend to their own customs, they should see God in everything. The one that the Muslims call Allah is the same as the one that Hindus call Vishnu, and Mhalsapathy's god Khandoba is also the same (verses 67–70). Also, Sai Baba reminds Mhalsapathy, his own god Khandoba was incarnated as a Bania, an upper-caste merchant, and married the low-caste shepherdess Banoo (verses 71–72). According to Gunther Sontheimer (1996), Khandoba, a local form of the god Shiva, had five wives. Two of these wives are most important in folk stories and in ritual worship: Mhalsa and Banoo (also known as Banai and as Banubai). Mhalsa came from a respectable, high-caste (Lingayat Vani) family and had an arranged marriage with Khandoba, while Banoo came from a low-caste shepherding (Dhangar) family and had a less socially respectable love marriage with Khandoba.[26] Thus, Sai Baba's point here, as Das Ganu recounts this incident, is that the god Khandoba himself was not particularly concerned with caste differences—so why should his devotee be?

Furthermore, Sai Baba continues in his sermon to Mhalsapathy, take the example of Chokhamela, the fourteenth-century Mahar (Dalit) poet-saint, who was more dear to Vithoba than the Brahmin priests, thus demonstrating that purity of heart is what matters (verses 75–76). Here Sai Baba refers to a popular Marathi legend about Chokhamela, in which Chokhamela had been denied entry into Vithoba's temple in Pandharpur due to his identity as an "Untouchable" Dalit. As he sat, dejected, on the bank of the Bhima River, Vithoba miraculously appeared before him. Chokhamela bowed happily and offered him some of his yogurt. But a Brahmin priest who overheard Chokhamela addressing his companion as Vithoba—thus seeming to profane God's name—slapped this companion on the face. Upon returning to the temple, however, the priest realized his mistake, for he saw that the temple image of Vithoba now had a reddened cheek from the blow and yogurt spilled on his robe.[27] At the conclusion of Sai Baba's short sermon, Mhalsapathy realized his spiritual superior in Sai Baba and fell prostrate at his feet, asking him to dwell in Shirdi permanently (verse 78). Here, in Das Ganu's telling, Mhalsapathy begins the narrative as a bad Brahmin, one mired in orthodox caste and communal exclusions, but ultimately transforms into a good Brahmin through Sai Baba's intervention, one able to see beyond caste and creed to recognize the spark of divinity within everyone.

As Das Ganu turns to the story of the Brahmin saint Vasudevanand Saraswati (commonly known as Shri Tembe Swami), he grows autobiographical. He recounts that the swami was meditating on the banks of the Godavari River near Rajahmundry, when Das Ganu and some friends approached him for darshan. As they bowed before him, the swami asked them about their travels. Upon learning that Das Ganu planned to return to Shirdi, the swami handed him a coconut and instructed him to present it to Sai Baba on his behalf. But when Das Ganu and his friends were en route, they ate the coconut, forgetting that it was a sacred offering. When they reached Shirdi and stood before Sai Baba, he asked for his coconut and then chastised them for breaking their promise. Awed and apologetic, they were ultimately reassured by Sai Baba, who told them that he could not remain angry with his children. Thus, on the surface, this tale seems intended to demonstrate Sai Baba's omniscience and paternal love for those who have faith in him—and indeed, that is how this story is presented by Dabholkar in chapter 51 of the *Shri Sai Satcharita* (verses 125–83). But Das Ganu uses this story to again think through issues of caste and community. When the swami learns that Das Ganu and his friends plan to visit Shirdi, he exclaims that although he is a Brahmin by caste, and Sai Baba is a Muslim, Sai Baba is his elder brother (verses 174–75). The swami elaborates, explaining that the caste distinction between Hindu and Muslim (Yavana) is superficial, only the outer covering of the same essence that abides within all (verses 176–78). In the *Shri Sai Satcharita*, by contrast, although the swami does declare that Sai Baba is his "brother," there is no didactic discussion of caste or community; rather, emphasis is on the ability of saints residing in different places to communicate with one another, mind to mind, as spiritual kindred for the guidance of their devotees (Dabholkar 2007, 847). Here, in Das Ganu's telling, although no explicit bad Brahmin acts as the foil of Vasudevanand Saraswati, the swami nonetheless is as an example of what a good Brahmin is like, counterposed to the bad Brahmins encountered in the earlier stories and to Brahminical Hinduism at large.

In chapter 53, Das Ganu presents his most extensive discourse on caste and community relations. He begins with the discovery of a *gurusthan* (literally, the seat of a guru) at the foot of the tree under which Sai Baba meditated and lived during his first years in Shirdi. This famous story is also related by Dabholkar in chapter 4 of the *Shri Sai Satcharita*, where the villagers are curious to know more about the mysterious young renouncer stationed under the tree, and the god Khandoba tells them to grab their pickaxes and strike the ground under the tree if they want answers to their questions. They do so and uncover to their amazement an underground meditation chamber with a wooden seat at its center and perpetual lamps burning. Khandoba tells them that Sai Baba, then approximately only sixteen years old, undertook penance for twelve years in this spot. But Sai Baba states that it is his guru's seat and should be preserved. The author, Dabholkar, expresses confusion, but attributes it to Sai Baba's playful mischief. Then, on Sai Baba's orders, the meditation chamber is sealed back up and becomes known as the samadhi (tomb) of Sai Baba's guru (Dabholkar 2007, 66–67). In Das Ganu's account, however, there is no mention of Khandoba; rather, Sai Baba himself tells the villagers to dig up the "tomb" under the tree. We are told that the villagers bickered among themselves, debating whether or not to dig, for some feared the consequences of digging in—and possibly defiling and being defiled by—an area that might be a Muslim burial ground. Sai Baba chides the bickering villagers, telling them that they should have faith in following the bhakti path, not enter into debates. Furthermore, the whole earth is a burial ground, he states, for all creatures arise from and return to the earth's soil. This metaphor of the earth as the common source of all varieties of creation is what binds together the many stories in Das Ganu's chapter.

Das Ganu then turns to Kabir, recounting the famous story of the debate that arose among the saint's Hindu and Muslim followers when he died. The Hindus wanted to cremate his body, while the Muslims wanted to bury it, each according to their tradition. Miraculously, his corpse transformed into a pile of assorted flowers, allowing each community to do as they wished with their share of the flowers. Hawley and Juergensmeyer note that this story "serves as a prime example of the way people fail to hear the prophet's message that God is one" (1988, 39). Das Ganu, however, has a different spin: he notes that while the Hindus threw their flowers into the holy Ganges River, the Muslims placed theirs in tombs throughout the country. One Muslim went to Shirdi from Delhi and placed flowers in the very tomb described above, under the tree. Sai Baba, aware of this, chose to reside at this very spot, which can grant the grace of Ram-Rahim. In using the term *Ram-Rahim*, Das Ganu explicitly sets forth an understanding of God as a single deity shared by Hindus (Ram) and Muslims (Rahim), as he does in his Hymn no. 2. Thus, just as a single essence, the earth, gives rise to different species of flowers, so does a single God, Ram-Rahim, give rise to different religious communities.

As the reincarnation of Kabir, Shirdi Sai Baba is wise enough to realize this underlying unity, and he can help his devotees realize it as well if they have faith in him and travel the bhakti path. To illustrate this, Das Ganu briefly tells the stories of several devotees who come from very different backgrounds but who all develop faith in Sai Baba after they encounter him. He explains that Sai Baba is able to appear as Shiva to Shaivas, as Vishnu to Vaishnavas, and as Parvardigar (Allah) to Muslims (verse 81). Among the many devotees mentioned in chapter 53, the one who receives the most attention is a Zoroastrian devotee by the name of Ratanji. Relating this story, Das Ganu waxes didactic about caste relations. Dabholkar also writes about Ratanji in chapter 14 of the *Shri Sai Satcharita*, and a comparison with Das Ganu's version reveals how central caste and community issues are in the latter.

Dabholkar describes Ratanji as a prosperous landowner and business-man who was despondent, despite his wealth, for he had no children. Das Ganu (appearing here as a character in Dabholkar's story) advised his friend Ratanji to go to Shirdi and pray to Sai Baba, asking him for the blessing of a son. Ratanji decided to heed this advice. In Shirdi, when Ratanji attempted to offer Sai Baba a monetary donation, or *dakshina*, of 5 rupees, Sai Baba told him that he had already received 3.14 rupees, and therefore Ratanji should deduct that from the 5. Ratanji was puzzled by this, since he had not previously been to Shirdi, but he did as instructed. Sai Baba then blessed him, telling him that God would see that his wish is fulfilled. Upon return-ing to his home in Nanded, Ratanji told Das Ganu of his conversation with Sai Baba and his puzzlement over the dakshina. After pondering a bit, Das Ganu realized that the amount must refer to what Ratanji had spent in host-ing a Muslim saint named Mowli Saheb. Looking at the accounting books, they saw that 3.14 rupees was exactly what Ratanji had spent on this hospi-tality. Dabholkar writes that Ratanji's faith grew deeper upon solving this puzzle. In due time, Sai Baba's blessing came to fruition and Ratanji became a father (Dabholkar 2007, 216–35). Thus the emphasis in Dabholkar's account is placed on Sai Baba's omniscience and his ability to reward his faithful devotees with worldly blessings.

The emphasis in Das Ganu's account is entirely different. Das Ganu describes Ratanji as a wealthy and pious Zoroastrian who had many friends from various castes and communities. Again, Das Ganu returns to his verdant metaphor, saying these friends are like flowers, each a different species with a different fragrance, but all arising from a shared source, the earth. The earth does not discriminate between the fragrance of roses and jasmine; rather, a garden is enhanced by the diversity and variety of flowers and fragrances in it (verses 113–21). He then contrasts this garden with modern Indian society, which is rife with discrimination as Brahmins and non-Brahmins embattle one another (verse 122). Brahmins claim that the Marathas (non-Brahmins) are idiotic and inferior upstarts, vying with them for position in society (verse 123). For the next sixty verses, from verse 124 to 183, Das Ganu presents the non-Brahmin critique of Brahmins in great detail.[28]

Das Ganu begins with a reference to the Vedic creation myth known as the Purusha Sukta, or Hymn of Man, found in Rig Veda 10.90. In this hymn a cosmic man, *purusha*, is sacrificed and from his various parts arise all of creation, including the four classes of society: Brahmins from the mouth, Kshatriyas from the shoulders, Vaishyas from the thighs, and Shudras from the feet. Channeling the non-Brahmin critique of the bad Brahmin who justifies his elevated status in society through such sacred scriptures, Das Ganu questions the caste hierarchy, saying that if Brahmins emerged from the mouth of the cosmic man, then they are parasites, worms, and as such are not worthy of respect or reverence (verses 126–32). The same goes for Kshatriyas: if they emerged from the arms, or armpits, then they are nothing more than lice (verses 136–38). Having challenged the Vedic origin story, he next turns to a consideration of morals, pointing out the vile and hypocritical conduct of upper castes as recorded in their own epic and Puranic stories. He notes that even as Brahmins and Kshatriyas are praised as heroes in this literature, it is also rife with incidents of sexual debauchery on the part of both Brahmins and Kshatriyas, citing as examples the mistreatment of women, including Draupadi, Tara, and Ahalya (verses 141–59). The upper castes are cunning, the argument continues, for they write their own scriptures to guard their own privileged status. But who truly deserves to be called superior? he asks in verse 168. Here the focus shifts to an examination of the essential roles performed by two Dalit castes, the Barber and the Sweeper. The Barber is essential to Hindu ritual, for his services are required at important rites of passage. The Sweeper is essential to Hindu society, for his services are required to keep the household and village sanitary. These castes are indispensible, not lowly (verses 169–75).

After airing this tirade, Das Ganu again returns to his verdant metaphor.

All of the varying species of flowers together enhance the beauty of the garden. They arise from the same earth, and they return to it after they have bloomed (verses 185–87). Like flowers, human society also has its varieties: Hinduism has its castes, Islam has Sunnis and Shias, Jains have Svethambars and Digambars, Christians have Protestants and Catholics (verses 188–90). Animals, too, come in a variety of species (verses 191–92). Thus, Das Ganu argues, such differences are natural and cannot be uprooted or removed. Instead, we must live harmoniously with one another and accept our differences, just as plants grow in harmony in a garden (verses 193–94).

Das Ganu pleads with Brahmins and non-Brahmins to stop abusing one another, arguing that this behavior will only end in mutual destruction (verse 195). In verses 197–207, he addresses non-Brahmins specifically, asking what would happen if they succeeded in trampling down the Brahmins and their institutions. He points out that in rejecting Brahminism, they would be bereft of the wisdom stored in Brahminical scriptures—knowledge of the solar and lunar cycles, astrology, medical wisdom, and a host of religious teachings, including those in the Bhagavad Gita and the works of the Marathi saints Jnaneshwar and Eknath. Then, turning to both non-Brahmins and Brahmins, Das Ganu reiterates that they must cleanse themselves of the filth of mutual hatred, or risk mutually assured destruction (verses 208–12).

Next, he addresses the Brahmins specifically, chiding them for misinterpreting the Vedic Hymn of Man. Das Ganu clarifies that this hymn does not stipulate a hierarchical social order with Brahmins at the top; rather, just as various parts (mouth, shoulders, thighs, and feet) together compose the body of the cosmic giant, so should the various castes be understood as composing one society. No part has any greater value than another—all are needed and must work together for the greater good; similarly, if one part attacks another, then all suffer (verses 213–15). Das Ganu then addresses his audience directly, decrying his misfortune in having to describe all of this, and lamenting how dark the era is. He beseeches those listening to band together in the face of such darkness, calling on them to bring light back into the world by joining together in mutual amity to follow in the footsteps of sadhus and saints (verses 216–33).

Finally, in verse 234, Das Ganu returns to his story of Ratanji. At Ratanji's house in Nanded, his friends from various castes and communities have gathered together, free from mutual hatred. They dine together—which is significant, because people of different castes and creeds eating together clashed with Brahminical orthodoxy—and Das Ganu states that it was during this communal meal that a wandering holy man called Mowli Saheb arrived. He was welcomed by all and fed, and then Ratanji honored him with a garland and a coconut at the end of the meal. In exchange, Mowli Saheb blessed Ratanji and told him to go to Shirdi to see the greatness of Sai Baba. Ratanji heeded his advice. On his arrival in Shirdi, Sai Baba asked Ratanji for dakshina, specifying an amount that he said was owed to him based on Ratanji's previous payment. As in Dabholkar's version, Ratanji was puzzled, since he had never been to Shirdi before. Returning home, Ratanji examined his account books and realized that the expenses of feeding and hosting Mowli Saheb exactly matched what Sai Baba said he had previously paid. Suddenly, Ratanji was filled with joy. Das Ganu concludes that the lesson of this story is that whatever money is spent for good purposes reaches Shirdi Sai Baba. Ratanji showed respect to a wandering saint by hosting and feeding him (much as Das Ganu hoped those in his audience would do for him as an itinerant kirtankar), alongside Ratanji's diverse group of friends, and this was a form of devotion to Sai Baba. Communal hatred is not good; but communal love earns Sai Baba's grace, and won Ratanji a son (verses 255–60).

Thus, whereas the emphasis in Dabholkar's account of this incident as told in the *Shri Sai Satcharita* is on Shirdi Sai Baba's omniscience and his ability to reward his faithful devotees with worldly blessings, especially the birth of sons, the emphasis in Das Ganu's version is on Sai Baba's message about the urgent need for Brahmins and non-Brahmins to unite. In the remaining verses of chapter 53, Das Ganu concludes his history of Sai Baba with his death in 1918, stating that though he is no longer physically present, he is imperishable and remains accessible from beyond the grave for all who turn to him in prayer.

BAD BRAHMINS, GOOD BRAHMINS, AND IN-BETWEEN BRAHMINS

In the *Bhaktasaramrita*, and especially in the story of Ratanji, Das Ganu presents a reformist critique of caste. The radical critique of caste, as seen, for instance, in the discourse of Dr. Bhimrao Ramji Ambedkar beginning in the late 1920s, argued that caste itself must be abolished to ensure the equality of all. Ambedkar rejected the argument that caste was justified because it is found in traditional Hindu scripture, provocatively stating that such scripture was an insult to the people and should be burned (Coward 2003, 46). Ambedkar's rejection of the caste system ultimately entailed a rejection not only of Hindu scripture but of Hinduism outright as inherently casteist. Prior to his death in 1956, Ambedkar converted to Buddhism in a public ceremony in which several hundred thousand of his Dalit followers also rejected Hinduism and became Buddhists.

The reformist critique of caste, on the other hand, generally argued that while untouchability was a corruption of Hinduism and needed to be abolished, caste itself was central to Hindu scripture, faith, and society. The problem was that caste had been misinterpreted over the centuries: rather than the hierarchical socioreligious system that had come into existence, caste had originally included all members of society as separate but equal components of the body politic. Therefore, caste itself did not need to be abolished; rather, Hindu society needed to be reformed in keeping with the ideal of traditional Hindu scripture. This position was most famously advocated by Mohandas "Mahatma" Gandhi, who wrote in his essay "The Ideal Bhangi" (originally published in his newspaper *Harijan* in 1936) that both the Brahmin and the Bhangi ("Untouchable" Sweeper caste) should be regarded as equal, for one sanitizes the soul while the other sanitizes the body of society. Gandhi stridently called on his fellow upper-caste Hindus to recognize Dalits (or Harijans, as he termed them) and low castes as their equals in society, writing, "Not till the invidious distinction between the Brahmin and the Bhangi is removed will our society enjoy health, prosperity and peace, and be happy" (1999, 127).

Das Ganu did not take the radical step of calling for the abolition of caste. Rather, like Gandhi, Das Ganu argued that caste divisions are inevitable in society but have been misinterpreted. Instead of the castes being ranked hierarchically, each should be valued for its unique contribution to society, just as each species of flower contributes to the beauty of the garden. The Sweeper and the Barber are just as essential as the Brahmin and the Kshatriya and should be valued equally. One can imagine that this reformist position would not satisfy those Dalits who did not want to follow their ancestral calling as latrine sweepers or barbers or whatnot, even if that line of work was suddenly to be held in higher social regard. This reformist position was also unsatisfactory to Ambedkar, for he sought equality not in terms of equal status of the castes but in terms of equal access to social, political, and economic opportunities (Coward 2003, 57).

Nonetheless, one must also appreciate how Das Ganu diverged from the dominant conservative defense of the caste hierarchy held by most Brahmin kirtankars, and by many upper-caste nationalists, in the early twentieth century. In her study of Marathi kirtans, Anna Schultz (2013, 51) notes that while the majority of rashtriya kirtankars in the early twentieth century favored a conservative and Brahminical brand of Hinduism (one that became "virulently chauvinist" by the onset of the twenty-first century), a minority of kirtankars articulated inclusive counterdiscourses, such as Vaman Abaji Modak and Gadge Maharaj. Das Ganu falls into this minority, as a Brahmin who articulated reformist and inclusive—though far from radical—visions for Indian society in his song-poems, performances, and writings. Utilizing the strategy of the Brahmin double, Das Ganu critiqued the "bad Brahmins" in his stories for their casteism, greed, lust, and hypocrisy but also highlighted "good Brahmins" for their sincerity in devotion and for embracing their fellow citizens across caste lines. Such a strategy had the advantage of allowing the non-Brahmins in attendance at his performances to hear their concerns acknowledged publicly, as Das Ganu channeled non-Brahmin critiques of Brahmins (as in the story of Ratanji), and allowing the "bad Brahmins" in the poems and stories to become the focus of non-Brahmin anger (and not Das Ganu himself as a Chitpavan Brahmin). It also had the advantage of not completely alienating those Brahmins in attendance by calling for a full-scale elimination of their privileged caste status, even as their caste superiority was criticized.

Both of Das Ganu's biographers, Damodar Athavale and B. V. Narasimhaswami, agree that Das Ganu was the most influential figure behind the spread of faith in Shirdi Sai Baba throughout the region of modern-day Maharashtra in the first half of the twentieth century. However, these two authors come to two very different conclusions about Das Ganu. For Athavale, Das Ganu is a guru and role model; he showed how to pursue a religious quest by overcoming obstacles based in society and in one's own inner nature, becoming progressively more selfless, free of desire, and full of faithful devotion in Sai Baba as guru and God. For Narasimhaswami, on the other hand, Das Ganu falls short of being a religious exemplar. Simply put, his faith did not measure up, and Narasimhaswami argues this was due to his prejudice as an orthodox Brahmin. The strongest example of the contrast between these two biographers' assessment of Das Ganu is found in their respective discussions of the events culminating in what is often called the Ganga Lila, or Miracle of the Ganges River (in Athavale's account the sacred river in question is actually the Godavari, which residents of this region equate with the Ganges).[29]

In Athavale's version, Das Ganu desired to take a purifying bath in the Godavari River. He went to Sai Baba for permission to leave Shirdi, but was denied. For several months, Das Ganu routinely made his request and was rejected, as Sai Baba said: "Go tomorrow, or the day after. What is the hurry?" On the day before an auspicious festival day, Das Ganu again entreated Sai Baba to allow him leave to bathe in the Godavari. Sai Baba replied: "Ganu, what is all this torment for? Is there added merit in bathing on special days? Don't you know one must be clean and pure within? The Godavari is always with us. Why do you sorrow in vain?" The next day, Das Ganu went for darshan with Sai Baba in the morning. Athavale reports that Das Ganu placed his head at Sai Baba's feet, when suddenly two streams of pure water—the Ganges and Yamuna Rivers—began to flow from Sai Baba's toes. Das Ganu collected the water in his hands and reverently sprinkled it over his head, experiencing as he did so an indescribable joy that exceeded that of bathing in the Godavari. Sai Baba asked him: "Are you satisfied, Ganu?" Athavale concludes that as a result of this miracle, Das Ganu's faith in Sai Baba "became firm" (Athavale 1955, 120–21).

In Narasimhaswami's account, Das Ganu asked Sai Baba for permission to go bathe in the sacred Ganges River. Sai Baba replied: "Ganga is here at my feet. Do not go." Dejected, Das Ganu fell silent. Sai Baba continued: "Come here. Hold your palm near my feet." Suddenly, a stream of water arose from Sai Baba's toes and filled Das Ganu's cupped hands. Das Ganu later reported to Narasimhaswami that he sprinkled this holy water over his head (Narasimhaswami 1954, 147–48). In *Life of Sai Baba*, Narasimhaswami takes issue with this gesture, writing that in 1919, shortly after Sai Baba died, Das Ganu was in Nanded, where a sadhu told him that he had too much egotism, *ahamkar*, as evidenced when Das Ganu sprinkled the holy water provided by his guru over his head rather than drinking it. "You sprinkled it on your head, but would not put it into your mouth, because you are a Brahmin and the Ganga was coming from (the feet of the mosque dwelling) Baba" (Narasimhaswami 1983, 144). Narasimhaswami agrees with this unnamed renouncer and concludes that despite this miracle, Das Ganu's faith in Sai Baba was not complete.

Thus, when it comes to interpreting Das Ganu's proclamation in his most famous hymn that "Shirdi is my Pandharpur, and Sai Baba is its God," his biographers come to two very different conclusions. For Athavale, this hymn is testimony to his guru's full acceptance of Sai Baba as not simply one of many Maharashtrian saints, but as God incarnate, following the Miracle of the Ganges River. For Narasimhaswami, on the other hand, this hymn is a hollow statement of faith. Narasimhaswami critiqued Das Ganu for ultimately failing to see Sai Baba as God due to his casteism, painting him as an elite Brahmin who, try though he might, could not escape his Brahminical heritage in order to awaken to a true understanding of who Shirdi Sai Baba was or what his teachings entailed. In Narasimhaswami's verdict, and in the verdicts of those following him, in the end Das Ganu was a Brahmin who could not fully accept a low-caste Muslim as God and who in his heart continued to prefer Vithoba over Sai Baba.

Ultimately, Narasimhaswami condemns Das Ganu's lack of faith in Sai Baba and attributes that spiritual failing to Das Ganu's orthodox conservatism. Athavale comes to the opposite conclusion, praising Das Ganu's firm faith in Sai Baba, and ascribing that spiritual achievement to Das Ganu's liberal ecumenism.[30] Unlike his biographers, my concern in this chapter is not with examining the degree of Das Ganu's faith in Shirdi Sai Baba. Instead, I am interested in understanding Das Ganu's historical role in spreading devotion to Shirdi Sai Baba and his unique interpretation of Shirdi Sai Baba's life and teachings. To fully comprehend that interpretation, however, we must examine his views on caste and communal prejudice, for they are intimately interwoven. Christian Novetzke notes that in nineteenth- and twentieth-century Maharashtra, there were numerous public and political figures from Brahmin backgrounds who "offered strident, although ultimately restricted critiques of caste that were posed with a 'reformist' rather than a radical sensibility" (2011, 232). Das Ganu was one of these figures, and he employed Shirdi Sai Baba in his critique, presenting him as a paternal figure who embraced all who came to him, no matter their caste or creed, and as an advocate for communal harmony. In the stories Das Ganu told and songs he sang about Sai Baba, he likened Shirdi to Pandharpur, where high caste and low, Shaiva and Vaishnava, Hindu and Muslim were all welcome to come together in one devotional community, and he regularly pitted good Brahmins against bad Brahmins, to criticize his fellow Brahmins' casteism as well as their greed, lust, and lack of true faith.

Nonetheless, Das Ganu stopped far short of offering a radical critique of caste. He nowhere suggests that caste should be abolished in its entirety. Instead, he adopts the reformist stance that castes must be valued equally for their unique contributions to society, not ranked hierarchically. Each flower should be valued for its unique appearance and fragrance. But—to continue Das Ganu's metaphor—how should these varying flowers interact? Should the roses and jasmine and other flowers be allowed to intermingle in a mixed garden, or should each species be planted in its own separate but equal subplot within the garden? In an ideal Shirdi or Pandharpur, should the different castes be allowed to intermingle in a mixed society, or should each caste maintain its own separate but equal space within society?

Although the Varkari pilgrimage to Pandharpur is famous for its inclusion of all castes, including Dalits, it has also been criticized for seeming to include lower castes only to exclude them. For instance, the Indian sociologist Irawati Karve wrote of her first experience on the Varkari pilgrimage to Pandharpur in 1962. Although a native Maharashtrian, she had not previously undertaken the pilgrimage because her family was not part of the Varkari community. She notes that this pilgrimage helped her get to know her Maharashtra anew every day as she walked behind the palanquin of the poet-saint Jnaneshwar: "I found a new definition of Maharashtra: the land whose people go to Pandharpur for pilgrimage. When the palanquin started from Poona [Pune], there were people from Poona, Junnar, Moglai, Satara, etc. Every day people were joining the pilgrimage from Khandesh, Sholapur, Nasik, Berar. As we neared Pandharpur, the pilgrimage was becoming bigger and bigger. All were Marathi-speaking people—coming from different castes, but singing the same songs, the same verses of Varkari cult, speaking to each other, helping each other, singing songs to each other" (Karve 1962, 22). Nonetheless, she also astutely observes that although all castes took part in the pilgrimage, caste separation was maintained in important ways: Brahmins ate separately from non-Brahmins and slept separately at night, even if they were part of the same walking group, or *dindi*. "Untouchables" not only ate and slept within their own group, they also formed their own separate walking group. Discussing her own walking group, divided between Brahmins and Marathas, she comments: "Every day I regretted the fact that one and the same *dindi* was divided into these two sections. All of the people were clean, and ate their food only after taking a bath. Then why this separateness? Was all this walking together, singing together, and reciting the poetry of the saints together directed only towards union in the other world while retaining separateness in this world? This question was on my mind all the time" (19).

Ambedkar made another critique. As noted above, in articulating his radical critique of caste, he ultimately rejected Hinduism outright. Christophe Jaffrelot (2005, 48) explains that Ambedkar's rejection of Hinduism included a rejection of the Varkari bhakti tradition in Maharashtra specifically; Ambedkar opposed his wife's wish to go to Pandharpur to pay homage to the Dalit poet-saint Chokhamela, arguing that despite the sanctity of a Dalit figure, she would nonetheless be refused access to the Vithoba Temple there because she was a Dalit. Though Dalits were allowed to form their own walking group and take part in the pilgrimage to Pandharpur for centuries, they were denied entry into the central Vitthal Rukmini Temple in Pandharpur. Their entry was only permitted beginning in 1950, following the fast to his death of activist Sane Guruji.

Reading Athavale's biography of Das Ganu, one catches glimpses of how Das Ganu was on both sides of the fence when it came to caste reform. Athavale devotes a whole chapter to highlighting Das Ganu's concern for reforming caste and gender inequities. However, in another chapter about Das Ganu's yearly travels between different cities to perform his kirtans, Athavale records that Das Ganu routinely went to Pandharpur every year at the time of Dasara (early to mid-October) and stayed there for approximately four months. He writes, "Until the year the untouchables were granted entry into the temple, Maharaj [Das Ganu] would perform ten kirtans before Goddess Rukmini in the night during the period of Navratri" (Athavale 1955, 207). We are left to draw our own conclusion here, namely, that from 1950 until the end of his life (or at least until the writing of the biography), Das Ganu chose not to perform his usual kirtans within the Vitthal Rukmini Temple in Pandharpur in protest against the entry of Dalits into that hallowed space.

Interestingly, the most famous advocate of the reformist position, Mohandas Gandhi, ultimately adopted the radical position that caste must be abolished. Harold Coward describes the efforts of both Ambedkar and Gandhi to combat untouchability, as well as the debates they engaged in with each another between 1920 and the time of India's independence in 1947. Coward (2003, 62) writes that after years of debates about the pros and cons of the radical versus reformist critiques of caste, Gandhi was persuaded by Ambedkar and began to call for the full repudiation of caste in the 1940s.[31] Unlike Gandhi, however, Das Ganu was apparently never persuaded to accept this radical position. While Das Ganu was certainly not the "bad Brahmin"—the orthodox, casteist, and hypocritical Brahmin—that Narasimhaswami concludes him to have been, neither was he the full-fledged "good Brahmin"—the kind who embraces his fellow citizens across caste lines—that Athavale concludes him to have been. Instead, Das Ganu fell somewhere in-between, speaking to both Brahmins and non-Brahmins and advancing a reform position that called for the transgression of some caste boundaries even as it called for the reinforcement of others. In Das Ganu's ideal Shirdi or Pandharpur, all castes are equally welcome—provided that they maintain their separate spaces.

CHAPTER 3

Shirdi Is the Future of Religion in India

NARASIMHASWAMI'S PLEA TO HINDUS

> So far as India itself is concerned, the future of religion in India is largely
> a question of the fusion of the two great trends which appear to be so
> widely different, namely, Hinduism and Islam.
>
> B. V. NARASIMHASWAMI, *LIFE OF SAI BABA*

B. V. Narasimhaswami (1874–1956) never met Shirdi Sai Baba face to face, and yet he became arguably the most influential person behind the explosive growth of Sai Baba devotion in the twentieth century. Narasimhaswami became a devotee of Sai Baba when he first set foot in Shirdi in 1936, eighteen years after Sai Baba had passed away. Although Sai Baba was no longer physically present, Narasimhaswami nonetheless felt an overwhelming sense of loving union with Sai Baba that demonstrated that he was still "alive" and accessible from beyond the grave. After accepting Sai Baba as his guru, Narasimhaswami spent the remaining twenty years of his life working to spread Sai Baba's name throughout India—especially southern India. To do so, he authored numerous books about Sai Baba's life and teachings, including *Life of Sai Baba*, *Devotees' Experiences of Sri Sai Baba*, and *Sri Sai Baba's Charters and Sayings*. Narasimhaswami also founded the

All India Sai Samaj in 1940, a nonprofit organization established to pursue Narasimhaswami's mission of *Sai prachar*, or propagating devotion to Shirdi Sai Baba. Based in Madras (now Chennai), Tamil Nadu, this organization had over four hundred branches, which together were responsible for establishing eighty Shirdi Sai Baba temples throughout India by the time of Narasimhaswami's death in 1956.

Narasimhaswami lived during the rise of the anticolonial struggle against British rule in India, and prior to his death he witnessed both the victorious granting of independence in 1947 and the simultaneous tragedy of the partition of India and Pakistan, accompanied by tumultuous bloodshed between Hindus and Muslims.[1] In this historical context, Narasimhaswami was drawn to Shirdi Sai Baba not only for the intimate emotional connection that he experienced with him but also for his composite identity. As a freedom-fighter-turned-renouncer, Narasimhaswami left behind his political offices when he took up the life of a renouncer, but he could not fully renounce his concern with the nation's political future. He hoped for a future in which India would be independent from British colonial rule and also at peace with itself, free of communal strife between Hindus and Muslims, so that its citizens could pursue meaningful lives while on earth and could strive to achieve liberation in the hereafter. Interpreting Sai Baba as a figure who was born as a Hindu Brahmin but who embraced both Hinduism and Islam in his personal life history, in his teachings, and among his followers, Narasimhaswami felt that Sai Baba was uniquely positioned to bring all of his devotees to a state of spiritual liberation and all Indians to a state of national unity. Throughout his writings, Narasimhaswami addresses a target audience of Hindus and champions Shirdi Sai Baba as the composite figure who will bring about a synthesis of Hinduism and Islam that will become the future religion of a united and peaceful India.

Yet Narasimhaswami has been criticized for presenting an overly "Hinduized" interpretation of Shirdi Sai Baba. Marianne Warren (2004, 13–14), for instance, credits Narasimhaswami with "almost single handedly introducing Sai Baba to South India," but she critiques his orthodox Hindu interpretation of Sai Baba, noting that the majority of his informants were Hindus, primarily Brahmins from Bombay, and that he made no effort to investigate the Sufi community when he was compiling Sai Baba's teachings. Antonio Rigopoulos (1993, xxv) similarly notes that Narasimhaswami "presents a Hinduized version of Sai Baba's life, overshadowing the Islamic influence and background," though he states that the comprehensiveness of his work makes it a central source. Smriti Srinivas, however, cautions that it is a mistake "to read Shirdi Sai Baba's story as simply one of 'Hinduization' or discuss only his appropriation by the 'Hindu' middle class." Rather, she argues that this is only "one strand of the narrative" (Srinivas 2008, 342–43). Through her important field research at Sai Baba temples in the Indian city of Bengaluru, she demonstrates how Sai Baba is understood differently at different temples: as an incarnation of Shiva and Dattatreya in the Rupena Agrahara Temple, built around 1970 and affiliated with the female renouncer Shivamma Thayee;[2] as an earlier avatar of Sathya Sai Baba in the Indiranagar Sathya Sai Baba Temple, built in 1988 and affiliated with Sathya Sai Baba; and as a deified Hindu guru in the Someshvarapura Shirdi Sai Baba Temple, built in 1968 by Narasimhaswami's All India Sai Samaj. Yet with regard to Narasimhaswami in particular, Srinivas comments that despite Sai Baba's "multiple heritages," he is now "imagined in a way that resembles a guru, even a Hindu deity, with alternative elements being pushed underground" in the temples of the All India Sai Samaj (228). The legacy of Narasimhaswami, therefore, is that Shirdi Sai Baba's "Sufi heritage has passed into a zone of cultural amnesia in the suburban landscape of believers" (233).[3]

Despite his importance to the historical growth of Shirdi Sai Baba devotion, and the criticism he has received for promoting a Hindu version of Sai Baba, no detailed analysis of Narasimhaswami and his writings exists. In this chapter, I examine Narasimhaswami's life and writings about Sai Baba, asking how Narasimhaswami, who was drawn to Sai Baba for his composite nature and saw him as the key to unity and amity across communal lines, could simultaneously be one of the primary figures responsible for "Hinduizing" Sai Baba. The answer, I argue, lies in understanding that Narasimhaswami believed that Sai Baba had two missions: the spiritual uplift of individuals and the temporal uplift of India. With regard to the former, Narasimhaswami saw Sai Baba as a guru who could lead individuals to God-realization through the exact program of guru worship that Narasimhaswami had successfully followed. Thus, while acknowledging that Sai Baba allowed disciples to worship him according to their differing religious upbringings, Narasimhaswami advocated a program firmly based in Hindu ritual tradition.

Scholars have focused on Narasimhaswami's discussion of Sai Baba's biography and his mission of individual spiritual uplift, criticizing the Hindu ritual path that Narasimhaswami advocated to attain God-realization. However, Narasimhaswami's discussion of Sai Baba's second mission, the temporal uplift of India, has been overlooked. Yet these two missions are inseparable in Narasimhaswami's writings. He conceived of God-realization as a transformative experience of loving union, not merely between guru and disciple, but between the individual self and the All-Self. Once one has awakened to God-realization, one sees the unity underlying everything. From this monistic standpoint, Narasimhaswami claimed that the essence of all religions is the same—love of God. It is over the "externals" that quarrels arise: temple versus mosque, this prayer versus that. Thus, in addition to the spiritual bliss this monistic experience entails, it also has a this-worldly effect, for quarrels can no longer stand when devotees experience an intimate, loving connection with one another. Narasimhaswami therefore set out to share his experience of God-realization through worship of Sai Baba so that other Hindus might experience it themselves. In so doing, he believed, they would become not only better, more spiritually awakened Hindus but also better Indians—and thereby save not only their own souls but the very soul of India, then divided by communal strife. Reaching out to his fellow Hindus, Narasimhaswami claimed that the future of religion in India entailed the synthesis or "fusion" of Hinduism and Islam into one community, joined in common love of Sai Baba.

This chapter argues that through exploring both of Shirdi Sai Baba's missions as Narasimhaswami understood them, we can better comprehend how Narasimhaswami's intention in spreading devotion to Sai Baba was not a right-wing Hindu effort to "Hinduize" a composite or Muslim figure; rather, his intention was a far more left-leaning effort to establish a new synthetic religion that would bring about a peaceful union between Hindus and Muslims in India. Only after exploring both of Sai Baba's missions as Narasimhaswami understood them can we then critically examine the limitations of Narasimhaswami's synthetic model and its implications for the future of religion in India.

BECOMING THE SOUTHERN SWAMI

Narasimhaswami was born Narasimha Iyer on August 21, 1874, in Bhavani town, Coimbatore District, Madras Presidency (now the southern state of Tamil Nadu). His parents, Venkatagiri Iyer and Angachiammal, were orthodox Hindu Brahmins devoted to the local god Sangameswar and goddess Bhavani, and they had as their family guru the Shankaracharya of Sringeri. According to his biographers, Narasimha received a strong religious upbringing from his parents, who taught him to partake in regular worship at the local temple; told him stories from the epics and taught him devotional songs; helped him to undergo the proper religious *samskaras*, or rites of passage, for a Brahmin boy; and took him to be blessed by the Shankaracharya of Sringeri as well as a local saint named Sorakkai Swamiji (Vijayakumar 2009, 25–28; Saipadananda 1973, 1–2; Varadaraja Iyer 1974, 2–5).

When Narasimha was a young boy, his parents moved to Salem, where his father was a pleader at law. Narasimha excelled at school, so his parents sent him to Madras for further education. He studied at the Madras Christian College, where he completed his intermediate schooling in 1890, then earned a bachelor's degree with distinction, followed by a law degree in 1895. Narasimha then returned to Salem, where he began practicing law. His biographer G. R. Vijayakumar (2009, 31-32) describes him as a successful lawyer whose debating skills earned him a large clientele and a sizeable income, but also as a compassionate lawyer who regularly took on the cases of those who could not afford court litigation. As Narasimha's legal practice and reputation grew, so did his family. He had been married to Seethalakshmi in 1890, when he was sixteen and she was ten years of age. Together they had five children: Venkataraman, Rajalakshmi, Saradambal, Jayaraman, and Savithri.

In the first decades of the twentieth century, Narasimha grew increasingly active in local and then national politics. He was elected to the Salem Municipal Council in 1902 and from 1904 to 1920 he served as chairman of the Salem Municipality. His biographers note that during these years he acquired a reputation for integrity, efficiency, and honesty (Vijayakumar 2009, 32; Saipadananda 1973, 3–4). As he turned his attention to national politics and the growing movement for Indian autonomy from British colonial rule, this reputation helped him get elected to further positions. Vijayakumar sums up Narasimha's nationalist activism during this period: "In politics he was an admirer and follower of the firebrand leader, Sri Bala Gangadhar Tilak, and was considered an extremist. This made him very popular and in 1914, he was elected to represent Salem, Coimbatore and Nilgiris in the Madras Legislative Council. He was also elected to the new Council established under the Montague-Chelmsford reforms. He continued to be a member of the Legislative Council till 1920 and, as a member of the Indian National Congress, he vigorously presented the national viewpoint on all issues that came up for consideration before the Council" (2009, 32).[4]

"Lokamanya" Bal Gangadhar Tilak (1856–1920) was a prominent leader of the Indian independence movement and one of its most outspoken proponents of Swaraj, or Home Rule. As a long-standing member of the Indian National Congress, the body dedicated to obtaining a greater share in governance for Indians, Tilak was known as the leader of the "extremist" wing that proposed direct revolution to obtain Swaraj, as opposed to the "moderate" wing that proposed a dialogic process with the British under the leadership of Gopal Krishna Gokhale.[5] In 1908, Tilak was arrested for sedition after defending the guerrilla tactics of two revolutionaries in his newspaper *Kesari*. He was tried, convicted, and sentenced to six years' penal transportation in Mandalay, Burma, which he served from 1908 to 1914. Tilak's eight-day trial was widely covered in the Indian press, for it revolved around the question of whether Indians had a right to freedom of the press as a civil liberty, in addition to the issues of violence and nonviolence, loyalty and sedition. The trial, and the resulting sentence that was widely perceived by Indians as unduly harsh, galvanized many burgeoning nationalists, including Narasimha. After Tilak returned to India in 1914, he began working with other prominent nationalists, including G. S. Khaparde, Joseph Baptista, and Annie Besant, the British Theosophist who was a champion of Indian independence. Together, they founded the All India Home Rule League in 1916 to demand self-governing Dominion status for India within the British Empire. Narasimha joined the league and teamed up with Besant, touring the Madras Presidency with her and conducting lectures to agitate for Home Rule (Vijayakumar 2009, 34; Varadaraja Iyer 1974, 5–6).

In 1917, as Britain was preparing for elections, the All India Home Rule League decided to try to persuade members of the Liberal Party in England to make an election issue of granting political independence to India. A delegation of three Indians was selected to sail to England, comprised of Narasimha Iyer, George Joseph, and Manjeri Rama Iyer. However, the delegation never arrived, for the British War Cabinet learned of the mission, detained the ship at Gibraltar, and arrested Narasimha and his colleagues. After fifteen days of detention, they were deported back to India (Vijayakumar 2009, 34; Saipadananda 1973, 4; Varadaraja Iyer 1974, 6). Although the mission was not successful, it nonetheless made Narasimha and his colleagues even more popular within pro-independence circles.

Though his biographers, particularly Vijayakumar, paint Narasimhaswami as an "extremist" and follower of Tilak, his evaluation of Tilak evolved considerably over the years. In the second volume of *Life of Sai Baba*, written in 1956, Narasimhaswami discusses his preference for

"Mahatma" Gandhi over Tilak, describing the former as an advocate of nonviolence and Hindu-Muslim unity. This discussion takes place in a chapter focused on G. S. Khaparde (1854–1938), an eminent lawyer and nationalist who was one of Tilak's closest associates. Khaparde fled to Shirdi in December 1910, seeking refuge at a time when many "extremist" nationalists were being rounded up and charged with sedition. He remained in Shirdi for a week on this visit and then returned several more times before Sai Baba's death in 1918: from December 6, 1911, to March 15, 1912; from December 29 to 31, 1915; on May 19, 1917; and for an unspecified number of days in March 1918 (Khaparde 2000, 113). During his visits to Shirdi, Khaparde kept a diary, wherein he records that Tilak accompanied him on his May 19, 1917, visit to Shirdi. Khaparde's discussion of the interaction between Sai Baba and Tilak is minimal, however, noting only that Sai Baba gave them *udi* (sacred ash) and told Tilak, "People are bad, keep yourself to yourself" (Khaparde 2000, 106–7).

Narasimhaswami provides a more in-depth discussion of this event. He states that the reason Tilak came to Shirdi was to seek Sai Baba's blessing for his efforts to advance Indian independence. Sai Baba's message to Tilak, as Narasimhaswami interprets it, was to advise Tilak to take a rest by resigning from the political scene. Narasimhaswami adds:

> Work on Tilak's lines had to end. Very soon the national work of reaching Independence was undertaken by a person who was not merely highly spiritually advanced but one whose method of activities, political and spiritual, ensured certainty of success, through the aid of not merely human beings inhabiting the country regardless of their distinctions of race, caste, or colour, but also through the aid of other nationalities and of God. Mahatma Gandhi was coming into the field and his lines were approved of both by Hindus and Muhammadans [Muslims] and his chances of success were therefore indisputably superior to Tilak's chances. (Narasimhaswami 1983, 334)

As early as 1920, Narasimha began to endorse Gandhi and his methods. That year, Narasimha was reelected to the Madras Legislative Council. However, that same year, Gandhi launched the Noncooperation Movement. Frustrated with the lack of progress toward Home Rule and the slaughter of many nonviolent Indians in the Jallianwala Bagh Massacre of 1919, Gandhi called upon all Indians to engage in a nonviolent boycott of British rule by refusing to buy foreign goods and resigning from government-run educa-

tional institutions, courts, and other government employment.[6] This movement gained widespread support throughout India, and Narasimha took
part by resigning his position on the council (Vijayakumar 2009, 35).
Although his resignation was motivated by politics, it was the first of many
moves Narasimha would make over the next several years to withdraw from
politics and public life in order to pursue the spiritual path.

According to Narasimha's biographers, a pivotal turning point occurred
in 1921 when his two youngest children, fifteen-year-old Jayaraman and
thirteen-year-old Savithri, drowned. Several months after their deaths, his
wife, Seethalakshmi, passed away, leaving him alone, since his three older
children were married adults. In his grief, Narasimha began to question why
God would allow such tragedy to happen. Ultimately, he came to believe
that these tragic events must have occurred to enable him to turn away from
the householder's life and toward a larger purpose (Vijayakumar 2009,
36–39; Saipadananda 1973, 5–6; Varadaraja Iyer 1974, 6–7). Writing of himself in the third person, he provides a brief autobiographical sketch of this
period in his life in the second volume of *Life of Sai Baba*:

> B. V. N. Swami [Narasimhaswami] was one of the foremost in the ranks of
> lawyers and political agitators, legislative councillors and Home Rule workers,
> when suddenly it pleased Providence to draw him away from all these by what
> appeared to be a terrible domestic calamity. In 1921, he had a sad bereavement
> by the loss of two of his children at one stroke through their accidental drown-
> ing. The blow was very severe but the giver of the blow, who is no other than
> Iswara [God] and, therefore, no other than Sai Baba, intended everything to
> have a special beneficial effect both to the person on whom the blow appeared
> to be inflicted and to the public. Swami who was then a grihasta [householder],
> and a political agitator, was drawn away from all this by the blow and he was,
> when in full possession of the powers of body and mind, made to use them for
> the largest spiritual purposes. Agitation for Home Rule for India and asserting
> the rights of the people in the Legislative Council and outside was no doubt
> service to the public. But the scope for effective work in all those directions
> was very limited, and there were other workers coming into the field with much
> greater energy and much better chance of turning out results. Therefore just
> at that time this author by his resolve not to take any further part in worldly
> affairs including political affairs was rightly drawn on to the religious and spir-
> itual field. Even before the bodies of the children were taken out from water it
> had dawned upon him that this dreadful thunderstroke had a meaning and that

Providence was directing him thereby not to use up his energies and attention in Law or politics and social or domestic affairs but to consecrate himself for the service of mankind by the search for God and the ascertainment and adoption of steps for realisation of God and the self. (Narasimhaswami 1983, 271–72)

In the next months and years, Narasimha systematically withdrew from his professional life. He had already resigned from the Madras Legislative Council, and one by one he resigned from his other professional obligations. In 1925, his final act was to return his legal certificate to the High Court. He then made final arrangements to become a *sannyasi*, or Hindu renouncer: he "distributed his wealth among his [living] children, cut off all his family ties and left Salem in September 1925 as a mendicant" (Vijayakumar 2009, 39). Henceforth, Narasimha Iyer went by the name of Narasimhaswami, though in the years to follow, he would also become known as the Southern Swami, the renouncer from Madras who left the south behind and wandered throughout India in search of his guru. Yet although Narasimhaswami took formal vows of renunciation and was consumed by the goal of attaining a personal experience of God-realization, he could not fully shed his former identity as a lawyer-turned-activist for Indian independence. His spiritual and philosophical writings remain infused with political concerns—most notably over the quest for independence and the relationship between Hindus and Muslims in newly independent India—and these concerns are intimately interwoven with his spiritual attraction to and his interpretation of Shirdi Sai Baba.

THE QUEST FOR A GURU: GO NORTH!

Narasimhaswami's belief that a guru was central to the spiritual journey was so strong that he spent eleven years roaming throughout India, visiting one holy person after the next, in the quest for his own guru, which he finally found in Shirdi Sai Baba. The central theme of the first book in Narasimhaswami's four-volume *Life of Sai Baba* is the guru. In this work, he discusses the significance of the guru path, or *guru marga*; the proper relationship between guru and disciple; and Sai Baba's role as the ultimate type of guru, a Samartha Sadguru. Narasimhaswami believed that book learning would only carry one so far toward the goal of God-realization: "God-realisation is a personal experience and cannot be obtained or explained through the written word. Those who are familiar with Hindu thought and in fact with religious thought generally, can realise the importance of a

Guru and absolute faith in a Guru for the quickening of spiritual growth" (1980, 8). He advocated following the guru marga, which he defined as "that form of Bhakti Marga [devotional path] in which faith in and devotion to the Guru is the only sadhana [spiritual practice] for achieving every end including salvation" (86).

But to follow the guru path, one must first find a guru, and this proved a challenge for Narasimhaswami. In 1925, after leaving his home in Salem, he traveled to the monastery in Sringeri that had been founded in the eighth century by the monistic Advaita Vedanta philosopher Shankaracharya, with which Narasimhaswami's family had long been affiliated. There, the Jagadguru Shankaracharya Sri Chandrashekhara Bharati Mahaswamigal (1892–1954) formally initiated Narasimhaswami into *sannyasa* (renunciation) and then directed him to go to Tiruvannamalai to join Ramana Maharshi (1879–1950), who was known throughout southern India as the Brahmin Swami. Narasimhaswami hoped to find his guru in Maharshi. During his three-year stay, Narasimhaswami recorded the biography of Maharshi and the lessons he learned from him, and he also spoke with other devotees and recorded their experiences.[7] These notes were compiled into the book *Self Realisation: The Life and Teachings of Bhagavan Sri Ramana Maharshi* (first published in 1931). In this work, Narasimhaswami writes that the "pith and core of Maharshi's teaching" is Atmadhyana, that is, meditation (*dhyana*) upon the self/Self (*atman*) in order to experience liberation in the form of God- or Self-realization, a nondualistic knowledge of the eternal divine Self within. The key question that Maharshi posed as a meditation device to Narasimhaswami, as to other devotees, was "Who am I?" This was the very question that set Maharshi on his own spiritual path in 1896, when as a teenager he had suddenly feared his own mortality and began to wonder to himself, "But with this death of the body, am 'I' dead? Is the body 'I'?" (Narasimhaswami 2010, 17).

As Narasimhaswami explains, meditating upon this question—Who am I?—leads to a series of questions about what is ultimately real: The body? The senses? One's thoughts? The intellect? "When object after object is eliminated with the remark, 'This is but an object, a possession of the Self, a thing which rises and falls, which changes, passes away and returns, and which is consequently not "I" and not the Real' . . . the intellect is playing its part and rendering service. . . . The final service of the intellect is to eliminate itself, saying 'I too am only the instrument of the subject and am not the subject'" (Narasimhaswami 2010, 215). Maharshi's teaching that this nondual realization is experienced by "diving within" opened the possibility of liberation to anyone willing to follow his method of meditating upon the Self. As Thomas Forsthoefel (2005) notes, this perennial stance was appealing to Indians from various backgrounds who would not traditionally qualify to become renouncers due to their gender, caste, or stage of life, as well as to non-Indians who were interested in the mystical quest for a universal enlightenment experience. Although Narasimhaswami had already been formally initiated as a renouncer, he too found this position appealing, noting with admiration that Shakta, Shaiva, and Vaishnava Hindus went to Maharshi, as did Muslims and Christians, each finding in him elements of their "true faith" (Narasimhaswami 2010, 210). In subsequent editions of *Self Realisation*, Narasimhaswami also noted that this position was appealing to westerners who also approached Maharshi, and he discusses over two additional chapters the example of the English journalist Paul Brunton (Narasimhaswami 2010, 255–72).

However, while the experience of Self-realization is available to all in theory, it requires that one go beyond intellectual theorizing and discursive reasoning to achieve that experience. As Narasimhaswami explains Maharshi's teaching, ultimately the nondual "pure Self" cannot be sensed by the intellect, for words fail to describe this limitless ultimate reality:

> We shall not try to describe, what is indescribable. Many thousands of seers have long ago declared that speech and thought retire baffled in their attempt to see, approach, and grasp the Self. . . . So one contents himself with description of the preliminaries for meditation and leaves the reader to realise the rest by Self-realisation. The mother when questioned by her little girl of five, what the joys and pains of maternity and childbirth are like, smiles and says: "Wait and see for yourself by your own experience." The "birth" of this Atman or its realization in one's self and all, as pure bliss, consciousness, existence can be understood only by actual realization. (Narasimhaswami 2010, 215–16)

To truly understand Self-realization, one must experience it. But while staying with Maharshi, Narasimhaswami was ultimately unable to make this leap from the intellectual pursuit of ultimate reality to the experiential. According to his biographer, Narasimhaswami therefore eventually sought Maharshi's permission to leave the ashram. Maharshi gave his blessing, saying: "I am not your Guru. Your Guru is waiting for you in the North. You will attain Realization from him" (Vijayakumar 2009, 46).

From Tiruvannamalai, Narasimhaswami next went to Hubli, where he spent several months with Siddharuda Swamiji. Then, from approximately 1930 to 1934, Narasimhaswami traveled throughout the region of modern-day Maharashtra, spending time in Pandharpur and other pilgrimage centers. During these years he spent time with many living saints, hoping anew that each saint he encountered would be his guru, and repeatedly having his hopes dashed. Narasimhaswami reached Meher Baba (1894–1969) in Meherabad toward the end of 1933, several years after Meher Baba had taken a vow of silence that he would keep until his death. Yet Meher Baba communicated with his devotees and even gave sporadic lectures through hand gestures and by pointing out Devanagari letters on a small alphabet board. When Narasimhaswami approached him for guidance, Meher Baba wrote (using the alphabet board) that he was not his guru, but gave him encouragement, writing, "Your Guru is waiting for you in the North" (Vijayakumar 2009, 57).

It was with Meher Baba (discussed further in chapter 5) that Narasimhaswami first learned of Shirdi Sai Baba. Meher Baba (1973) advanced a theory of "involution," the inward journey across seven planes of consciousness that the individual self (atman) must travel toward the divine Self (*param Atman*) within before attaining Self- or God-realization. Like Ramana Maharshi, Meher Baba also described ultimate reality as a nondual state that could ultimately only be experienced to truly be known. In the sixth plane of consciousness, the mind perceives God to be omnipresent and ultimately, in the seventh plane, the mind and God, or the "seer" and the "seen," are united as one (Meher Baba and Stevens 1998, 61).

To aid humanity on this journey, Meher Baba had proclaimed that five Sadgurus, or Perfect Masters, live in each age. These five Perfect Masters are God-realized individuals who simultaneously possess both individual human consciousness and God-consciousness, so they can span the seven planes of consciousness. They then use their advanced spiritual perception and powers to aid the advancement of others. In addition to the five Perfect Masters, there is also the Avatar, the original or Supreme Perfect Master who incarnates again and again through the pull of the Perfect Masters to help humanity on its path toward God-realization. Meher Baba claimed to personally be the Avatar, and he identified the five Perfect Masters living in his lifetime as Hazrat Babajan of Pune, Hazrat Tajuddin Baba of Nagpur, Narayan Maharaj of Khedgaon, Sai Baba of Shirdi, and Upasni Maharaj of Sakori. Meher Baba had encounters with each of these five figures, though he was most influenced by Upasni Maharaj, with whom he spent seven years in Sakori before establishing his own ashram at Meherabad in 1923.

Shirdi Sai Baba passed away in 1918, Hazrat Tajuddin Baba in 1925, and Hazrat Babajan in 1931. Thus, of the five Perfect Masters identified by Meher Baba, only Narayan Maharaj and Upasni Maharaj remained alive for Narasimhaswami to consult with as potential gurus. Narasimhaswami had already visited Khedgaon and met Narayan Maharaj, who had told him that he would eventually find his "flawless diamond" of a guru and then pointed him in the direction of Meher Baba (Vijayakumar 2009, 56). And so Narasimhaswami next traveled north to Sakori to meet Upasni, with whom he would spend the next two and a half years. As had been his pattern with Ramana Maharshi, Narasimhaswami recorded the biography of Upasni, the lessons he learned from him, and the experiences of other devotees at the ashram. These notes were compiled into the book *Sage of Sakuri* (first published as a booklet in 1934).[8]

Upasni Maharaj (1870–1941) advocated faith and good works over the intellectual quest for God-realization and thus helped Narasimhaswami to focus more intently on the path of devotion, or *bhakti marga*. In *Sage of Sakuri*, Narasimhaswami writes that Upasni required "blind faith" of his devotees:

> He wanted that they should be deeply devoted to and put implicit faith first
> in their Guru—surrendering their will and their all to him, and next in their
> Ishta-Devta, i.e., the particular form in which God has appealed to them. They
> should not merely try to turn their mind and heart to these. As mind and heart
> seldom work except in material ways cognizable by the senses, they are directed
> to be almost always doing something in furtherance of their goal—to reach
> their Guru-God. This something, of course, must be good works, unselfish
> beneficial works and works in consonance with the Swadharma of the doer.
> (Narasimhaswami and Subbarao 1966, 107)

Narasimhaswami notes that although God-realization is the ultimate goal, Upasni Maharaj urged his followers not to focus on that goal, stressing that they should read and repeat the sacred words of Hindu scriptures but "without troubling themselves about their meaning" (Narasimhaswami and Subbarao 1966, 106). Instead, it is better to engage in repetitive devotional acts that allow one to calm the mind, acquire faith, and accumulate merit. These acts included repeating sacred words, performing ritual *puja* (worship) of

Upasni as their guru, and serving their guru by preparing food. Narasim-haswami writes that he had witnessed the success of this method:

> The writer has watched the effect of these repetitions and constant listening
> to these words. The colony is small and one hears these sounds from any part
> of it, night and day. These electrify the very air of the Ashram and produce a
> religious ozone which purifies the heart and dispels doubt, care, and the lower
> urges of our nature. At times, in specially sensitive souls, there is the sudden
> appearance of God, the Ishtadevata. With such an appearance, some reach the
> high water mark of their spirituality; and ever keeping up or trying to keep up
> the presence of God in their soul, their spiritual career is assured, and their life
> has served its purpose. (Narasimhaswami and Subbarao 1966, 111)

During his stay in Sakori, Narasimhaswami found that several devotees had attained at least momentary glimpses of nondual union with God through their faith in Upasni Maharaj. However, Narasimhaswami was not one of these individuals. Nor could he simply place blind faith in Upasni and accept him as his personal guru. In fact, he grew disheartened by some of Upasni's practices and teachings. Particularly troubling was the teaching of *kanya daan*, the gifting of girls for religious merit. As Narasimhaswami explains in *Sage of Sakuri*, Upasni taught that the "giving or 'Daan' of a girl by her parents or by herself, if adult, to a perfect Sat-Purusha, who has attained realisation, ensures the Uddhara-Gati or salvation from the cycle of births and deaths not only of the girl herself but of 21 generations of ancestors on her father's and 21 on her mother's side" (Narasimhaswami and Subbarao 1966, 134–35). Aside from noting that this view was "peculiar to [Upasni] Baba" and had not been taught by other religious figures past or present (132), Narasimhaswami's treatment of this issue is brief and even-handed in this work.

In his later writings, however, Narasimhaswami reveals more details about this teaching, noting in *Life of Sai Baba* that Upasni Maharaj acquired twenty-five wives through this practice: "Acting upon these declarations of Upasani, some devotees presented their wives to him and some (rather a large number) gave away their daughters to him in marriage so that they might live with him, and that is how he got such a large number as 25 wives or satis by the end of his career" (1983, 293). Narasimhaswami also reveals his discomfort with this practice, describing Upasni's inability to let go of his attachment to women and wealth as a "defect" in his character: "Humanity is frail and frailty attaches even to persons who reach great heights like Upasani Baba. That is the one lesson we may draw from the defects noticed above. To go beyond that and either lose respect for him or to treat him and his institutions with disregard, contempt, or hatred would be totally unwarranted and harmful to the persons harbouring such feelings" (297–98). According to Vijayakumar, when Narasimhaswami arrived in Sakori, Upasni was facing a court summons and the possibility of a jail sentence if convicted of polygamy, and he viewed the arrival of this lawyer-turned-renouncer as providential. Narasimhaswami was persuaded to defend him in court and ultimately succeeded in earning an acquittal. However, once the legal work was finished, Narasimhaswami decided to move on in the further quest for his guru (Vijayakumar 2009, 58–62).

Although Narasimhaswami did not find his guru in Upasni Maharaj, Upasni did point Narasimhaswami toward Shirdi Sai Baba. In *Life of Sai Baba*, Narasimhaswami credits Upasni with drawing him and countless others to Sai Baba:

> It was Upasani that drew him [Narasimhaswami] out of his distracting currents and fixed him on to Sai Baba. Without that, so many years or decades of work in Sai literature and Sai devotion and so many efforts to spread Sai faith throughout the length and breadth of this country by 600 or 700 lectures all over India in incessant tours and publication of innumerable pamphlets, books and journals could not be accomplished. Even now the movement which had overflowed the limits of Maharashtra is markedly the result of Sri Upasani's attracting this author. And if today Sai movement has far overflowed its original banks and promises to reach the farthest corners of the country if not of humanity through the latest works like the present work, Sri Upasani must be given much of the credit for this result. (Narasimhaswami 1983, 276)

Upasni Maharaj stayed with Sai Baba in Shirdi from 1911 to 1914. During his first year there, Sai Baba accepted Upasni as his favored student, proclaiming that there was no distinction between them and that he would help Upasni to attain God-realization and become a Sadguru over the next four years (Narasimhaswami and Subbarao 1966, 39). However, Upasni left Shirdi without Sai Baba's permission before finishing his fourth year of studentship, a fact that Narasimhaswami (1983, 284) said invalidated any claim that Upasni was Sai Baba's legitimate successor. Nonetheless, Upasni claimed to have attained God-realization during his time in Shirdi under the tutelage of Sai Baba. At the height of Upasni's fame in the 1920s and early 1930s, before his legal difficulties, he drew the attention of thousands who trekked to Sakori to meet him, including Mahatma Gandhi, or who waited for hours in line to pay homage to him during his visits to various cities (228). In his emphasis on the devotional path and the centrality of faith in himself as a guru, Upasni routinely cited his own experience of God-realization through contact with his guru, Shirdi Sai Baba, and in this way promoted Sai Baba's name along with his own.

In writing *Sage of Sakuri* in 1934, Narasimhaswami extolled the virtues of Sai Baba and briefly described his miracles, his divine or near-divine status, and his appeal to devotees of diverse religious backgrounds: "Devotees of all religions found that he [Sai Baba] could see anything taking place at any place or time—in the past, present or even distant future; that nothing ever spoken by him was false or falsified; that he could himself appear at any place, do anything he wanted and disappear; and that he used these powers (which they could only describe as Omnipresence, Omniscience and Omnipotence) as the guardian angel of those who surrendered themselves to him as their sole refuge, out of pure mercy and love—but never for pecuniary or other despicable reasons" (Narasimhaswami and Subbarao 1966, 31). Yet despite such high praise for Sai Baba, Narasimhaswami did not consider visiting Shirdi in his quest to find his guru, for he was seeking a living guru. His biographer records that at the close of his time in Sakori, Narasimhaswami was despondent, having spent the past eleven years searching for a guru. He had decided to stop wandering from place to place and return to Madras when "a Pathan"—a Muslim—suggested that he visit Shirdi first. Narasimhaswami replied curtly: "Sai Baba has attained 'Mahasamadhi' eighteen years ago in 1918. A darshan of his samadhi will not benefit me in any manner. I have already visited dargahs of Hazrat Baba Jan, Tajuddin Baba, and Khwaja Moinuddin Chisty Sheriff. None of them has made any impact on me" (Vijayakumar 2009, 65). Nonetheless, Narasimhaswami followed the man's advice and traveled north several kilometers, arriving in Shirdi in the late morning of August 29, 1936. There, at the tomb of Sai Baba, Narasimhaswami found his guru at long last.

SHIRDI SAI BABA AS THE SAMARTHA SADGURU

In *Life of Sai Baba*, Narasimhaswami notes that persons who are not yet fit to be disciples, that is, "those without humility, reverence, patience, receptivity and other virtues, or the proper attitude towards great saints," must have *satsang* (associating with goodness),[9] "they must move with bhaktas [devotees] and fit themselves for further progress. When they are fairly fit, they will get their Guru" (1980, 81). In Narasimhaswami's case, it took eleven years of active searching as a full-fledged renouncer before he was "fit" enough to find his guru. Finally, and much to his surprise, he found that guru in Shirdi Sai Baba. After he arrived in Shirdi on August 29, 1936, he went to the *samadhi* (tomb) of Sai Baba to pay homage. This was a life-changing experience, which he describes as a moment of silent communion in which Sai Baba reached out to him, "radiating thought": "A person seated before such a Mahatma [great soul] feels that his whole being is permeated, controlled, communed with and moulded by the Mahatma without the use of a single word and without direction that any book should be studied or any practice should be followed" (xii).

Narasimhaswami calls this method of silent communion with and instruction by a guru the "Dakshinamurti method," referring to a manifestation of Shiva in the form of a divine guru named Dakshinamurti who instructed his disciples and helped them to attain liberation through silence. Various renouncers, including Ramana Maharshi and Meher Baba, adopted this method and took vows of silence for extended periods. Although Shirdi Sai Baba is not known to have taken such a vow during his lifetime, here Narasimhaswami invokes this traditional method of austerity to explain how Sai Baba could communicate with him directly, infusing Narasimhaswami's being with his presence. "In our present day civilisation," says Narasimhaswami, "we have only understood conveyance of thought by speech. But with persons of the coming race or the fully developed human being that is represented by Baba, one of the most elementry [*sic*] powers is to convey thought and impulse to action without utterance of a single word" (1980, xii). This is significant because it enables Narasimhaswami to explain how Sai Baba can continue to function as a guru even though he passed away in 1918.

Narasimhaswami argues that Sai Baba is still available in his afterlife: "Baba is still a Guru, a Personality, a Divine Personality, not a mere abstraction, and can be seized by those who are in dead earnest" (1980, xiii). Narasimhaswami conceives of Sai Baba as a special type of guru, the Samartha Sadguru, which he defines in this way: "He who teaches about God or Sat is called Sadguru. He who uses *all his siddhis and superior powers* to carry the shishya [disciple] right up to the goal is called 'Samartha Sadguru'" (78).

Such figures have attained God-realization during their lifetimes and remain available even after they have left their bodies behind to aid others in attaining God-realization. Narasimhaswami argues that although Sai Baba has passed away, he can still use his superior powers to appear in embodied form, thereby reaching those who prefer to connect to a guru in human form as well as those who prefer to worship a formless being: "Being Nirakara [without form], he could be Sakara [with form] at any time whether he was in the flesh or beyond the flesh (i.e., after Mahasamadhi). Thus he serves as the ideal Guru, though he is not in the flesh, as he can and does appear in his old form to deal with his old and new devotees. Several people felt and feel that a Guru who is not in the flesh does not suit them, as others feel in the exactly opposite way. But by Baba's grace, all these have been drawn by him to his feet" (1980, 125–26). One can speculate that in the aftermath of Upasni Maharaj's legal troubles, Shirdi Sai Baba also served as the ideal guru for Narasimhaswami in that in his afterlife condition he was unlikely to be tainted by scandals of the flesh.[10]

Throughout his writings, Narasimhaswami repeatedly returns to his grounding in Advaita Vedanta philosophy to explain the nature and mission of Sai Baba as the Samartha Sadguru. Narasimhaswami asks what it means to attain God-realization and what relationship a God-realized being such as Sai Baba has with God. He raises this topic several times in his four-volume *Life of Sai Baba*, noting that many Hindu devotees identify Sai Baba with God and view him as an incarnation of God on earth (Narasimhaswami 1980, 262). Is Shirdi Sai Baba, then, God? The answer he arrives at is both yes and no. In his chapter "Nature and Functions of Baba," in volume 1, Narasimhaswami notes that Sai Baba himself seemed to make conflicting claims, at times stating that he was human and at other times stating that he was divine. Narasimhaswami explains such contradiction away, saying that it depends on the stance of the beholder: "Seen with ordinary eyes, Baba was a man and a poor fakir living in a dilapidated Mosque, but seen with the eye of devotion, Baba was God or a Guardian Angel" (193).

In this discussion, and elsewhere in his writings, Narasimhaswami (1980, 190) compares Sai Baba with Krishna, implying that just as Krishna was the human incarnation of Vishnu, so Sai Baba is an aspect of God: "What happened to Sri Krishna is what happened to Sri Sai Baba also. The vast mass took him to be a mere man, a begging fakir who was putting up in the Shirdi Mosque. And his nature was dedused [*sic*] from these premises that he was a beggar intent on getting his food and was wasting his time doing nothing useful to anybody. This was the exact opposite of the truth. But the mass did not know the truth at first." He goes on to explain that from the perspective of the devotee, "he is certainly God or a '*Vibhuti*.' Those who know enough of facts about him find that he knows everything everywhere at any time, that he has power to do anything everywhere, that he has power to control the movements and the heart of creatures, and even the elements of nature like rain, fire, etc., that he had a mastery of the knowledge of the past, present and future, even innumerable centuries away from the present, and that he had the highest moral principles of selflessness, service and love to all including the meanest beings." But, Narasimhaswami notes, not everybody has the ability to see this in Sai Baba, so he "was both God and not God" (195–96). Similarly, in volume 4, Narasimhaswami notes that Sai Baba is said to be a divine incarnation by some and not others. So, he concludes, "the best thing to say is that Sai Baba had in him the all-round perfection of divine qualities in such a manner as to fulfill our idea of God" (Narasimhaswami 1982, 84).

Ultimately, Narasimhaswami suggests, such questions and debates are pointless, for to truly know what God is, one must experience God-realization. When this happens, one immediately realizes there is only one All, only one Self: "In getting Baba as a Guru, one is helped on to the Supreme realisation of Jiva Brahma Aikya [identity of self and All-Self]. Those who refer to Baba as a single Guru or saint with a particular shape in one place are indulging in their tendency of materialisation, localisation, and fragmentisation. The real fruit of Baba's influence is perceiving him as the All—everything including one's old Guru, one's Ishta Devata [personal deity], and oneself" (Narasimhaswami 1980, 127). Just as Sai Baba began to help Narasimhaswami experience God-realization during his first visit to Shirdi through silent communion, he can help countless others as well: "Thus [Sai] Baba's answer to the question 'What is God' is that the question cannot be answered in words of course, as the real truth about God is one to be felt at heart. One should grow into God and then only he knows God. It is only by developing the little spark of Love that Baba will ignite in your heart, and blowing it into a name, that you can be transformed into a mass of love. God is love, nothing but love. . . . No other answer to the question 'What is God' is worth having" (Narasimhaswami 1982, 58–59).

Narasimhaswami felt utterly transformed by the "little spark of love" that he believed Sai Baba had ignited in his heart that day in Shirdi. For the remaining twenty years of his life, he pursued the guru marga with faith in and devotion to Sai Baba as his personal guru. Narasimhaswami believed that his experience was replicable: just as he had experienced God-realization through his devotion to Sai Baba, so could others. And through this communion with Sai Baba, they too would be transformed into masses of love. Furthermore, this transformative experience was not solely a spiritual one but had very significant worldly consequences: "If a person once realises that he is not this organism and this body, but is something very much wider, which may be the result of Baba's training him to pitch himself into all others' hearts and identify himself with those souls, then the present 'necessity' and the desires and aversions formerly prevailing with oneself, all drop off. The scales fall from one's eyes. All values are different. The world looms as something totally different from what it did. One sets about it and acts in a different way" (Narasimhaswami 1980, xiv). Thus, Narasimhaswami characterizes Shirdi Sai Baba's mission as the Samartha Sadguru as twofold: "the uplift of mankind" in both religious and political realms, noting in the first volume of *Life of Sai Baba* that "a study of this work describing [Shirdi Sai Baba] will shower upon the readers incalculable benefits both spiritual and temporal in this world and beyond" (9).

SHIRDI SAI BABA AND THE SPIRITUAL UPLIFT OF INDIVIDUALS

With regard to Shirdi Sai Baba's first mission, the spiritual uplift of individuals, Narasimhaswami saw Sai Baba as the Samartha Sadguru who could lead individuals to God-realization through the exact program of guru worship that Narasimhaswami had himself successfully followed. Narasimhaswami praised Sai Baba for allowing his disciples to worship him according to their differing religious upbringings: "Sai allowed the Hindus to adopt their puranic method of worship and treat him either as an Avatar or Ishtadeva or a Gurudeva, as they liked, while he allowed the Muslims approaching him to read their Koran and the Shariat at the Mosque and to join his flock as his devotees, treating him merely as an *Avalia* or a saint with remarkable powers" (1980, 57). However, while acknowledging that devotees could worship Sai Baba in whatever manner they chose, Narasimhaswami argued that the pursuit of the guru marga was the most efficacious method, for he had tangible proof that it worked in his own experience of God-realization. In addition, he maintained that the guru marga had the benefit of being approved of by Sai Baba in the final years of his life.

Although in principle anyone could turn to Sai Baba in pursuit of the guru path, as noted above one had to be "fairly fit" from a moral standpoint to find one's guru in Sai Baba. Narasimhaswami discusses the qualifications and disqualifications of *shishyas*, or disciples, writing that it all boils down to two key qualities: "*Nishta* (faith) and *Saburi* (patience) are the qualifications and their absence the disqualifications in a shishya" (1980, 108–9). Nishta, faith in the guru, is the first requirement of a disciple, and those lacking in faith encompass a wide variety of moral deficits: "Atheists, scoffers, flippant persons, women hunters, combative persons, passionate natures, hypocrites, cruel-hearted and wicked people in general, or those reveling in sin, are, as a rule incapable of pure and strong faith and so are unfit either to be Gurus or shishyas" (111). Narasimhaswami writes that when one's faith has been tested by Sai Baba and found to be true, only then can one begin the process of attaining God-realization. Sai Baba tests his devotees through various means, sometimes in person when they come to see him in Shirdi, at other times through visions (112–17). A person with faith is described as having the fullest respect for the guru, being free of self-conceit and worldly attachments and ready to serve the guru (118). After passing this test of faith, Sai Baba then begins to refine the disciple to prepare him or her for God-realization, which may occur in this lifetime or may take multiple rebirths to attain.

Saburi, patience, is the second requirement of a disciple. It took Narasimhaswami eleven years of active seeking before he found his guru, thus he was very aware of how long it could take to minimize attachment to worldly affairs and shed one's ego to develop faith. He writes of his own experience, "Fullest faith and surrender cannot easily get into a man's heart after he has spent 40 years, i.e. the best part of his life at the bar, in politics and in the world" (Narasimhaswami 1980, 119.) Not only can it take many years in one's current lifetime to find a guru, but even after finding Sai Baba and becoming his disciple, it can still take many lifetimes before becoming refined enough to experience God-realization. The techniques used for refining the disciple are said to vary, depending on each disciple's individual needs. However, according to Narasimhaswami, the best technique is ritual worship of Sai Baba as the Samartha Sadguru, grounded in Brahminical orthopraxy.

In *Life of Sai Baba*, Narasimhaswami describes how the worship of Sai Baba grew more complex in the first years of the twentieth century as Hindu devotees sought to systematize their worship of Sai Baba in keeping with temple traditions by hiring a priest and composing devotional hymns. He explains that although Sai Baba despised all the pomp (Narasimhaswami 1980, 41), he nonetheless allowed followers to worship him "with the prescience that it would be the means for providing temporal and spiritual benefits to millions of individuals and also the means of solving Indian's national problems of communal and religious unity" (55). Narasimhaswami explains that worship is essential to the quest for God-realization because it is the key to progressing down the guru path; through worship, "one gradually progresses with lower and external forms till his inner kernel of devotion attains maturity and perfection" (48). Narasimhaswami then outlines a nine-point program of ritual worship, which he says must be attended to and followed because it is found in the Bhagavata Purana and was stressed by Sai Baba:

> The nine modes are, 1) Sravana, listening to accounts of the deeds of Gods, his Avataras and saints; 2) Kirtana of Vishnu—reciting these or repeating God's names and praise; 3) Smarana—constantly recalling these, especially uttering God's names; 4) Padasevanam, falling at the feet of God, saints etc.; 5) Archana—(formal) worship, e.g., with flowers, water, food, scents, all the 16 upacharas, etc.; 6) Vandana, prostration before God and the saints; 7) Dasya— e.g., service, doing every work for God or saint; 8) Sakhya—remaining in the company of God or Saint; and 9) Atma Nivedana—i.e., surrender of the self— i.e., forgetting oneself entirely in the contemplation of God after formally offering the self as a gift to God. (Narasimhaswami 1980, 48–49)[11]

Of special significance to Narasimhaswami were the first three points on the list: praising God through stories, songs, and chanted meditation upon his names. In Hindu puja traditions, the recitation of a deity's names— *namastotram*—is typically composed in poetic Sanskrit verse and consists of 100, 108, 1,000, or 1,008 names. According to Constantina Eleni Rhodes (2010, 83), in premodern Hindu traditions the enunciation of a namastotram was thought to activate "the various aspects of the deity's vibratory essence," thereby rendering the deity present to receive the devotee's praise and to bless the devotee in exchange.

This idea of rendering the deity present through the namastotram was applied to Shirdi Sai Baba by Narasimhaswami, who composed the *Shri Sai Ashtotharam* (108 names of Shri Sai) in Shirdi in 1936–37 as a token of his devotion to his newfound guru. Written in Sanskrit, this namastotram entails 108 verses in praise of Sai Baba. Narasimhaswami shared his composition with Das Ganu Maharaj (discussed in chapter 2) and other devotees then present in Shirdi, who then began to chant the verses in their daily prayers. Soon, the Shri Saibaba Sansthan Trust formally incorporated the verses into the daily service at the Samadhi Mandir. Narasimhaswami reportedly viewed this as evidence that Sai Baba had accepted his devotion (Vijayakumar 2009, 67). During the final two decades of his life, Narasimhaswami arranged to have the *Shri Sai Ashtotharam* printed in pocket-sized editions, which he distributed for free wherever he traveled as a way of spreading the name of Sai Baba and encouraging daily meditation upon and worship of him. The *Shri Sai Ashtotharam* has received widespread acceptance within the community of Sai faithful. Today, the poem is known by heart by millions of devotees who chant it as part of their regular prayers. It continues to be part of the daily puja schedule at the Samadhi Mandir in Shirdi and is included in either the daily or weekly puja schedules of a majority of Shirdi Sai Baba temples throughout India and around the world. In these temples, the poem is commonly referred to as *archana*, "praising" in the form of formal worship of the image of Sai Baba installed in the temple and involving the offering of flowers, water, food, and so on, along with chanting the 108 verses.

Narasimhaswami opens the *Shri Sai Ashtotharam* with the following verses:

1. Homage to Lord Sai.
2. Homage to Lakshminarayan.
3. Homage to Krishna, Rama, Shiva, and Hanuman.
4. Homage to Sheshashayi.
5. Homage to Him who resides on the banks of the Godavari.
6. Homage to Him who dwells in the hearts of his devotees.
7. Homage to Him who resides in the hearts of all.[12]

In these first lines, Narasimhaswami is not just praising multiple Hindu deities. He is equating Sai Baba with the Hindu pantheon by proclaiming that these deities—Vishnu in multiple forms (Lakshminarayan, Krishna, Rama, and Sheshashayi), Shiva, and Hanuman—are names and forms of Sai Baba. He then says that Sai Baba also took physical form and dwelled along the Godavari River and yet is simultaneously unmanifest, dwelling in immaterial form, not only in the hearts of his devotees, but in the hearts of everyone.

In these simple verses, we find a compact distillation of Advaita Vedanta philosophy as Narasimhaswami had come to understand it through his personal experience of God-realization in Shirdi. At the core of his understanding is the belief in the nondual nature of ultimate reality, whereby the self within is the same as God, which is also the universal All-Self. Shirdi Sai Baba is therefore not only the guru who leads one to that All, but is himself that All, which is located within us and all around us. In *Life of Sai Baba*, Narasimhaswami would later expand upon this, arguing that when understood from this monistic perspective, Sai Baba was both formless and with form. This sentiment is reiterated in later verses of the *Shri Sai Ashtotharam*, when Narasimhaswami pays homage to "Him who manifests in many forms and in the form of the Universe itself" and "Him who is formless and unmanifest" (verses 64–65).

The next verses continue to praise Sai Baba's divine nature, noting among other things that he is eternal, and thus beyond the boundaries of time and death (verses 9–15), and that he is the supporter of all living things and of the universe (verses 17–18). The poem next praises Sai Baba for the protection he offers his devotees (verses 19–20), and then it considers the various benefits that these devotees gain by worshiping him. Devotees may receive a bounty of worldly benefits, including food, clothing, health, wealth, sons, friends, family, and aid when in distress. The list begins to incorporate more otherworldly concerns beginning in verse 29, which praises Sai Baba as the one who "bestows worldly pleasures, salvation of the self, heavenly bliss, and ultimate union." In the next verses, Sai Baba is praised for his ability to deliver to his devotees limitless love, ultimate truth, bliss, and eternal happiness (verses 31–35).

After listing the worldly and spiritual bounties to be reaped by worshiping Sai Baba, the poem next praises Sai Baba as God, using various epithets, including Supreme Lord, Param Brahman, Param Atman, embodiment of Supreme Knowledge, and Father of Creation (verses 36–40). The next verses then praise Sai Baba's intimate connection with his devotees, describing him as a parent who provides security from fear and is bound to them by love (verses 41–48). Sai Baba is able to destroy the karma of past deeds, opening up the pathway to liberation (verses 49–51). The remaining verses are largely dedicated to praising Sai Baba's various qualities. He is described as truthful, virtuous, all-powerful, invincible, beautiful, subtle, helpful, pure, and all-knowing. Notable among these latter verses are number 97, which pays homage to Sai Baba as "Him who preached and practiced the equality and oneness of all religions," and numbers 98–99, which pay homage to Sai Baba as Dakshinamurti, a form of Shiva, and as Sri Venkateswara, a form of Vishnu. In these three verses we have a concise statement of Narasimhaswami's belief, which he later spells out in greater detail in the volumes of *Life of Sai Baba*, that Sai Baba is both an intra- and inter-religious unifier. Narasimhaswami views Sai Baba as an intra-religious unifier for his ability to unite both Shaiva and Vaishnava Hindus in conjoint devotion to him, once they come to the monistic realization that God is both Shiva and Vishnu, both Dakshinamurti and Sri Venkateswara. Similarly, he views Sai Baba as an inter-religious unifier because he accepted devotees from multiple religious backgrounds and taught them that God is both the Hindu God and the Muslim God. Seen from this monistic view, all religions are part of a larger united devotional community dedicated to the one true God. The final verses of the *Shri Sai Ashtotharam* read:

107. Homage to Him who consolidates the true path of amity, unity, and understanding among all people.
108. Homage to the Samartha Sadguru, Lord Sai.

Here, Narasimhaswami concludes by declaring Sai Baba to be a beacon of inclusivism, whose primary work as the Samartha Sadguru is to unite people in the loving harmony of shared devotion.

Narasimhaswami maintains that meditation upon Sai Baba as the Samartha Sadguru is absolutely necessary to experience God-realization. While he acknowledges that any form of meditation could work in theory, he advocates Hindu ritual in particular as the best program of action to help one progress toward the goal of surrendering the self within God. He believes that daily recitation of the *Shri Sai Ashtotharam* in praise of Sai Baba, either at home or in the temple, will help devotees experience Sai Baba's presence from beyond the grave, just as Narasimhaswami experienced it himself in his first moment of silent communion with Sai Baba in Shirdi in 1936. From this first experience of Sai Baba's presence, one's devotion will grow as one continues to meditate upon Sai Baba:

That is how worship begins, and grows. Gradually . . . it leads the worshipper higher and higher so that he understands his own self and the Supreme self more and more until the Jiva [self] is absorbed in the Paramatma [All-Self]. There is a considerable distance of time, stages, and a vast amount of effort between the beginning of worship and the highest achievement; and Baba worship had and has all stages in it, and sorts of worshippers. Baba who first objected to his worship, did by his own Antarjnana or prophetic vision foresee or ordain what was to follow, namely, not only individual benefits to millions but also national benefit, and ultimately benefit to the cause of religion itself for the sake of humanity. That is why, he gradually promoted and then developed his worship, in spite numerous obstacles. (Narasimhaswami 1980, 32)

Ritual worship, then, is central to the guru marga as Narasimhaswami understands it. Such worship is the means by which individual disciples come to experience the union of their individual selves with Sai Baba as the Samartha Sadguru, and in so doing experience the nondual nature of ultimate reality.

For devotees seeking more intensive worship of Sai Baba, Narasimhaswami also composed the *Shri Sai Sahasranamam* (1,000 names of Shri Sai Baba). Like the *Shri Sai Ashtotharam*, the *Shri Sai Sahasranamam* can be chanted informally in one's home and is also chanted as part of formal temple puja. In addition to composing and printing textual devotional material about Sai Baba, Narasimhaswami also focused on visual devotional material. He was well aware of the importance of visual imagery in Hindu ritual tradition, where *darshan*, seeing the divine image and being seen by the deity in exchange, is central to home and temple puja. Thus, to facilitate the journey down the guru path, he also arranged for the printing of posters of Sai Baba and even for the creation of jewelry featuring images of Sai Baba. His biographer writes that Narasimhaswami had these items produced in Madras but also shipped them to Shirdi for pilgrims to purchase outside the Samadhi Mandir:

Narasimha Swamiji arranged for printing of Sai Baba's pictures on a mass scale. These pictures were useful for creating devotion for Sai Baba. Rao Brothers in Triplicane, Madras, produced pictures of Sai Baba from tricolour blocks on art paper in card size and cabinet size. The Tripurasundari Jewellery works in Mint Street, Madras, made lockets in circular and star designs, in small, medium and big sizes and in gold plate and nickel. Every locket contains a picture of Sai Baba on one side and a deity on the other side. Around the picture of Sai Baba are minted in Tamil the famous saying of Sai Baba—"Why fear when I am there." They also made rings, buttons and pendants containing Sai Baba's figure in bust and tiny silver *padukas* [footprints]. Devotees were quite enthusiastic in purchasing these items. This generated a lot of income for the All India Sai Samaj, which in turn was helpful in its expansion. (Vijayakumar 2009, 86)

Given the importance that Narasimhaswami placed on darshan, in addition to namastotram, to render the presence of Sai Baba, when he founded the first All India Sai Samaj temple dedicated to Shirdi Sai Baba in Mylapore, Madras, in 1953, he had a poster of Shirdi Sai Baba installed within the inner sanctum for ritual worship.[13]

Ritual worship of and meditation upon Shirdi Sai Baba as the Samartha Sadguru, along with patience and faith, are the means by which Narasimhaswami experienced God-realization. He therefore set forth this method, which he referred to as the guru path, as the means by which others could also receive Sai Baba's blessing of spiritual uplift. He describes this spiritual uplift as a monistic state of blissful God-realization known as *satchitananda*, wherein the disciple realizes that his inner spirit is identical with both guru and God as the All. But spiritual uplift is only half the picture. Narasimhaswami believed that this monistic experience of God-realization had temporal benefits as well, arguing that ritual worship of Sai Baba was the means by which individuals could attain the spiritual bliss of satchitananda and India could attain the temporal bliss of peaceful union as an independent nation.

SHIRDI SAI BABA AND THE TEMPORAL UPLIFT OF INDIA

With regard to Shirdi Sai Baba's second mission, the temporal uplift of India, Narasimhaswami saw Sai Baba as the Samartha Sadguru who could "unify all faiths by acceptance of him as the common Gurudeva" and thereby establish national peace (1980, 62). Central to this second mission was the conception of Sai Baba as a composite figure. Unlike Das Ganu Maharaj, who maintained that Sai Baba was born to Muslim parents (as discussed in chapter 2), Narasimhaswami insisted that Sai Baba was born to Hindu Brahmin parents. Yet Narasimhaswami agrees with Das Ganu that Sai Baba studied with both a Muslim *fakir* and a Hindu guru. Thus, while he maintains a high-caste Hindu identity for Sai Baba, Narasimhaswami simultaneously characterizes him as a composite figure who embodies both Hinduism and Islam. For instance, Narasimhaswami (1980, 26–27) states that Sai Baba "had both Hindu and Muslim features in his body and in his actions and practice" and had both Hindu and Muslim gurus who provided him with religious initiation and instruction as a young man. Because of Sai Baba's composite nature, Narasimhaswami believes that he is the ideal figure to bring together members of multiple faith communities in India, especially its two largest communities, Hindus and Muslims:

> The only thing that could bring Hindus and Muslims together was a weird, saintly personality acting as a Guru or God-Man, absolutely neutral, allowing all sects, religions and creeds to have their own ways, and yet bringing them all to a common platform, namely, devotion to that saintly personality and enabling them to see that the differences are petty and ridiculous—unworthy of serious men of jnana or realisation. Sai Baba was such a person. In him, divine qualities, obviously superhuman powers combined with even-minded beneficence were so patently manifested that all alike, Hindus, Muslims, Christians, etc., who came to know about him felt that they were before a higher influence and that they could all approach and reach God through him, that he was the high water mark of saintliness or Godliness or God-head and they willingly made him their Gurudeva or protector. (Narasimhaswami 1980, 56–57)

Narasimhaswami conceives of the "weird, saintly personality" of Shirdi Sai Baba in explicitly nationalistic ways. In the chapter "Baba's Mission" in the first volume of *Life of Sai Baba*, he writes that Sai Baba will unify India through "the building up of one common central religion or faith" and in so doing will solve "India's National problem of unifying conflicting groups" (Narasimhaswami 1980, 179; see also p. 63).

In the years leading up to Indian independence, tension between the Hindu majority and the Muslim minority swelled amid debates about how an independent India should be governed and the role of majority and minority religious communities in said governance. In 1947, when independence arrived at long last, it came with the partition of the subcontinent into India and Pakistan. This partition unleashed unprecedented communal bloodshed between Hindus and Muslims.[14] Narasimhaswami began writing his four-volume *Life of Sai Baba* in 1953–54, during which he was painfully aware of the divisive civil discourse over the place of religion in the newly established republic of India. Because of Sai Baba's composite nature and his ability to bring together in shared devotion members of multiple faith communities, especially Hindus and Muslims, Narasimhaswami argued that Sai Baba was instrumental to the peaceful cohabitation of Hindus and Muslims in the newly independent and pluralistic nation of India. Indeed, he wrote that Sai Baba "added to Gandhiji's plan of work" by secretly working on the hearts of all in the interest of unity (Narasimhaswami 1980, 153).

Addressing Hindus as his primary audience—and as the majority religious community in India—in *Life of Sai Baba* Narasimhaswami first turns to the topic of Hindu divisiveness. He notes that Hindus are not unified in and of themselves and therefore are often in conflict with one another across sectarian lines. In the chapter "Unification and Purification of Hinduism," in volume 1, he argues that the "essential substratum of all these faiths called Hinduism" is the monistic belief in God, or Param Brahman (Narasimhaswami 1980, 64). Sai Baba taught his Hindu followers that the Real is one, and therefore no matter what one calls it or what form of it one worships, ultimately the names and forms are insignificant, and there is no need for discord over such details. Vaishnavas, Shaivas, Shaktas—all of these Hindu groups should unite in the recognition that they worship different forms of the same divinity.

Furthermore, Narasimhaswami argues, this belief in God, or Param Brahman, is the common core not only of Hinduism but of all religions. He explains:

Baba, therefore, drew the attention of all his bhaktas [devotees] to the fact that whether you called your God, Siva or Vishnu, he is the Supreme Power that is responsible for the creation, maintenance, and the withdrawal of the world, and he gives you all that you need and finally the highest bliss at his own feet. This, being the central essence of all Theism, is or should be the central plank for unifying all branches and sects of Hindus and also unifying Hinduism with Islam and other theistic religions. In fact world unity of religions can be achieved mainly on this basis. (Narasimhaswami 1980, 67)

Here, Narasimhaswami positions Sai Baba as both an intrafaith unifier and an interfaith unifier. Narasimhaswami believes that Sai Baba put into practice this principle of seeking unity by bringing together Hindus from various regions and sectarian backgrounds, as well as devotees from other religious traditions:

Those who came to him saw in him their only God, recognised him as their Guru Deva (and that was the highest religious sentiment that they had) and there was no possibility of their tearing themselves off into divisions, though

their original loyalties were in other respects maintained. Baba hated intoler-
ance and made people tolerate each other's views and peculiarities. He did not
allow the Hindus under him to fight against the Muslim devotees. He removed
asperities and made them work in unison as fellow-devotees, as brothers in Sai
faith. Thus he worked out not merely the unification of Hinduism but also the
unification of Hinduism with the other great religion in India, namely, Islam.
(Narasimhaswami 1980, 68–69)

In volume 4 of *Life of Sai Baba*, Narasimhaswami expands on this discussion of religious unification in two further chapters. In "Sai Baba and
Future of Religion," he delves into his theory that the essence of all religions
is the same. It is over the "externals," the peripheral details, that religious
adherents quarrel: temple versus mosque, this form of prayer versus that
form. But the essence is the same, and for Narasimhaswami that essence is
not only God but love of that one God: "Let every person sit quietly directing
his mind to the greatness of God and the grand qualities of God and allow
himself to be lost in them. Then there is no possibility of his quarrelling
with any other person or any other person quarrelling with him. The result
of contemplation of love for God is Love. If we go into the essence of religion, that is, if each tries to concentrate on God, the result will only be love
and harmony and not a jarring set of crusades among people trying to
trample on one another" (Narasimhaswami 1982, 88). By bringing Hindus,
Muslims, and others together in Shirdi and uniting them in their common
love of him, Sai Baba set in motion a future in which the religious externals
would be shed in favor of one synthetic religious community of Indians who
together would "form the foundation of India's main religion of the future":

So far as India itself is concerned, the future of religion in India is largely a
question of the fusion of the two great trends which appear to be so widely different, namely, Hinduism and Islam. The differences have led frequently to the
breaking of heads and burning of temples, and recently even the breaking-up
of the political unity of the country. So, the achievement of something like a
basis for the unity of Hinduism and Islam is itself a very great and momentous
task and may be justly viewed as affording a solution to the country's problem
of fusing the two into one. (Narasimhaswami 1982, 84–85)

In the chapter "Sri Sai and National Unity," Narasimhaswami continues
this theme by explaining that Sai Baba worked to encourage Hindu-Muslim

unity in three specific ways: his composite personhood, teachings, and personal example. As noted earlier, Narasimhaswami describes Sai Baba as having both Hindu and Muslim features in his body. In this chapter he provides further examples of this composite physicality, including a story of Sai Baba calling his followers "worthless fellows" for debating whether he was born a Hindu or a Muslim, and then stripping naked and challenging them to figure it out. Those present could not agree whether he had been circumcised (marking him as Muslim), nor whether his ears were pierced (marking him as Hindu) (Narasimhaswami 1982, 100). However, just a few pages later, Narasimhaswami contradicts himself when he writes, "There is not a particle of doubt that Baba's ears were bored," as corroborated by Marthand Mhalsapathy, indicating Sai Baba's birth to Hindu Brahmin parents (104). Nonetheless, Narasimhaswami continues by explaining that just as Sai Baba embodies a composite identity, so do his teachings. Sai Baba studied with Hindu and Muslim gurus, and he encouraged his followers to read scripture and engage in ritual practices from both traditions (107–8). Finally, in his personal example he demonstrated how to allow the "principle of love" to pervade in Shirdi by accepting all who came to him, with an open heart (109).

Narasimhaswami links this threefold method of encouraging Hindu-Muslim unity to an explicitly nationalist agenda, writing that Sai Baba was a freedom fighter who served in the Rani of Jhansi's army and fought against the British during the Indian Rebellion of 1857.[15] Although Sai Baba had presumably left politics behind by the time of his arrival in Shirdi as a renouncer, Narasimhaswami states that he "always encouraged patriotism" and that he encouraged Hindu-Muslim unity not only as an act of communal solidarity but as an act of patriotism: "As to the question of Hindu-Muslim unity, any person carefully studying the subject would see that Hindu-Muslim unity is the one great desideratum to make India strong and prosperous. Baba also saw it, and so, he laid the foundations of Hindu-Muslim unity" (Narasimhaswami 1982, 103).

For Narasimhaswami, then, Shirdi Sai Baba is a Samartha Sadguru who remains available even after the death of his physical body to guide devotees along the guru path to God-realization. God-realization, as he conceived of it, entails a transformative experience of loving union that words ultimately fail to fully describe. This loving union is not merely between guru and shishya, or God and devotee, but between the individual self and the All-Self that exists in everyone and everything. Thus, once one has awakened to God-realization, one sees the unity underlying everything. This monistic experience of salvation involves both spiritual bliss and a tangible, this-worldly effect, here and now, erasing divisions as devotees of Sai Baba experience loving union and realize their interconnectedness. Narasimhaswami thus set out to share his path to God-realization, so that other Hindus might experience it themselves and in so doing save not only their own souls but the very soul of a communally fractured India.

NARASIMHASWAMI'S MISSION: SAI PRACHAR

Narasimhaswami's experience in Shirdi taught him that Sai Baba was still available, even after his death, to serve as a guru and to guide his followers to God-realization. As he had done while studying in Tiruvannamalai under Ramana Maharshi, so in Shirdi did Narasimhaswami converse with other devotees of Sai Baba, in an effort to gain a more thorough understanding of Sai Baba's life and teachings. He compiled notes into his three-volume *Devotees' Experiences of Sri Sai Baba*, which was first published in 1940. In the preface to the first volume, Narasimhaswami encourages readers to turn to Sai Baba, claiming that he continues to guide those who approach him with love toward both spiritual liberation and national peace.

Narasimhaswami (2008, i) cites the example of Narayan Asram, profiled in chapter 5 of the first volume, to demonstrate Sai Baba's ability to bring devotees to the monistic experience of loving union with the guru that is God-realization: "The holy Swami Narain [Narayan] Asram reveals how he was enabled by Baba to enjoy the mystic bliss of perceiving that all things are but his own self—that difference is really non-existent. The reader may be assured that such high advaitic flights are by no means confined to the older devotees that were privileged to see Baba in the flesh. The modern devotee can still derive similar and even higher benefits by concentrating his love on Baba." Narasimhaswami then cites the example of Abdullah Jan, profiled in chapter 9 of the first volume, to demonstrate Sai Baba's ability to bring devotees to a state of loving union with their fellow citizens: "The other statements in this part speak for themselves and show how far Baba helped in overcoming the unfortunate differences between the two communities of India. The case of Abdullah Jan who came from beyond the Himalayas, with the view that Indians—especially Hindus—are the natural enemies and prey of stronger northern races, and was so deeply changed by contact with Sai Baba as to regard Hindus as his brethren and internecine quarrels as destructive of the country's welfare, is by no means a solitary exception but typical of whole groups" (ii).

In *Devotees' Experiences*, Narasimhaswami aimed to document the array of spiritual and temporal benefits that devotees had received through their devotion to Shirdi Sai Baba. To compile these accounts, he began by interviewing devotees who were still present in Shirdi in 1936 and had known Sai Baba before his death in 1918, including Das Ganu Maharaj (discussed in chapter 2) and Abdul Baba (discussed in chapter 1). He then traveled to Bombay and throughout Maharashtra to collect statements from others who had had personal contact with Sai Baba. Finally, he began to record the statements of those who had not had personal contact with Sai Baba but whose lives had been transformed by him from beyond the grave. In all, Narasimhaswami interviewed seventy-nine devotees in 1936, the majority of whom were Hindu. As he toured throughout western India, accompanied by Das Ganu and M. B. Rege, he also held devotional gatherings to spread the faith. However, the more accounts he collected, the more Narasimhaswami felt that he needed to publicize the information so that those living beyond western India could also look to Sai Baba. To reach potential devotees in the south, he began publishing these accounts in the Madras *Sunday Times* in 1936–37, prior to releasing the collection of accounts in book form. By this means, he said, "the initial work of creating among the devout public all over India an interest in Sri Sai Baba got off to a very good start" (Saipadananda 1973, 27).

Narasimhaswami grew convinced that his personal mission in life was to engage in Sai prachar, propagating devotion to Shirdi Sai Baba. He believed that Sai Baba approved of his mission, writing that the meeting in early 1936 with Narayan Purushottam Avasthi, the man who would introduce him to sixty of the devotees he would interview for *Devotees' Experiences*, was "proof of Sri Sai Baba's grace flowing towards me" (Saipadananda 1973, 25). In the fourth volume of *Life of Sai Baba*, Narasimhaswami (1982, 23–24) writes that he realized that Sai prachar was the work allotted to him by Sai Baba himself, and that the ongoing visions and appearances of Sai Baba that other devotees had witnessed since 1918 were "a stunning proof that Sai is living, that Sai responds to prayer, and that Sai Baba wishes that all should come to know of his glory and benefit thereby, especially because once they see that Sai is living and answering prayers, and is helpful, vast masses, hundreds, thousands, and lakhs of people will get Sai faith, and that will build up their future." In 1939, Narasimhaswami returned to Madras, the home base from which he would spend the remaining seventeen years of his life working to grow the community of Sai faithful.

In Madras in 1940, Narasimhaswami founded the All India Sai Samaj. As discussed in chapter 1, the Shri Saibaba Sansthan Trust was founded in Shirdi in 1922 with a mission of organizing the daily ritual activities at the Samadhi Mandir and providing accommodations for pilgrims in Shirdi. In 1940 the Trust did have a Bhakta Mandal, or association of Sai devotees, but Narasimhaswami thought that its scope was too limited, as its primary activity was to send *udi* (sacred ash) to registered devotees three times a year, and it had no goals for expansion of its mission or geographic presence (Vijayakumar 2009, 82). The mission of Narasimhaswami's All India Sai Samaj, on the other hand, was to disseminate Sai devotion throughout the country. To accomplish this, Narasimhaswami focused on several key activities: publishing books, magazines, pamphlets, images, and other devotional matter about Sai Baba; organizing lecture tours to build devotional communities throughout India; and establishing temples for the worship of Sai Baba beyond the Samadhi Mandir in Shirdi.

Narasimhaswami was a prolific writer, publishing numerous English-language books on Sai Baba during the final two decades of his life. In addition to the three-volume *Devotees' Experiences of Sri Sai Baba* (1940), his other major publications include *Who Is Sri Sai Baba of Shirdi?* (1939), a booklet providing an overview of Sai Baba's life and teachings; *The Wondrous Saint: Sai Baba* (1939), a booklet focused on Sai Baba's alleged miracles; *Sri Sai Baba's Charters and Sayings* (1939), a compilation of the teachings and statements made by Sai Baba to his devotees as collected in Narasimhaswami's interviews; and the four-volume *Life of Sai Baba* (1955, 1956, 1957, and 1969, the final two volumes published posthumously). Narasimhaswami also composed devotional poems in Sanskrit, most notably the aforementioned *Shri Sai Ashtotharam* and *Shri Sai Sahasranamam*. In addition, Narasimhaswami started the monthly magazine *Sai Sudha* in early 1940. Here, Narasimhaswami published in serial form many of the narratives that appeared in *Devotees' Experiences*, as well as the lectures he gave on Sai Baba to gatherings as he toured the country, making them available in English, Tamil, and Telugu.

From his base at the All India Sai Samaj in Madras, Narasimhaswami also prepared lecture tours that took him throughout India, spreading word of Shirdi Sai Baba. On these tours he visited with small gatherings of Sai worshipers in the homes of devotees and addressed audiences of curious onlookers in parks and other public arenas. He lectured about Sai Baba's life and teachings and led the singing of devotional hymns. He handed out pocket-sized editions of the *Shri Sai Ashtotharam*, udi from Shirdi, and pictures of Sai Baba to anyone who would take them. Although he focused primarily on southern India, he also visited major cities throughout the north, including Bombay, Delhi, Allahabad, Banaras, and Calcutta. His biographer P. S. Varadaraja Iyer paints Narasimhaswami as a wandering renouncer, spreading Sai faith during this final phase of his life:

> A short figure, covered in a long shirt, and single dhoti going round the waist like a lungi, broad forehead, fronting a head almost bald, [Narasimhaswami] carries a cloth bag that comes down from the shoulder and walks briskly along. The bag holds small packets of 'Udi' from Shirdi, copies of pocket size Ashtotharam on Sai Baba compiled by him and pictures of Sai Baba in card size— these are his gifts to the sick and sorry that accost him for relief and the gifts work wonders. As he passes on the Udi he mutters "Baba Paripoornaprasada siddhirasthu [May there be the perfection that is Baba's abundant blessing]."
> (Varadaraja Iyer 1974, 1)

As he traveled throughout the country, Narasimhaswami also established branch offices of the All India Sai Samaj. Reports submitted by these branch offices about their activities were regularly published in *Sai Sudha*, alongside Narasimhaswami's travel itineraries. His biographer Vijayakumar reports on the success of these lecture tours in growing the Sai Baba movement: "By 1950 he had built seventy-five *Upasamajams* [branch offices] affiliated to the All India Sai Samaj and a network of thousands of sincere Sai devotees. Over fifteen Sai Baba temples were built all over India as a result of Narasimha Swamiji's extensive tours and many more were under construction. A band of volunteers readily assisted him in Sai prachar work and Sai Baba, who was confined only to Shirdi uptil [*sic*] 1936, had now moved over to the entire country" (2009, 101).

Narasimhaswami held an All India Sai Devotees' Convention in Madras on May 16–19, 1946, to plan for future growth. In addition to Narasimhaswami and other local volunteers, approximately two hundred delegates attended from outside of Madras. Together they engaged in daily prayer to Sai Baba (in Sanskrit, Tamil, Telugu, and Hindi), discussed the activities of various branches, and listened to speeches by several dignitaries in the movement, most notably a handful of Sai Baba's original devotees, including Das Ganu Maharaj and Marthand Mhalsapathy. In his presidential address to the convention, Narasimhaswami encouraged the branches to engage in active service that would promote communal harmony in their cities. Specific activities that he encouraged included feeding the poor, starting free boys' and girls' schools, and opening medical facilities for those in need. The convention ended with a charitable ceremony at which over a thousand were served free food. After this first convention, conventions were held annually throughout the late 1940s and 1950s, each hosted by a branch of the All India Sai Samaj located in a different city (Vijayakumar 2009, 104–6).

As devotion spread and more donations came in to the All India Sai Samaj, Narasimhaswami purchased land to establish a permanent building in Mylapore, Madras. Prior to this, the Samaj had functioned in rented or borrowed spaces for its day-to-day business, with devotional gatherings held on Thursdays in the houses of devotees. In 1952 the Samaj moved into the new building, and its temple was initiated on October 19, 1953. In the final years of Narasimhaswami's life, these facilities continued to expand, with the purchase of additional land and the construction of a large hall for lectures and devotional gatherings, a library, a hospital, and hostel amenities for visitors (Vijayakumar 2009, 100–101, 110).

On October 19, 1956, Narasimhaswami passed away at the age of eighty-three. In the decades following his death, he has become a sanctified figure within the All India Sai Samaj and is often deemed the "apostle" of Shirdi Sai Baba by its members.[16] At the All India Sai Samaj quarters in Madras, a marble *murti* (statue) of Narasimhaswami is installed in his cottage, which was turned into a shrine and meditation hall where devotees can pay homage to him, in addition to worshiping Sai Baba within the temple. Narasimhaswami is also worshiped in other branches, as his biographer describes: "At all the *Upasamajams* [branches] affiliated to the All India Sai Samaj, devotees worship Narasimha Swamiji" (Vijayakumar 2009, 116).

At the time of Narasimhaswami's death in 1956, there were over four hundred branches of the All India Sai Samaj, which were together responsible for establishing 80 Sai Baba temples throughout India (Vijayakumar 2009, 108). Forty years later, in 1995, there were 1,003 Shirdi Sai Baba institutions affiliated with the All India Sai Samaj throughout India (Srinivas 2008, 232). Narasimhaswami was successful in his mission of spreading Sai Baba's message far beyond Shirdi, particularly throughout the southern states of India. Indeed, through Narasimhaswami's efforts, the All India Sai Samaj

grew so successful so quickly that some members of the Shri Saibaba Sansthan Trust in Shirdi became alarmed by its momentum during the latter
years of Narasimhaswami's life. Suspicious of Narasimhaswami's motives,
they began to spread word that he was not an official representative of the
Trust and was not to be trusted. In the fourth volume of *Life of Sai Baba*,
Narasimhaswami includes an apologia chapter on Sai prachar, wherein he
briefly makes note of this conflict and reasserts the validity of Sai prachar
as his mission that was sanctioned by none other than Shirdi Sai Baba, and
therefore presumably needs no sanction by the Trust:

> On principle there is absolutely nothing wrong in publishing and broadcasting
> Sai's great merits. This was not at first properly understood, and leading gentle-
> men, the trustees of the Shirdi Sai Sansthan, set their faces deliberately against
> all prachar, thinking especially that it was wrong on principle. It was about
> 1934 that the broadcasting of Baba's good qualities in "Sunday Times" was
> started by the "Southern Swami" [Narasimhaswami] who was pulled by Baba
> to himself through Upasani. When this work was going on in 1940 Baba sud-
> denly thrust large sums of money into the hands of the Southern Swami, and
> the work gained ground. But suddenly just a handful of the influential people
> amongst the Sai Sansthan set their faces against propaganda and published in
> a number of language newspapers in Bombay State that the Southern Swami
> was not to be trusted, and that he was doing propaganda for his own private
> purposes, and that propaganda was never favoured by Baba. All these have
> since been found to be incorrect even by the Shirdi Sai Sansthan and in their
> later publication by Gunaji they have practically withdrawn their aspersions.
> So far as their aspersions on the Southern Swami go, there is Baba to look after
> the Swami and his name. But so far as the Swami's propaganda is concerned,
> it might be mentioned that Sai Baba has shown that it is he that carries on the
> propaganda and really not the Swami. (Narasimhaswami 1982, 21–22)

As Narasimhaswami hints in this passage, some members of the Trust
were concerned that Narasimhaswami did not have altruistic motives and
was seeking only to profit from the sales of his books and pilgrims' souvenirs. The press releases issued by the Trust to various newspapers warned,
"This Madrasi Sadhu is doing all this for gaining money. Nobody should
believe him" (Vijayakumar 2009, 87). In time, however, the members of the
Trust became convinced that Narasimhaswami was not accumulating personal wealth but was pouring all income from book sales and donations

back into expanding devotion to Sai Baba through the All India Sai Samaj. As devotion to Sai Baba skyrocketed, the Trust witnessed an upswing of pilgrims arriving at Shirdi, particularly from the southern states. Vijayakumar notes the resulting financial implications and rehabilitation of Narasimhaswami's reputation with the Trust: "As a result of Narasimha Swamiji's work princely revenue was received by the Shirdi Sansthan from pilgrims from various parts of the country. The Shirdi Sansthan nominated Narasimha Swamiji as a member of the Executive committee of the Sansthan" (Vijayakumar 2009, 113). Narasimhaswami declined the nomination due to his ailing health but deputed his disciple Radhakrishna Swamiji (d. 1980), also known as Saipadananda, to serve in his stead and to effect a rapprochement between the All India Sai Samaj and the Shri Saibaba Sansthan Trust in recognition of their shared interest in propagating devotion to Sai Baba.

Today, Narasimhaswami's books are sold in the bookstore run by the Trust at the Samadhi Mandir in Shirdi, and tour bus after tour bus filled with devotees from the southern states arrive at the pilgrimage complex on a daily basis.[17]

NARASIMHASWAMI AND THE FUTURE OF RELIGION IN INDIA

As previous scholars have asserted, a close look at Narasimhaswami's writings reveals that he did "Hinduize" Shirdi Sai Baba, both ritually and biographically. With regard to ritual, Narasimhaswami believed that Sai Baba was the Samartha Sadguru who could lead individuals to God-realization through the exact program of guru worship that Narasimhaswami had himself successfully followed. This entailed the nine-point program of ritual worship found in the Bhagavata Purana, including among other elements of Hindu puja, the recitation of the names of the divine and a visual exchange with the divine. Thus, the temples founded by the All India Sai Samaj all promote the worship of Sai Baba through these traditional Hindu ritual means. With regard to biography, Narasimhaswami contradicted Das Ganu Maharaj in insisting that Sai Baba was born to Hindu Brahmin parents.

Rather than lamenting that Narasimhaswami "Hinduized" Sai Baba in these ways, I maintain that far more interesting and productive questions to ask are why Narasimhaswami, who was born into an orthodox Hindu Brahmin family, would turn to the unorthodox figure of Shirdi Sai Baba, and what his goals were in promoting devotion to him. As this chapter has shown, by exploring both of Sai Baba's missions as Narasimhaswami understood them, we can more fully appreciate that Narasimhaswami's intention in spreading devotion to Sai Baba was not a Hindu nationalist effort to "Hinduize" a composite or Muslim figure; rather, his intention was a more liberal effort to establish a new synthetic religion that would bring about a peaceful union between Hindus and Muslims in India. We can also more fully and critically examine the limitations of Narasimhaswami's synthetic model and its implications for the future of religion in India.

At many points throughout his writings, Narasimhaswami specifically addresses a Hindu audience, calling upon Hindus at large, and orthodox Brahmins in particular, to turn to Shirdi Sai Baba to bring about both their own spiritual uplift and the temporal uplift of India. Examining a six-page appendix at the end of the first volume of *Life of Sai Baba* helps us to better understand what is at stake in Narasimhaswami's claim that Sai Baba was born a Brahmin (Narasimhaswami 1980, appendix 4). Narasimhaswami tackles this biographical issue directly in this appendix, addressing this short section to those orthodox Hindus who object to worshiping Sai Baba on the grounds that he is Muslim. He presents a multifaceted argument for accepting Sai Baba as the Samartha Sadguru. The first point he makes is grounded in the need for direct experience: darshan with Sai Baba will melt all such worries away, just as it did for Narasimhaswami himself. But orthodox Hindus who feel that they cannot approach a non-Hindu guru for darshan need not worry, for Sai Baba was in fact born to Brahmin parents.[18] After reassuring hesitant Hindus that Sai Baba was Brahmin, Narasimhaswami then claims that although he was Hindu because he was Brahmin by birth, and studied with a Brahmin guru, he was also Muslim because he was raised by a Muslim fakir, lived in a mosque, and commonly passed as a Muslim.

Narasimhaswami next encourages his readers to look beyond caste and creed, arguing that Sai Baba's indifference as to whether people called him a Hindu or a Muslim is proof of his spiritual advancement, for caste is one of the eight attachments that Hindus are supposed to shed when taking refuge with a guru. Finally, Narasimhaswami concludes by citing passage after passage from authoritative Hindu scriptures—including the Manusmriti, the Mahabharata, and the Chandogya Upanishad—to remind his Hindu readers that the true definition of a "Brahmin" is not one of birth or parentage, but of conduct. Properly chastised, these orthodox Hindus should now stop focusing on the question of Sai Baba's personal identity as either Hindu or Muslim and start focusing on their own conduct in pursuing the guru marga to God-realization.

Narasimhaswami was convinced that Shirdi Sai Baba was the Samartha Sadguru who could unite in loving bliss all who turned to him. As more and more Hindu devotees accepted Sai Baba as their guru, they would not only find the spiritual bliss of satchitananda, peaceful union with God, but also the temporal bliss of peaceful union with their neighbors. Given the communally fractured state of South Asia during the years leading up to and immediately following independence and partition, Narasimhaswami felt a sense of urgency to spread Sai Baba's name and teachings. Thus, after accepting Sai Baba as his guru in 1936, Narasimhaswami spent the remaining two decades of his life engaged in Sai prachar, working to spread devotion to Sai Baba and grow the community of Sai faithful to help usher in the new national order that he envisioned, in which all Indians would be peacefully united together under the banner of Sai Baba.

Narasimhaswami (1982, 92) therefore believed that in promoting devotion to Shirdi Sai Baba, he was not promoting any one religion over another, but was promoting True Religion—the essence of all world religions—while letting go of all the unnecessary externals that adherents of differing religious traditions too often fight over: "Do not stress the external observances. Externals no doubt differ. But stress the essence of all religions, namely, the approach to God and the achievement thereby of the satisfaction of your various needs and the conquest of various obstacles for the elevation of your nature gradually further and further upward, till you lose your self by contact with the feet of God." The future of religion in India meant leaving behind the nonessential externals of Hinduism and Islam, including the communal bloodshed of mid-twentieth-century India, in exchange for the shared essence of these religions, the loving union of self with God and neighbor.

In his discussion of syncretism in the Indian context, Peter van der Veer argues that frequently, when Indian culture is claimed to be basically tolerant because it is pluralistic, that claim "often has a distinctively Hindu flavour" upon closer examination (1994b, 209). He cites the example of the philosopher and former president of India, Sarvepalli Radhakrishnan, who identified the essence of all religions with the Hindu nondual experience of the universal Self and then proclaimed this shared experience to be the "spirit of India." This spirit of India would ultimately unite not only all Indians but all of humanity, providing the key to global peaceful coexistence through its ability to "unify each individual in himself and bind us all together by the realization of our common condition and common goal"

(Minor 1995, 500). Van der Veer challenges scholars of religion to critically examine such syncretistic or synthetic claims, even when they are well intentioned: "I fully sympathize with any attempt to stop the communal violence in India, but it might still be important to examine critically the notion of the essentially tolerant and pluralistic character of Indian civilization." This is particularly so, he argues, because such claims can and have been used by those who seek to marginalize the place of Islam and Muslims in India by asking Indian Muslims to either accept their essential Hinduness or to leave for Pakistan (van der Veer 1994b, 202–4).

At a time when Hindu nationalists from one end of the Hindu spectrum were arguing stridently against secular pluralism and for an independent Hindu nation, Narasimhaswami moved to the other end of the spectrum to argue for a pluralistic nation united in devotion to Shirdi Sai Baba. In his utopian vision, Sai Baba devotion would arise as a new religious offspring: a synthesis of the two most prominent religions in India, a "fusion of the two great trends which appear to be so widely different, namely, Hinduism and Islam" (Narasimhaswami 1982, 84). This future religion would be the saving grace of the Indian nation, he believed, healing its deep communal rift. But in considering the limitations of Narasimhaswami's synthetic model, and its implications for the future of religion in India, it is important to consider the ways in which his vision retains a "distinctively Hindu flavor." This is found not only in the biographical claim that Sai Baba was born to Hindu parents, or in the liturgical claim that Hindu ritual is the best means for worshiping Sai Baba and attaining God-realization, or in the philosophical claim that the essence of all world religions is equivalent with nondual Hindu Advaita Vedanta philosophy. It is also found in the partisan claim that Hinduism is at its core more tolerant than Islam.

Narasimhaswami repeatedly and specifically addresses Hindus with his plea to look to Shirdi Sai Baba, believing that to build the future of religion in India he had to start with his fellow Hindus. Although he acknowledges that some orthodox Hindus will be hesitant to embrace Sai Baba because of his composite nature—and chides them for this attitude while simultaneously reassuring them that Sai Baba is a Brahmin Hindu—he believes that orthodox Muslims will be even more hesitant to embrace Sai Baba. This he chalks up to the more tolerant nature of Hinduism compared to Islam, which accounts for the ability of Sai Baba's "weird, saintly personality" to appeal to more Hindu disciples than Muslims: "More Hindus would naturally go to a Muhammadan [Muslim] saint who is not found to be an iconoclast and who is exercising his powers beneficially to all devotees than Muslims to a Hindu saint. A few Muhammadans, who had known Swami Vivekananda's work like Rajab Ali Mohamed of Bombay, appreciated Baba, and so had no prejudices, like the cultured and educated Hindus. But as for the others, their attitude towards Baba could not easily attain to the devotion of the Hindu devotees" (Narasimhaswami 1978, 159–60).

Thus, although Narasimhaswami seems to have deeply valued Sai Baba's composite identity, and was genuinely committed to promoting communal harmony between Hindus and Muslims, he simultaneously maintained that the unifying and tolerant teachings of this composite figure are essentially Hindu at their very core—and that Hindus are therefore the most receptive audience for these teachings. Islam, thus, does not stand alone in any meaningful way as a contributing partner in a synthetic mixture of religions in Narasimhaswami's vision of the future of religion in India. Instead, in the manner of the flawed "biological" model of syncretism as defined by Tony K. Stewart and Carl W. Ernst (2003, 587), the mixture of Hinduism and Islam that Narasimhaswami envisions ultimately cannot "breed true"; it disaggregates by showing itself to be less a blend of two equal parents and more a product of one dominant parent, Hinduism. Despite Narasimhaswami's deep-seated interest in promoting a future for India that would eliminate communal antagonism through devotion to the composite figure of Shirdi Sai Baba, the future religion that he presents is in many key ways less a synthesis or "fusion" of Hinduism and Islam, and more a liberal recasting of Hinduism anew under Shirdi Sai Baba as the Samartha Sadguru.

CHAPTER 4

Shirdi Is for Unity in Diversity and Adversity

BOLLYWOOD'S PLEA TO THE NATION

O the savior of the helpless, Lord Shiva,
I do not know the way of puja and bhakti,
I only know your name.
Hail, hail Lord Sai.

FROM THE "O DUKHIYON KE DATA" SONG
IN THE FILM *SHIRDI KE SAI BABA*

Prayers on my lips, tears in my eyes,
Hopes in my heart, yet my pockets are empty,
O Sai Baba of Shirdi!
A petitioner has arrived in your court.

FROM THE "SHIRDIWALE SAI BABA" SONG
IN THE FILM *AMAR AKBAR ANTHONY*

IN his 1972 study of the Sai Baba movement, Charles White reported that Shirdi Sai Baba was "coming to be regarded as a major incarnation" in Bombay (now Mumbai), where posters of him were widely displayed and a temple had recently been built. White predicted that in coming years, Sai Baba might "acquire the kind of pan-Indian devotion that figures like Sri Aurobindo and Sri Ramakrishna have" (1972, 868). Indeed, Shirdi Sai Baba devotion has increased dramatically throughout India in the decades since White's study, as evidenced by the establishment of new temples and street shrines dedicated to Sai Baba throughout the country. In Mumbai alone there are now dozens of temples and hundreds, perhaps thousands, of street shrines to Sai Baba, a dramatic increase over the one temple mentioned by White. In a recent article on Shirdi Sai Baba's history and presence in Mumbai, William Elison writes that the streets of Mumbai today are full of unauthorized religious structures: "The principal structures of this sort are small shrines of brick, stone, or concrete, and it is safely stated that, while shrines dedicated to various Hindu gods and Muslim, Christian, and Buddhist objects of veneration are easily met with, the most common occupant of such installations in downtown Mumbai is Sai Baba" (2014, 160).[1] White's prediction was correct. However, what White did not predict was the role that Hindi cinema, popularly known as Bollywood for its headquarters in Bombay/Mumbai, would play in furthering the expansion of Sai Baba devotion from the late 1970s onward.

The first film about Shirdi Sai Baba was the 1955 Marathi *Shirdiche Sai Baba*, a small-budget black-and-white mythological film directed by Kumarsen Samarth and produced by Nandadeep Chitra. It premiered at Bombay's famous Majestic Theatre and featured a soundtrack composed and directed by Pandurang Dixit, which included two hymns written by Das Ganu Maharaj (discussed in chapter 2).[2] This film about Sai Baba's life and miracles won the second All India Certificate of Merit at the National Film Awards held in 1956 (Rajkamal Kalamandir's Hindi *Jhanak Jhanak Payal Baje* received the first All India Certificate of Merit; Satyajit Ray's Bengali *Pather Panchali* won the President's Gold Medal for the best Indian feature film of 1955). Despite this critical acclaim, as a regional film *Shirdiche Sai Baba*'s viewership was limited to the Marathi-language audience in western India. It was not until more than two decades later that Shirdi Sai Baba would appear on screen in Hindi-language films, reaching a substantially larger audience throughout India.

Priya Joshi and Rajinder Dudrah write that the paradox of 1970s Indian cinema is the coexistence of a cinematic golden age at the same time as the country's most tarnished political moment. As a state of emergency was declared in 1975, posing a serious threat to democracy, Hindi cinema "encountered daring new talent in writing, directing, and acting. New scripts, new topoi, and new kinds of engagement with 'India' emerged in popular film that, in the estimation of some, have not been matched in any decade since" (Joshi and Dudrah 2012, 1). To understand why Shirdi Sai Baba emerged as a Bollywood "hero" in 1977, we must examine the changes taking place in both Indian society and Hindi cinema at this time.

The decade of the 1970s tested India's commitment to democracy and pluralism. In June 1975, when the High Court found that Indira Gandhi's 1971 reelection as prime minister was tainted by corruption and therefore invalid, political activist Jayaprakash Narayan called for her resignation and a nonviolent "total revolution." Rather than resign, Indira Gandhi declared a state of emergency on June 26, 1975, during which civil liberties were suspended; the press was censored; parliamentary elections were postponed; opposition political parties were banned; and tens of thousands of the prime minister's opponents were jailed, including Jayaprakash Narayan (Metcalf and Metcalf 2002, 250). Indira Gandhi declared the emergency, she said, not to keep herself in office but to safeguard the country. Her 1971 campaign had used the slogan "Garibi Hatao" (Abolish Poverty) in an effort to reach out to India's rural farmers and villagers, many of whom had faced starvation when crops failed after the 1965–66 drought, as well as India's urban slum dwellers, many of whom were unable to find full-time employment. Seeking to reach these same constituents once more, Indira Gandhi now promoted a "new spirit of discipline and morale," and her administration coined slogans (displaying them in Hindi and English) such as "Discipline Makes the Nation Great"; "Talk Less, Work More"; "Be Indian, Buy Indian"; and "Efficiency Is Our Watchword" (Guha 2007, 492).

Two groups in particular were alienated by the efforts of Sanjay Gandhi, Indira's younger son and political heir-in-training, to "safeguard" the country during the emergency: the poor, especially the low-caste; and Muslims, notably those in northern India. Significantly, these very groups had been Indira Gandhi's strongest supporters (Guha 2007, 522).[3] One of these efforts was slum removal. Supposedly to beautify Delhi and remake it into a modern city, Sanjay ordered a massive demolition of old Delhi, sending bulldozers into a congested area of informal residential settlements ("slums"), established residences, and small businesses in the Turkman Gate and Jama Masjid areas. Hundreds of thousands of people were dislocated, the majority of them working-class Muslims, and at least a dozen died when police opened fire on those protesting the demolition of their homes and the forced resettlement of their community (Metcalf and Metcalf 2002, 251; Guha 2007, 510–11).

A second effort was family planning. To limit India's population growth rate, Sanjay Gandhi spearheaded a family-planning program that endorsed compulsory sterilization for men who had fathered two or more children. He set high targets for each state, which were achieved through widespread coercion, including withholding government employees' paychecks until they underwent surgery; refusing to renew truck drivers' licenses without a sterilization certificate; and refusing to allot slum dwellers a resettlement plot without a sterilization certificate. Stories abound of poor men being rounded up in police vans and forcibly sterilized. In Muzaffarnagar in October 1976, Muslim artisans and laborers were targeted "with particular relish" under the directive of the local Hindu district magistrate; when a scuffle broke out between those promoting sterilization and their potential victims, the police were called in and they shot more than fifty people (Guha 2007, 513).

Facing increasing domestic and international pressure, the prime minister suddenly freed her political opponents in January 1977 and announced that elections would be held in March, thereby ending the state of emergency. When the election took place, Morarji Desai of the newly founded Janata Party defeated Indira Gandhi in a landslide (though she would be reelected prime minister in 1980), ending the Congress Party's political reign in India since independence in 1947. In these 1977 elections, Indira Gandhi notably lost the support of northern Indian Muslims, lower castes, and the poor. In the wake of these elections and the fragmenting of Congress Party loyalty, politics in India would become increasingly diverse with the rise of numerous religious, caste, and class-based political parties.

Scholars of Hindi cinema have argued that the mid-1970s were a golden age in Indian cinema precisely because of the nation's political turmoil at this time. M. Madhava Prasad writes that the "recuperation of the commercial film industry from the crisis of the Indira Gandhi era required a reconstruction of its cultural base and a reform of its mode of address" (1998, 139). He argues that the new mode of address entailed a subaltern hero, best exemplified by the working-class "angry young man" persona of Amitabh Bachchan as portrayed in the hit films *Zanjeer* (1973), *Deewar* (1975), and *Sholay* (1975). As a subaltern hero who rallies the working classes and the dispossessed, Bachchan's character was able to reach beyond the middle-class audience of earlier Hindi films to mobilize a new cultural base consisting of the proletariat and other marginal sections of society. Thus, Prasad

(1998, 138–59) argues, Hindi cinema in the 1970s witnessed the rise of a "populist aesthetic of mobilization," where the angry young man played by Bachchan acts as an agent of national reconciliation and social reform by violently enacting a transition from feudal to populist power.[4] Philip Lutgendorf notes that this populist aesthetic of mobilization manifested in other cinematic forms in addition to the angry young man played so well by Bachchan. In particular, he writes, the 1975 mythological film *Jai Santoshi Maa* "represents part of a larger picture of non-elite assertiveness and agency, but with specific relevance to an audience unaddressed by films like *Deewar* and *Sholay*: an audience mainly consisting of lower-middle-class women" (Lutgendorf 2002, 35).

In 1977, two Hindi films were released that featured Shirdi Sai Baba. One was the mythological *Shirdi Ke Sai Baba*, in which Sai Baba is the lead character and the narrative retells stories of the miracles associated with him; the other was the blockbuster *Amar Akbar Anthony*, in which Sai Baba played a small but crucial part. Though drastically different films that presumably targeted different audience demographics, both set forth a pluralist interpretation of Sai Baba as the patron saint of the nation who is able to unite multiple religious communities into one shared devotional community. These two films also gave a populist interpretation of Sai Baba as the patron saint of the downtrodden who is able to soothe their anger and help them organize to attain a happy ending. This chapter examines the pluralist and populist interpretation of Sai Baba put forward in these two films, which together helped spread awareness of and devotion to Shirdi Sai Baba among the Hindi film-watching public throughout India from the late 1970s onward.

SHIRDI KE SAI BABA

Shirdi Ke Sai Baba (1977) was directed by Ashok Bhushan and starred Sudhir Dalvi as Shirdi Sai Baba. This film is part of the mythological (or mythodevotional) genre of popular Indian cinema, a genre that dates to the very beginning of India's film history and is frequently described as unique among world cinemas. One of India's first filmmakers, D. G. Phalke, is often credited with the birth of not only the mythological genre but Indian feature filmmaking more broadly. Phalke released *Raja Harishchandra* in 1913, a fifty-minute feature film based on an episode from the Mahabharata epic. Following this film, he produced dozens more that were also based on

Hindu epic and Puranic stories.[5] As Rachel Dwyer (2006, 15) notes, the mythological genre was thus the founding mode of Indian cinema and one of the most productive genres of the country's early cinema. Whereas Dwyer defines the mythological genre narrowly, to include only films that depict tales of Hindu gods and goddesses, heroes and heroines, as told in the Sanskrit Puranas and epics, other scholars of Indian cinema define the genre more broadly, to include films that recount the legendary biographies of *bhakti* (devotional) poet-saints.[6] A hallmark of the mythological film genre (including devotionals) is the emphasis on *darshan*, the act of seeing and being seen by the divine that is central to Hindu worship. In mythological films, this entails an aesthetic of frontality that arises out of earlier visual media and portrays the divine object of attention directly facing the viewer, so that the viewer-devotee can look into the eyes of the divine figure.[7] Films further foster darshan through an array of cinematic editing techniques, including zooming in on the face of the divine figure, pausing for an extended close-up of the divine figure's face and eyes, and interspersing shots of the divine figure with shots of the devotee to model the exchange of glances central to *puja* (ritual worship).

Despite the mythological genre's foundational presence in Indian cinema, the output of such films (including devotionals) declined as other genres (the social, historical, stunt film, etc.) arose from the 1920s through the 1950s (Dharap 1983). Philip Lutgendorf (2002, 14) notes that by the 1970s, mythological films were frequently viewed as "downmarket and vernac [vernacular]" when compared with social films, marketed toward viewers who were more rural and less educated than the urban, English-speaking audience that attended social films. Mythological films were also frequently box-office flops. Yet in 1975, one became an acclaimed blockbuster success: *Jai Santoshi Maa* (directed by Vijay Sharma). The other blockbusters of 1975—*Sholay* and *Deewar*—were "masala" (mixed spice) films featuring multiple stars and incorporating just a bit of everything into the blend: drama, romance, comedy, action, song, and dance. They were both "expensive and slickly made by the standards of the industry, and both featured Amitabh Bachchan, the male superstar whose iconic portrayal of an 'angry young man' would dominate the Hindi screen for the next decade. Female characters were marginal to both, and this was not surprising given that their target audience was young urban males, who strongly identified with their themes of honor and revenge" (Lutgendorf 2002, 10). Unlike these films, *Jai*

Santoshi Maa became a superhit among lower-middle-class women, in particular, because it addressed their aspirations and suggested that a happy ending could be found for marital and familial woes through ritualized devotion to the goddess of satisfaction, Santoshi Ma. Significantly, Santoshi Ma was a little-known Hindu goddess prior to this film's success. But as people flocked to movie theaters in both major urban centers and smaller provincial towns, temples and shrines to this goddess began appearing in many parts of India, and more and more women began to participate in her ritual worship (Lutgendorf 2002).

Released just two years after *Jai Santoshi Maa*, the film *Shirdi Ke Sai Baba* sought to capitalize on this renewed surge of interest in mythological movies. Its creators marketed it to a dual audience: The vernacular Hindi-speaking public was the primary target audience, as seen, for instance, in the use of Devanagari credits and the relative lack of English in the dialogue. But the film also targeted a more educated, urban audience of both men and women by including a framing story of an upper-middle-class urban family, with its educated doctor husband who voices skepticism about the relevance of holy men in an age of science. Although *Shirdi Ke Sai Baba* did not become an instant blockbuster, it did eventually secure a sizeable viewership (though largely on the small screen, rather than in theaters, as discussed below), and it inspired many spin-offs. More importantly, *Shirdi Ke Sai Baba* has contributed substantially to the increasing worship of Shirdi Sai Baba, who at the time of the film's release was still relatively little known outside the states of Maharashtra, Andhra Pradesh, and Tamil Nadu.

Shirdi Ke Sai Baba opens with an extended darshanic montage: the Samadhi Mandir in Shirdi, a marble statue of Sai Baba, and an array of popular photographs and posters of Sai Baba. This opening lasts for several minutes and situates the film in the mythological genre, with Sai Baba as the subject of devotion, while also inviting the viewer to mentally prepare for the visual communion with Sai Baba that will ensue throughout the film. The framing narrative then begins, wherein a distraught Pooja (Hema Malini) races to the hospital to see if there has been any change in the condition of her son, Deepak. The doctor (Rajendra Kumar), who is also Pooja's husband and the boy's father, tells her that there is no cure for Deepak's type of blood cancer, and it is time to take the boy home to live out his final days. As the devotional song "Sai Baba Bolo (I)" plays, Pooja wanders into her neighborhood Sai Baba temple, where the priest (Manoj Kumar) gives her some *vibhuti* (sacred ash) from Shirdi to place on her son's tongue. As she does so, the pace of the song speeds up, ending in a burst of devotional fervor as young Deepak opens his eyes and exclaims, "Baba! Baba!" He tells his surprised parents that they must take him to Shirdi, for Baba has called him there. This sets the stage for the family's visit to Shirdi, accompanied by the priest, where the skeptical doctor asks to be told about this miracle worker Sai Baba: Who is he? Is he Hindu or Muslim? And can he really cure his dying son?

The film then turns to its core narrative, which features Shirdi Sai Baba as the "hero" and depicts one miraculous incident (*lila*) after the next to demonstrate the growing devotion of his community of followers in Shirdi during his lifetime—and presumably to encourage such devotion to grow in the contemporary viewing audience. Social commentary is interspersed throughout these scenes, emphasizing the need for unity in diversity among India's religious communities; for eradicating caste bigotry; and for helping the downtrodden, especially the poor, the sick, and the lowly in society. The theme of religious unity in diversity first arises with the question of Sai Baba's own religious identity; the question the doctor asked of the priest— Is Sai Baba Hindu or Muslim?—is revisited in an early episode that relates Sai Baba's arrival in Shirdi as a young man with Chand (also known as Chandbhai).[8] Chand, who is wandering through the forest searching for his runaway horse, is awestruck upon meeting Sai Baba and witnessing him produce a hot coal out of thin air to light his *chillum* (a type of pipe). When Sai Baba, seated in meditation under a tree, recites a short passage from the Quran, Chand says to him: "So you are a Muslim. I am also a Muslim." Sai Baba next recites a verse from Hindu scripture, leading Chand to ask in confusion, "Are you Hindu?" In response, Sai Baba turns to gaze at him, and a close-up that lingers on Sai Baba's face allows viewers to witness the divine stars in his eyes. Chand promptly apologizes for falling into the Hindu-versus-Muslim mind-set. Pleased with this response, Sai Baba nods his approval and helps Chand find his lost horse. In this way, viewers are instructed about the inappropriateness of the question of religious identity, learning through Chand's example that they must overcome this dualistic mode of thinking.

This topic of religious unity in diversity takes on overtly nationalistic tones in several later episodes, when such dualistic thinking is shown to be divisive and part of the mind-set of the film's villains. Whereas our hero Sai Baba is portrayed as a figure who is himself a composite blend of Hindu and Muslim traits (for instance, he recites Hindu and Muslim scripture) and who actively works to unite Hindus and Muslims in his community, such unity is portrayed as threatening to two distinct groups in the film. On the one hand are the Brahmin priests, who seek to protect their orthodox hold on the village, and on the other hand are the indigenous officers in the employ of the British Raj, who seek to protect the colonial hold on the nation. Both groups of villains argue that the union of Hindus and Muslims will not bring peace and prosperity to India but will instead further divide Hindus and Muslims by causing a riot to erupt between the two communities. By the film's conclusion, however, both groups of villains have been converted to devout followers of Sai Baba and are thus persuaded of the value of unity in diversity for their own spiritual progress as well as the progress of Shirdi and the nation at large.

The first villain to appear in the film is an orthodox Brahmin priest and *vaid* (healer) named Kulkarni (Birbal). He rejects Sai Baba as untouchable *fakir kachara* (literally, ascetic garbage) and forces the other Brahmins to bathe in order to purify themselves after coming into contact with him. He also persuades the village *panchayat* (council of elders) to ostracize villagers who have accepted Sai Baba, arguing that Sai Baba is the enemy of the village, for he will eventually cause a riot by constantly saying "Allah, Allah" to Hindus and "Ram, Ram" to Muslims. Those who have been ostracized turn to Sai Baba for advice, who tells them to focus on the children in the village and teach them not just to read about love and nonviolence but to practice these values in their actions. Repeatedly, Kulkarni seeks to thwart Sai Baba: he persuades the oil vendors not to donate oil to Sai Baba to light the mosque at night, he hires thugs to beat up Sai Baba, and he presents a poisonous cobra to Sai Baba as a religious offering. But Sai Baba's miracles prove more powerful than Kulkarni's mischief: Sai Baba lights his oil lamps with water, he sets the thugs' clubs aflame and scares them off, and he transforms the snake into a garland of flowers. After Kulkarni is bitten by the very snake with which he tried to poison Sai Baba, and then is healed through his wife's faith in Sai Baba and some vibhuti, he finally ceases his assault and becomes a believer in Sai Baba. Thus, Kulkarni and his Brahmin sidekick, who are both initially presented as doubting opponents, come to worship Sai Baba and believe that instead of further dividing the village's Hindus and Muslims, his teachings will unite them.

A similar story arc occurs with the second group of villains, the officers of the colonial government. Like Kulkarni, Das Ganu Maharaj (discussed in chapter 2) first appears in the film as a very disagreeable figure—a corrupt police officer working for the British Raj who would rather compose lewd songs and boss his underlings around than do honest police work. His superior officer, Nana Saheb Chandorkar, is a hard-working and—initially—loyal officer of the British government. Based on reports that a strange man in Shirdi is saying "Allah, Allah" to Hindus and "Ram, Ram" to Muslims, Chandorkar is ordered to investigate whether this man is trying to create trouble for the British. He sends Das Ganu to Shirdi to look into the situation. Das Ganu leaves for Shirdi, saying that he will test Sai Baba with his uniform as well as a girl's anklets. Das Ganu figures that he will quickly be able to out the fakir by using a carrot-and-stick approach, dangling both the lure of a beautiful dancing girl and the threat of a police investigation. But much to his surprise, he finds Sai Baba to be the real deal. Not only is Sai Baba not tempted by the dancing girl, but he converts her on the spot (though not until after she has performed a tantalizing dance number for film watchers to behold), thereby saving her from the accrual of further bad karma that would arise from a lifetime of lascivious dancing. Sai Baba then calls upon Das Ganu to do the same: to leave his profession, which makes him engage in corrupt work for the colonial government, and to focus on composing devotional hymns rather than lewd verses. As holy water miraculously springs from Sai Baba's feet (the Miracle of the Ganges River), Das Ganu bows in reverence, accepting Sai Baba as his guru and uttering that Shirdi is where the holy Ganges and Yamuna Rivers truly flow.

Eventually, Das Ganu convinces Chandorkar to visit Shirdi. Chandorkar confesses that while he is by no means an atheist, he is skeptical of living saints and fakirs. As Das Ganu leads Chandorkar through the village to meet Sai Baba, Das Ganu launches into the song "Sumer Manva." This song sequence seeks to reassure Chandorkar—and with him the film's viewers—that Sai Baba is a divine persona by explaining that divinity is not different from the five elements; divinity is everywhere, but goes unrecognized by most of us. It also seeks to establish Sai Baba as a figure whose message of loving unity extends to members of all the major religions of India. As Das Ganu's procession arrives before Sai Baba and the chorus urges devotees to "think of the five elements with pure thoughts," Sai Baba raises his hand in greeting. Above each of his five fingers a different symbol appears: the Hindu Om over the thumb, the Christian cross over the index finger, then the Buddhist wheel, the Muslim crescent moon and star, and finally the Zoroastrian torch. The next verses of the song exclaim:

This is the vessel of oneness,
The door of supreme peace.
He gives a divine message,
He gives a divine chant.
Hail, hail Lord Sai avatar!

Persuaded to bow before Sai Baba, Chandorkar's doubts lift after Sai Baba blesses him and promises that his barren daughter will bear a son within the year. Thus, like the village Brahmins, the officers of the colonial regime are initially presented as doubting opponents but come to worship Sai Baba and believe that instead of further dividing Hindus and Muslims his teachings will unite them. Such unity, they come to see, will not cause a communal riot, though it may indeed spell trouble for the British.

Two scenes make especially explicit the suggestion that the unity of Indians of all creeds is needed to defeat the British and attain independence. The first occurs when Sai Baba singles out G. S. Khaparde, who is standing amid a crowd of devotees, and asks him how such a brave freedom fighter as himself has arrived in Shirdi.[9] Khaparde presents Sai Baba with the *Gita Rahasya* as an offering from its author, Bal Gangadhar Tilak—then imprisoned on charges of sedition—who requests his blessing. Sai Baba takes the book and reverently holds it to his forehead (as opposed to setting it at his feet where flowers and other offerings are placed), and then he explains to his followers—expressly shown in this scene to be Hindu and Muslim— that the Bhagavad Gita and the Quran must not be defiled but must be held up with great respect. Furthermore, he continues, there will come a day when Tilak's *Gita Rahasya* (his commentary on the Bhagavad Gita) will reach every home and be read everywhere. In this scene, the film calls upon Hindus and Muslims to respect one another's religious traditions and to set bickering aside so that the two communities can join together in a shared mission to free India from colonial rule. By endorsing the *Gita Rahasya*, here Sai Baba seemingly endorses Tilak's call to action—including armed insurrection—against the British. Given the film's release date, this endorsement is made to seem providential, suggesting to its 1977 audience that Sai Baba—who died three decades before independence—knew through divine insight that India would prevail against the British and that the revolutionary Tilak would deserve to be praised in households throughout the nation for his efforts to secure India's freedom.[10]

The second scene occurs later in the film, when two men arrive in Shirdi from afar hoping for darshan with Sai Baba. One is a Muslim and the other a Sikh; the Muslim is severely wounded, with bloody bandages on his head and arm. Upon arriving, they learn that Sai Baba appears to have died three days earlier—though as the viewer will soon discover, he has only entered into a seventy-two-hour-long *samadhi*, or meditative state. In a song sequence, the villagers sing their heartfelt praise to Sai Baba, asking him to speak, to open his eyes, and to return to them. Das Ganu begins the song "Sai Baba Bolo (II)," and as it continues other devotees join in, one by one, including the two visitors. The lyrics praise Sai Baba in Hindu, Muslim, and Sikh phrases, calling him Sai Ram and Sai Shyam, Allah Sai and Moula Sai, Nanak Sai and Gobind Sai, with each devotee using terms of endearment for sacred figures from within their own religious traditions. The camera alternates between close-ups of the devotees' faces and Sai Baba's face, but the latter's closed eyes forestall the desired darshanic exchange of glances. Finally, as the pace gets faster and faster, the song ends when Sai Baba miraculously awakens, at long last opening his eyes and closing the darshanic circuit by blessing the assembled devotees—and the film's viewers— with his glance. In the visitors' audience with Sai Baba following his awakening, Sai Baba asks why the police are pursuing them. They explain that they are freedom fighters working to uproot the British Raj. As police invade the village, Sai Baba replies that they will not be able to accomplish anything if they are caught. He then gives the men his blessing and helps them escape. When questioned by the police about whether he has seen two traitors, Sai Baba laughingly replies that indeed he has, pointing to himself and to Chandorkar, thereby revealing that neither he nor the ranking colonial officer present is loyal to the British.

Thus, the concern raised by both groups of villains in the film—that the union of Hindus and Muslims will only prove divisive in the end—is demonstrated to be false. Instead, the union of Indians across religious lines is shown to be the cure to the divisiveness that plagues Shirdi and the colonial domination that plagues India at large. Furthermore, Sai Baba is shown to be the one person who can accomplish this union of Indians. The final song in the film, "Tuhi Fakir," celebrates Sai Baba's inclusiveness. It is sung by a blind beggar who has led a life of sin—he drank, gambled, strangled his wife, and fled from the police. He arrives in Shirdi with his son when Sai Baba is nearing the end of his life. Stating that he has paid for his crimes by serving time in jail and being struck blind, the beggar now seeks redemption. In these verses he praises Sai Baba, saying that Sai Baba's thousands of hands are available to any who take his name in faith. As the villagers of Shirdi join in song behind the beggar, demonstrating their religious diversity as a community and their united faith in Sai Baba, the verses liken Sai Baba to figures revered in Hinduism, Sikhism, Islam, and Buddhism:

When I look upon you from one side you look like Krishna,
When I look upon the other side you look like Durga.
You've got the smile of Guru Nanak on your face,
You've got the glow of Muhammad on your face.
You are the rosary of the name of Rama,
You have the enlightenment of Gautama.

The song then praises Shirdi as a pilgrimage place that is welcoming to members of all religious traditions, declaring Sai Baba's abode to be the "ocean of mercies" from which all religions fill their pitchers. After the song concludes, the beggar miraculously regains his sight, and Sai Baba tells him to return to his village and start his life anew, with the knowledge that Sai Baba will always be in his heart.

As the elderly Sai Baba passes away, the film returns to the framing narrative in its final moments. The priest's voice explains that Sai Baba's *murti* (statue) resides in the temple in Shirdi. The camera pans across the temple, the Dwarkamai mosque, and various images of Sai Baba while the priest tells Pooja and the doctor that the fire first lit by Sai Baba in the mosque years ago still burns, the rock Sai Baba sat on is still present, and Sai Baba is also still here. Miracles still happen, not only in Shirdi, but wherever Sai Baba's devotees are. As the temple bell rings, signaling the start of puja, the priest invites Pooja and the doctor to bring Deepak inside. But as Pooja turns to her son, she finds him missing. She and her husband run through the streets of Shirdi, calling out for their son. But the priest is calm in the face of their panic: he bows down in prayer to Sai Baba and then confidently leads them into the temple, where Deepak is found sitting at the feet of the murti of Sai Baba. Upon seeing his mother, he runs to her, exclaiming that Sai Baba had taken his hand and brought him here. With a knowing smile, the scientist-turned-priest (himself a converted skeptic) asks the doctor how he can explain this miraculous healing of his son. In response, the doctor also bows down in prayer before Sai Baba. As the devotional hymn's refrain rings out in Hindi, "Sai Nath, you have thousands of hands," film viewers are left with a final image of the murti of Sai Baba in the Samadhi Mandir, beneath which is written (in English) one of Sai Baba's 11 Sayings, "If you look to me, I look to you."[11] The film's closing image promises its viewers that through the darshanic exchange of glances both individual and nation can be touched by one of the many hands of Sai Baba and transformed for the better.

Showing versus Telling the Story of Sai Baba

The opening credits of *Shirdi Ke Sai Baba* proclaim that the film is based on two hagiographic sources: the *Shri Sai Satcharita* by Govind Rao Dabholkar (discussed in chapter 1) and *Devotees' Experiences of Sri Sai Baba* by B. V. Narasimhaswami (discussed in chapter 3). However, immediately following is a disclaimer, in Hindi, acknowledging that the film is a fictionalized presentation of Shirdi Sai Baba's life and teachings: "In order to present in its fullest form Baba's message to humankind, some new names and statements have been relied upon to help complete the incomplete portions of the story." The film does take several substantial liberties with these textual sources, some of which explicitly emphasize Sai Baba as a nationalist icon who advocates a united and pluralist independent India.

Take, for instance, the film's recounting of Sai Baba's seventy-two-hour samadhi. In this scene, the Hindus, Muslims, and Sikhs of the village are all shown uniting as one devotional community—with the exception of the villain Kulkarni and his sidekick—to sing "Sai Baba Bolo (II)." Present for this song are not only all of the villagers but also the visiting Muslim and Sikh freedom fighters, who receive Sai Baba's blessing after he awakens. But in the version of this incident in the *Shri Sai Satcharita*, no freedom fighters are present. Furthermore, the Hindus and Muslims of Shirdi are not united through their shared devotion; rather, for a full thirty-six hours they debate what to do with Sai Baba's corpse, each community claiming him as their own and insisting that their own funereal traditions be followed (Dabholkar 2007, 719–20, 723–24). Similarly, while the film shows Sai Baba endorsing Tilak's *Gita Rahasya* and simultaneously calling upon Hindus and Muslims to respect one another's traditions so that they might band together to secure India's freedom, the texts paint a different picture. The *Gita Rahasya* receives only a very brief mention in chapter 27 of the *Shri Sai Satcharita*, in a discussion of devotees bringing various scriptures to Sai Baba to seek his blessing for their ongoing study and spiritual development. Dabholkar (2007, 444) explains that in this way, Sai Baba gave his blessing over many different texts, including the *Gita Rahasya* when it was presented to him by Bapusaheb Jog (not Khaparde). In the *Shri Sai Satcharita*, then, the *Gita Rahasya* is just one among many devotional scriptures, and there is no discussion of a nationalist agenda.[12]

Other departures from the film's textual sources seem to have been introduced to meet cinematic conventions. Most notably, the depiction of Kulkarni as the film's lead villain is significantly different from his presentation in textual hagiographic sources, but it meets Hindi cinema's requirement that the hero must confront a villain.[13] In this film, of course, the confrontation is a battle of faith rather than a physical brawl, but the orthodox priest Kulkarni's recurring opposition to the rather unorthodox Sai Baba, and Kulkarni's eventual conversion to become a devotee, serves to dramatically highlight Sai Baba as the true hero of this mythological flick.

The filmic Kulkarni is based on a historical figure, Laxmanrao Kulkarni Ratnaparkhe, also known as Laxman Mama, who was a resident of Shirdi and did serve as a priest, ayurvedic healer, and astrologer. However, little of his portrayal in the film beyond these basics is found in the textual sources. For instance, the *Shri Sai Satcharita* (Dabholkar 2007, 82) presents the miracle of the oil lamps in chapter 5. In this source, the village grocers decided that they were tired of giving daily handouts to Sai Baba, so one day they all refused when he came begging. Sai Baba returned to the temple, calmly mixed the little bit of oil he had with water, and then used this solution to light his candles, which miraculously burned all night long. No mention is made of Kulkarni. In Narasimhaswami's (1980, 21–24) longer discussion of the same incident, he explains that it was this miracle that first caused many villagers to begin worshiping Sai Baba; again, no mention is made of Kulkarni. But in the film, Kulkarni becomes the instigator behind the oil vendors' conspiracy of refusal. He is shown conducting Lakshmi puja in an oil vendor's shop, while trying to pry as much money out of the vendor as he can, when a young Dalit girl, Vidya (who is also not mentioned in the film's textual sources), comes to beg for oil on behalf of Sai Baba. Angered at the appearance of this "Untouchable" in the midst of his ritual worship, Kulkarni tells the vendors she is an obstacle to proper worship and sends her away without oil. When Sai Baba then comforts the teary Vidya by miraculously lighting the candles in the mosque, she breaks into the song "Deepavali Manaye." Thus, Sai Baba is shown to be the more genuine religious figure, in contrast with the greedy and caste-conscious Brahmin priest, Kulkarni.

Similarly, the film portrays Kulkarni as Sai Baba's lead skeptic and opponent during Sai Baba's seventy-two-hour samadhi. While the other villagers band together to sing "Sai Baba Bolo (II)," asking Sai Baba to return to them in a show of faith and unity, Kulkarni is so eager to dispose of Sai Baba that he digs a grave himself. When Sai Baba awakens from his meditation, he not only blesses the two freedom fighters, as discussed above, but also chides Kulkarni for digging the grave and tells him to fill it back in before he himself falls into it. Chapter 43 of the *Shri Sai Satcharita*, however, tells a very different story of Kulkarni's role in this incident. Kulkarni is instead presented as so devout that he receives a special vision from Sai Baba in his dream, calling him to attend to his morning worship. While others fail to attend the morning puja, assuming that Sai Baba is dead, Kulkarni heeds the vision and arrives, as usual, at dawn with his puja accoutrements. The text praises Kulkarni for his unfailing display of ritual devotion, noting that he "was scrupulously exact in the discharge of all religiously enjoined acts, and words. After taking a bath in the morning and putting on clean, washed clothes, he would take Baba's *darshan*. He would then wash Baba's feet, apply sandalwood paste and consecrated rice, offer Tulsi leaves, flowers, etc., and after waving lights, burning incense and offering *naivedya*, he would offer *dakshina* in the end. Then, prostrating in obeisance with prayers, he would take Baba's blessings and thereafter, offer *prasad*, and apply sandalwood paste on the foreheads of all" (Dabholkar 2007, 719). Called by Sai Baba in his vision, Kulkarni followed the same ritual on this morning, but rather than feeling his usual joyful affection for Sai Baba, he was reportedly filled with grief, fearing that Sai Baba had died and that this would be the last time he could perform his puja (Dabholkar 2007, 720).

Thus, in the *Shri Sai Satcharita* text, Kulkarni is a model Hindu devotee of Sai Baba; but in the film *Shirdi Ke Sai Baba*, Kulkarni is cast as an orthodox and bigoted rival of Sai Baba. By the end of the film, of course, the villainous Kulkarni is transformed into a devotee, and Sai Baba's spiritual generosity is dramatically highlighted as Kulkarni begs at his feet for forgiveness after being miraculously cured of snakebite. And yet, though transformed into a believer, Kulkarni never quite becomes a model devotee. At the end of the film, Kulkarni holds a meal in Sai Baba's honor to show his devotion. A beggar arrives, and Kulkarni rudely throws him out, demonstrating that despite his newfound faith he is unable to completely leave his old orthodox habits and biases behind. The beggar is Sai Baba in disguise, testing Kulkarni's faith and finding it still lacking. Again, Sai Baba chides Kulkarni, instructing him to always give food to anyone who is hungry and knocks on his door. This lesson is immediately followed by another, directed to a devotee who takes excessive pride in his many pilgrimages to temples and mosques in the quest for enlightenment. Sai Baba chides him for falsely claiming that he had no cash to spare when a poor man asked for help to buy medicine for his ailing mother. Religion, Sai Baba explains, begins within one's own heart and with compassion for one's neighbors. Enlightenment is not to be found in a temple or a mosque; it is not to be found by adhering to orthodoxy or orthopraxy.

Though cinematic convention may dictate the need for a villain, it does not dictate that the villain be an orthodox Brahmin. Repeatedly throughout *Shirdi Ke Sai Baba*, there are examples of Kulkarni and other elite, upper-caste, and upper-class Hindus who are bigoted, greedy, or have sinned in various ways. In this way, the film suggests that Hinduism needs to be reformed—as Kulkarni and the other Hindus ultimately are—to be rid of such prejudicial and selfish thought and practice. And it suggests that Shirdi Sai Baba is the agent of such reform, able to bring about a village/nation that is united in its diversity across not only religious lines but also caste and class barriers. During the song "Dam Dam Dam Damroo," Sai Baba's growing number of Hindu devotees take him on a procession through the village, carrying an umbrella over him as a sign of his exalted status. A wandering Hindu ascetic named Somdev looks on, skeptical of such fanfare, which smacks of hypocrisy to him given Sai Baba's status as a fakir. As the villagers march, they sing about the drum playing and the gong ringing, requesting, "Sai Nath [who is] Lord Shiva, hear it play." Somdev confronts Sai Baba in the mosque after the song ends, only to become a believer when Sai Baba calls him to task for his own hypocrisy. Sai Baba explains that his own actions as a renouncer are not hypocritical, but generous, for it does not matter to him where he lives or what he wears; he gladly accepts whatever his devotees offer to him. However, he points out that Somdev became a renouncer not for genuine spiritual reasons but out of cowardice after his wife passed away, leaving two young children behind. Nonetheless, Sai Baba blesses the ascetic with a vision of himself as Krishna, redeeming him for abandoning his children. As a devotional *bhajan* (hymn) to Vishnu begins to swell in the background, Somdev drops to his knees in obeisance.

Shortly thereafter, a dispute breaks out in the village when a Brahmin angrily refuses to accept a girl as his daughter-in-law after her impoverished family is unable to provide a dowry. That same Brahmin then suffers from a stroke and is paralyzed. When his son comes to Sai Baba seeking help, Sai Baba explains that his father had sinned and this must be corrected. As the son turns around, he finds the shunned bride-to-be standing before him, and the two hold hands. The song "Sai Bhola Bhandari" begins as Sai Baba gives sacred ash to the paralyzed Brahmin. The lyrics equate Shiva and Sai Baba, proclaiming each to be the "treasurer of miracles." The song relates the story of the demon Bhasmasur, whose powers grew so great through his penance to Shiva that he became a threat even to Shiva, and only Vishnu—taking the form of the enchantress Mohini—could save Shiva. The song ends by praising Shiva's generosity, stating that he grants the requests of all of his devotees. During the song, the Brahmin recovers from his paralysis, signals his approval of his son's union, and joins the bhajan. This healing serves as proof that Sai Baba's vibhuti has worked and that Sai Baba, like Shiva, is a source of miracles who grants the wishes of his devotees (even those who have sinned).

Repeatedly in *Shirdi Ke Sai Baba* it is the lowly in caste status, the poor, the sick, and women who are shown to be wronged by those with status and power in society, particularly Hindu Brahmins and renouncers. "Untouchables" are repeatedly shunned; impoverished beggars are denied food even when it abounds in the homes of the wealthy; lepers are denied even their humanity, let alone basic medical attention; and wives are ignored even when in the right. These same characters are also those who have sincere faith in Sai Baba. By acknowledging the injustices these groups face, Shirdi Sai Baba becomes the balm that soothes them, and the film suggests that through ritual worship of Sai Baba, the poor, the sick, the lowly—those who have a right to be angry—can ultimately attain justice and happiness. Yet while seemingly aimed at a lower-class vernacular audience, the film does not foreclose a viewership of upper-class and caste Hindus. All is not lost for those with status and power, as the examples of Kulkarni, Das Ganu, Somdev, and the unnamed Brahmin father demonstrate. The framing story is especially important in this regard, for it features a well-educated and upper-class Hindu family, as well as a Hindu priest, who are not vilified before being redeemed, contrary to how Kulkarni and other Hindu elites are treated within the core narrative. In this way, *Shirdi Ke Sai Baba* leaves open the possibility that upper-caste and upper-class Hindus can also be model devotees, turning to Shirdi Sai Baba with sincere devotion after learning

more about him, even as the film champions the devotion of the marginalized and dispossessed.

Sai Baba's Message of Unity, Service, and Rights

Shirdi Ke Sai Baba did not achieve blockbuster status and was not ranked
among the top ten films of 1977. Indeed, based on its box-office revenue it
was ranked the thirty-first best-selling Hindi film of the year, officially making it a flop—as most mythological films were in the 1970s. Nonetheless,
over time the film has attracted a substantial following, especially after its
transition to the small screen. Although Doordarshan, the Indian government-run television network, was first introduced in 1959, it did not reach
the average home until the mid-1980s. In the mid-1980s and early 1990s,
television expanded dramatically in different parts of India, with the number of transmitters increasing from 26 in 1982 to 523 in 1991 (Mankekar
1999, 5). In 1984, the first entertainment serial was broadcast, enthralling
the audience, and other tremendously successful serials quickly followed,
most notably Ramanand Sagar's famous mythological *Ramayan* serial,
which aired from January 1987 to September 1990 and captivated viewers
across the nation in an unprecedented way.[14] Doordarshan also began airing Hindi movies once a week, and it first broadcast *Shirdi Ke Sai Baba*
nationwide in 1988. At the same time, video cassette recorders (VCRs) arrived
on the Indian market, allowing people to record the televised film broad-
casts and then share the video cassettes. K. Moti Gokulsing notes the widespread rise of video cassette businesses in the 1980s: "Young entrepreneurs
started investing in VCRs and set up video 'parlours' where people could
watch film cassettes for a small fee. This concept was gradually extended to
renting out VCRs (sometimes along with a colour television set) with cassettes. Even people living in shanties were soon hiring cassettes—often a
dozen—to watch along with family and friends over the weekend. These
video libraries mushroomed in the mid-1980s, in large towns and small"
(Gokulsing 2004, 16). As *Shirdi Ke Sai Baba* aired on Doordarshan in 1988,
it was recorded by countless such entrepreneurs across the nation and
stocked on the shelves of many of these video libraries.

Although hard statistics for the viewership of *Shirdi Ke Sai Baba* on the
small screen are impossible to come by, given the informal nature of the video-
viewing market, my research with Sai Baba devotees suggests that the film
was both widely viewed by devotees and instrumental in bringing many new
Hindu devotees into a relationship with Sai Baba. For instance, C. B. Satpathy

(discussed in greater detail in chapter 5) writes in his testimonial memoir, *Shirdi Sai Baba and Other Perfect Masters*, about the significant impact the film had on him. In the late 1980s, Satpathy was living in New Delhi, where he worked as an officer in the Indian Police Service. At this time, he became increasingly curious about Sai Baba, whose image he began to encounter everywhere—photographs of Sai Baba hung in neighborhood shops, friends and acquaintances wore rings and lockets that pictured his likeness, taxis and rickshaws sported bumper stickers with his face and sayings. One day Satpathy decided to rent *Shirdi Ke Sai Baba* to learn more:

> There is a video shop in Palika Bazaar near my house, from where I used to occasionally collect video cassettes. I do not remember the exact date, but it was sometime in November 1989. I went to the shop to collect a certain film cassette. It was not available. I scanned most of the cassettes, but none was appealing. Suddenly I saw a cassette on Shirdi Sai Baba produced by Manoj Kumar. I enquired about the cassette from the owner, who told me that children love it for the many miracles of Shirdi Sai Baba that have been shown therein. The word "miracle" also stimulated some interest in me. (Satpathy 2001, 25)

Satpathy notes that at this time he had an intellectual curiosity about miracles, but no faith in them. Yet this would all change with the viewing of the film: "When I heard about the miracles of Shri Sai Baba of Shirdi, I decided to see the film. Little did I know at that point of time, that yet another miracle was about to take place. My life would stand transformed in a matter of a few hours" (Satpathy 2001, 27).

This "miracle," as Satpathy describes it, entailed his personal transformation during the viewing of *Shirdi Ke Sai Baba* from a curious skeptic to a true believer in Sai Baba. He watched the miraculous episodes that make up the first half of the film rather routinely, but he was overtaken by a "strange feeling" during the samadhi episode in which Sai Baba is shown leaving his body and appearing dead to the world for three days before reviving. As he watched this scene, Satpathy reports that the image of his late father's face repeatedly appeared over that of Sai Baba's. Pausing the video, he tried to understand what was happening—was it just a coincidence because the two men looked alike? But no, that could not be it, for their appearance did not really match. Deciding that this was a call from on high, that he was "being literally dragged to appear before Him," Satpathy packed and left for Shirdi early the next morning (Satpathy 2001, 28). He describes the peace he felt at the moment of mutual acceptance as he gazed upon the murti of Sai Baba in Shirdi: "Divine glory poured forth from His face, from every pore of His body. He appeared to gaze at me. There was a hint of a smile at the corner of His lips. What is happening to you?, I asked myself. The inner voice echoed— this is the moment for which you have been waiting since your birth. A strange sense of separation and also reunion swept over me like giant tidal waves in succession. Everything felt so divine. Those few moments were more intoxicating than all the liquor in the world" (31).

Like Satpathy, many of the Hindu devotees of his generation whom I interviewed credited the "darshanic pull" (to use the words of one such devotee) of *Shirdi Ke Sai Baba* with bringing them into a ritualized relationship with Sai Baba. Many reported feeling an instant connection with him upon first viewing the film, which not infrequently occurred by happenstance rather than intent—turning on the television at just the right time to witness one of the film's miracles, or visiting a friend's house just as the family was sitting down to watch the movie. Such happenstance, however, was in hindsight understood to be divine guidance. Some devotees admitted to repeat viewings of the film—one woman told me she must have watched it at least fifty times in one year, bringing the video cassette home after work every Thursday—in the quest to become more familiar with Sai Baba's life and miracles. As is common practice with mythological films and televised serials in India, many Hindu viewers engage in ritualized behavior while watching the film, offering flowers or incense before the screen while taking darshan with Sai Baba.[15] In 2008, as I was living in the Defense Colony neighborhood of New Delhi while on a research sabbatical, a neighbor learned of my interest in Sai Baba and invited me to join her to view *Shirdi Ke Sai Baba*, which she lauded as "the greatest film ever made." Prior to starting the film, she placed her copy of the *Shri Sai Satcharita* and a small jar of vibhuti on a tray, along with some sweets. She then carefully placed the tray on a small table positioned in front of the television set, so that they could "soak up" Sai Baba's presence during the screening.[16]

A widow then in her late sixties, and an ardent devotee of Shirdi Sai Baba, my neighbor had first seen the film in late 1990, just months after her husband had passed away. As we watched the scene in which Kulkarni's lamenting wife sings the devotional song "O Dukhiyon Ke Data," begging for Sai Baba to heal her husband from snakebite and bring him back to life, my neighbor confessed that she had initially found the film very off-putting because of this episode: "First Baba tells her that karma is karma, even he can't stop its fruit. But then he tells her that if she is devout enough then she has the power to save her husband. So she sings this song and Kulkarni, that bad man, he is saved at the end of it. He wakes up. [Long pause.] But my husband, he died. I prayed, too, of course, to my family god when my husband was ill, but still he died. So I felt after watching this that I was to blame, that my devotion was not strong enough."

But then, over the next few weeks, she kept thinking about the earlier scene in the movie in which Baijamma passed away. Sai Baba had loved her dearly—she was like a mother to him, but even he could not save her life. In this scene he does revive Baijamma, momentarily, to reassure her that though karma must play out now, she will be at his side in her next lifetime. My neighbor credited the film—and this scene in particular—with changing her life by helping her to accept her husband's death and find a purpose again rather than wallowing in sorrow and self-blame. She began to make weekly visits to the nearby Shirdi Sai Baba temple on Lodhi Road, took her first pilgrimage to Shirdi, and became active in the temple's social welfare activities. As we watched the film together, she sang along with the bhajans and occasionally wiped her eyes with her handkerchief. At the film's end, she muttered a quick prayer, placed a small pinch of sacred ash on each of our foreheads, and then put a sweet *halwa* in each of our mouths. "You see," she concluded, "it is the greatest film ever made."

Both Satpathy and my neighbor felt such an intimate, personal connection with Sai Baba upon viewing *Shirdi Ke Sai Baba* that they were drawn into his devotional circle. They made pilgrimages to Shirdi, visited Sai Baba temples, and sought out the community of other devotees. In addition to being attracted by Sai Baba's "darshanic pull," they also reported feeling drawn to the film's portrayal of Sai Baba as a pluralist and populist figure. For instance, as my neighbor became more involved in the devotional community at her nearby Sai Baba temple, she began to engage in more and more *seva*, or charitable service activities, particularly those that benefitted the families of patients seeking medical treatment at the All India Institute of Medical Sciences (AIIMS) in New Delhi:

> In the film, Baba says that we must share our food when we have it with those
> who are hungry, and share our money when we have it with those who need
> to buy medicine. So we are working to do this. You know, when a patient is in
> AIIMS with cancer, they come here from far away for specialty treatment. The

treatment is subsidized for the poor, so they can get the medical attention they need. But often they cannot afford a place to stay while they are here, or even enough food to eat. Sometimes even the patient cannot stay in the hospital, if there are no beds available. So the families of the patients, and even some patients, they sleep on the pavements at AIIMS. We help by doing *annadaan* [food charity] every week and provide other sorts of medical aid and services to these families.

This devotee found solace in such service, explaining to me that it helped her transition into her life as a widow by finding a purposeful existence after losing her husband to cancer. Furthermore, she believed that such service also enriched her life by making her a better citizen:

Before I became involved in this seva, I was very isolated. I wasn't aware of my isolation then, I didn't see it that way, but I only met with my family and with friends living in Defense Colony or other such [upper-class] enclaves. But people come to AIIMS from across the country, they are of every religion, every caste, they are rich and poor. Cancer, illness, can strike anyone. It is not picky about your caste or your *dharma* [religion]. So in this way I have met people that I never would have before. Baba has brought me to them, he has taught me not to ignore people because they are from a different community. So like this all of us must come together. This is what Baba teaches, "Sabka Malik Ek" [Everyone's Lord Is One].

C. B. Satpathy, too, felt a call to service, one that ultimately led him to retire from the police force to focus on founding temples to Shirdi Sai Baba and pursuing the spiritual path full-time.[17] In an interview with Satpathy, he stated that many people—like himself—first turn to Sai Baba because of the miracles associated with him, and they think he may fix their problems with some miracle: he may heal them, give them a child, pay their debts. But ultimately, they come to understand that Sai Baba is not about miracles:

Either everything is a miracle, or nothing is. It is as simple as that. But assimilation, that is the main thing. . . . The root principle is this—do you fear God, or do you love God? All religions fall into one category or another. Either love God, or fear God. If the teaching is to love God, to love everyone, then assimilation—not contradiction—can happen. Today, we are very materialistic, here in India and around the world. But there must be some love, some humanity left. Or else, where is the happiness? We find this love in Sai Baba. To cut across all religions in nineteenth-century India—this could not have been easy. Sai Baba did this. He built no personal property, he had no heir. He was not materialistic. He served and he died. This is the appeal. He is a role model in this way. We too should not be so materialistic. We too should serve and then die.[18]

As our conversation continued, Satpathy said that *Shirdi Ke Sai Baba* is important because it gets this right: the film is not about Sai Baba's miracles, though it does depict many of them. Rather, its core message is one of love and service: "*Shirdi Ke Sai Baba* shows how Baba assimilated everyone together, Hindus, Muslims, Sikhs. And it shows how he loved all the people throughout his lifetime, it did not matter if they were high caste or low, or if they were big or small. He served everyone, and then he died. Serve and then die, that is the real miracle."[19]

In speaking with many other devotees at Sai Baba temples in urban India (including Mumbai, New Delhi, and Bengaluru), I found such sentiments common. People from similar middle- or upper-class and upper-caste backgrounds often told me that offering loving service in Sai Baba's name was the way to reform India into a more just and unified country. As one devotee in Bengaluru (formerly Bangalore) explained, referencing the episode in *Shirdi Ke Sai Baba* when Sai Baba takes on the guise of a poor beggar to test Kulkarni: "When bellies are empty, families fight, but when bellies are full, the whole family can sleep peacefully. It is the same in the country as in the family. When there is hunger there cannot be peace. So Baba teaches that we must offer seva to fill the bellies and to bring peace. This is the final lesson he gave to Kulkarni, that he must feed the beggar at his door. So that is why we do annadaan every Thursday at the temple, to feed the beggars at our door."[20]

However, devotees from the lower classes and castes that I interviewed at the same temples did not espouse a "serve and then die" attitude. Instead, they frequently interpreted Shirdi Sai Baba's message not as a call to service but as a call for the recognition of rights. A repeated theme in my conversations with these devotees was the urgent need for basic human rights, particularly the right to a living wage, to housing, to food and water, and to health care. They felt that Sai Baba's teachings called for a more just society wherein a person was evaluated based on his or her deeds, rather than caste, class, gender, or religion. Sai Baba set the example himself, they told me, by welcoming devotees from all backgrounds if their faith was sincere, by sharing his food with those who were hungry, by redistributing to his devotees money that came to him in the form of *dakshina* offerings, and by curing lepers who were denied proper medical attention, among other acts.

When conversations turned to *Shirdi Ke Sai Baba*, many of these devotees immediately recalled scenes that spoke to these issues. Particularly powerful to many was the (fictitious) character Vidya, a poor "Untouchable" girl with a recurring role in the film. One devotee in Mumbai, a Dalit himself, said that he viewed her as the model devotee:

> In the film, Vidya is the best devotee, far better than Kulkarni, even though she is Dalit and he is Brahmin. She is the one who comes to Baba as a child and loves him her whole lifetime, while Kulkarni keeps rejecting him. She begs oil for him daily, and is abused by Kulkarni and the merchants who do not give oil to her because of their bias. She grows up, she has children, and she thanks Baba for them, yet Kulkarni still cannot see who Baba really is. Her faith is purer than his. The message is that our society will be better when people are not judged by their caste, but by what is in their hearts.[21]

Speaking of this same character, a female devotee who was also a Dalit commented:

> The priest Kulkarni, he won't help Vidya when she comes to him seeking medicine for her father on his deathbed. But Baba, he gives her vibhuti and tells her to also visit [the Hindu god] Khandoba. But when she tries, she isn't allowed into the temple. So Khandoba comes to her and gives her a vision of him. This lowly woman gets the vision that even Kulkarni doesn't get, and her father is healed. Dalits are denied access to medicine, to religion, to education, even to life. But Baba points out the injustice of this, the need to change these old ways of thinking if we want to move forward as a society.[22]

AMAR AKBAR ANTHONY

The blockbuster *Amar Akbar Anthony* was also released in 1977. Directed by Manmohan Desai, who directed many hits in the 1970s and 1980s, including *Dharam Veer* (1977) and *Coolie* (1983), *Amar Akbar Anthony* perhaps best exemplifies Desai's trademark "multi-starrers centering around mistaken identity, lost and found siblings, and highly improbable feats" (Ganti 2004, 103). The star-studded cast of *Amar Akbar Anthony* includes Vinod Khanna as Amar, Rishi Kapoor as Akbar, and Amitabh Bachchan as Anthony, three young brothers who are tragically separated from their birth parents and from one another through a series of misfortunate events. After their separation, each brother is adopted, and they grow up in three different homes as members of three different religions: Amar is Hindu, Akbar is Muslim, and Anthony is Christian. They meet again as adults in the culminating scene of the long opening sequence: Amar, Akbar, and Anthony are each found to share the blood type of an accident victim, and they all agree to give blood for the elderly blind woman's recovery. Unbeknownst to them, the enfeebled victim, Bharati (Nirupa Roy), is their birth mother, and as Philip Lutgendorf (2014) comments, the scene in which they donate blood is "one of the film's most memorably overdetermined visuals." The three sons give their blood through a direct transfusion, with their beds positioned directly under windows framing (respectively) a Hindu temple, a Muslim mosque, and a Christian church as their mother lies in a fourth bed positioned at their feet. Here, the three brothers must join together to heal their wounded mother. Because each brother represents one of India's three major religious traditions, the scene suggests that India's religious communities must also join together to heal a communally fractured Mother India. Shirdi Sai Baba's role in *Amar Akbar Anthony* is brief but crucial to the reunion of the entire family, and thus to the film's larger metaphorical message about national unity.[23]

The film's primary villain is Robert (Jeevan), the criminal boss who employed Kishanlal (Pran), the husband of Bharati and father of the three boys. Robert's hard-hearted actions caused the turn of events leading to the family's separation, and Kishanlal (who thinks his wife is dead) has sworn vengeance for the death of his wife and loss of his sons by kidnapping Robert's only daughter, Jenny (Parveen Babi). Years later, Robert kidnaps Bharati (who thinks her husband and sons are dead), wrongly assuming that she has been in contact with Kishanlal and has knowledge that will lead him to Jenny. The kidnapped Bharati manages to flee from the car as it overturns in an accident. Running from the scene of the crash and blindly feeling her way about the landscape, she moves in the direction of music that she hears in the distance. Cue the song sequence "Shirdiwale Sai Baba" (O Sai Baba of Shirdi), a *qawwali-bhajan* hybrid performed by Akbar (sung by playback singer Mohammad Rafi), who stands in the center of a shrine and leads a congregation in singing this devotional hymn before a large murti of Shirdi Sai Baba. The lyrics proclaim that the devotee stands before Sai Baba with

Prayers on my lips,

Tears in my eyes,

Hopes in my heart,

Yet my pockets are empty.

As the congregation repeats the chorus "O Sai Baba of Shirdi! / A petitioner has arrived in your court," Bharati is shown inching closer and closer to the shrine. As she enters the sacred compound, Robert and one of his henchmen follow her in hot pursuit, but a cobra leaps in front of them and denies them entry. Here, Sai Baba—who is frequently associated with snakes for his reputed ability to heal snakebite—is shown to be at work responding to the needs of the genuine petitioner, Bharati, who has indeed arrived at his doorstep empty-handed but—as we shall soon see—not without prayers, tears, and hopes.

Although *Amar Akbar Anthony* is not a mythological film, it draws upon the standard cinematic convention in Hindi mythological and devotional films by emphasizing throughout this song sequence the darshanic exchange of glances between the divine figure and the devotee. The camerawork is flashy, drawing attention to itself by repeatedly zooming in on the face of the devotee (first Akbar and then Bharati), then zooming in on the face of Sai Baba from the point of view of the devotee, and then offering a shot/reverse-shot of the devotee (sometimes from just over Sai Baba's shoulder) to show the devotee from Sai Baba's viewpoint. This sequence is made even more obvious by the use of extreme close-ups that linger on the faces and eyes of the divine figure and the devotees for several seconds. Lutgendorf has noted that this ubiquitous convention in mythological song sequences in Hindi cinema invites the film viewer to assume "both positions in the act of *darshanic* intercourse, thus closing an experiential loop that ultimately moves (as most Hindu loops do) toward an underlying unity" (Lutgendorf 2002, 28). Visually, then, the film invites the viewer to identify with Akbar and Bharati in their devotion to Sai Baba but also to identify with Sai Baba in his reciprocal attention directed toward his devotees. The divine figure and the devotee are here united in one darshanic loop, suggesting through this "visual theology" that the devotee and the divine are part of one larger, nondual ultimate reality.

Visually, in this song sequence, the film also suggests an underlying unity between Islam and Hinduism in two interrelated ways. First, it presents both Akbar and Bharati as devotees of Shirdi Sai Baba, thus suggesting that Sai Baba is equally receptive to Muslims (Akbar) and Hindus (Bharati), drawing no distinctions between them in terms of their faith (the congregation in the background also consists of Hindus and Muslims, as well as men and women). Second, it presents the shrine as a composite space for devotion by employing both Muslim and Hindu religious imagery in a visual display that Lutgendorf (2014) describes as "unembarrassed syncretism." As Akbar sings the devotional song, he is shown standing in front of a *mihrab*, the prayer niche in the *qibla* wall of a mosque that indicates the direction of Mecca. This wall is painted green, the color associated with Islam in South Asia, and the Muslim crescent moon and star hang from the ceiling. A few seconds later, Bharati stumbles up the stairs and enters the shrine, which is topped with a saffron-colored flag, the color associated with Hinduism. She is shown facing Sai Baba and bowing to him in prostration, next to a statue of the bull Nandi, the *vahana* (vehicle) associated with the Hindu god Shiva who frequently stands guard at the doorway of Shaivite temples. The Sai Baba shrine, then, is half Sufi *dargah* (tomb shrine) and half Hindu temple. Both Muslims and Hindus are equally welcome to enter its doors as genuine petitioners, to become members of one community united in shared devotion to Sai Baba.

The song's lyrics similarly emphasize Sai Baba's connection with his devotees, drawing out the theme of unity in several ways. First, the lyrics complement the visual theology that underlines the unity of devotees and the divine through a mutual bond of love. For instance, Akbar uses the metaphor of a garden in his verses, likening humanity in all its variety to the flowers and Sai Baba to the gardener. Just as the flowers need the loving care of the gardener to flourish, so the gardener needs the flowers for his garden to thrive. Second, the lyrics emphasize that a variety of different people are united with one another through their shared bond of devotion to Sai Baba. Akbar stresses that Sai Baba is loved by—and in turn loves—Hindus and Muslims, the wealthy and the poor, those with social status and those without:

> People are so different, yet all are dear to you,
> You listen to everyone's petitions, and you remember each and every one,
> Be it a big person or a small one, no one ever returned disappointed,
> You are a support to the rich, and you provide means of survival to the poor,
> The tale of all of your compassions can't be narrated by Akbar.

Third, the lyrics tell us that families torn asunder will be reunited under the loving gaze of Sai Baba. Akbar and the congregation sing these words again and again:

The one who has been abandoned by all others,
Has been embraced by you.
You make the separated ones meet,
And you light up the extinguished lamps.

While they are singing, flames of light suddenly appear in Sai Baba's eyes and then transfer to Bharati's own eyes. The camera blurs out of focus and then quickly refocuses on Sai Baba, enacting for the viewer the miraculous return of Bharati's eyesight, the lighting up of her extinguished lamps. As Bharati gazes upon Sai Baba with grateful tears in her eyes—for she is now able to take his darshan—and Akbar appeals to Sai Baba to turn these dark nights of sorrow into festivals of love and light, like Eid (celebrated by Muslims) and Diwali (celebrated by Hindus), Bharati experiences a vision. While looking at Sai Baba, she sees an image of her three sons, lost to her so many years ago, each gesturing her to come forward. The prostrate Bharati dramatically scoots across the floor of the temple, approaching Sai Baba as the congregation frenetically repeats the song's chorus over and over, and then she collapses at his feet.

The family's reunion unfolds after Bharati's encounter with Shirdi Sai Baba, who makes the separated ones meet, just as the lyrics of "Shirdiwale Sai Baba" proclaim. First, Bharati realizes that Akbar is her son when he takes her home to help her escape from Robert. There she sees a photo of Akbar as a young boy, taken with his adoptive father, and recognizes Akbar as her own boy, Raju. Next, Amar and his birth father, Kishanlal, are reunited when they independently revisit the family's former home and recognize one another. Finally, Anthony and Kishanlal are reunited when Anthony confronts Kishanlal about the mistaken belief that he killed his adoptive father. As all parties finally piece together the puzzle of their true identities, the film ends on a happily-ever-after note when the three boys come together to foil Robert's diabolical plans and see that he is imprisoned, and then they together embrace their birth mother and father in a big family hug before riding off into the sunset along with their three new brides.

Thus, in *Amar Akbar Anthony* Shirdi Sai Baba functions as the deus ex machina who appears as the patron saint of the family unit. Through his intervention, Bharati is healed of both her blindness and her heartache when her sundered family is reunited. After the three brothers learn their true identity, they band together in the final song sequence, "Amar Akbar Anthony." Here, they not only outwit and defeat the villains but do so in

FIGURE 4.1. Shirdi Sai Baba making the separated ones meet. Film still from *Amar Akbar Anthony.*

costumes that visually proclaim Akbar's and Anthony's religious identities: a bearded and fez-wearing Akbar is dressed as an elderly Muslim tailor; Anthony is dressed as a robed and collared Catholic priest; Amar is comically dressed as a one-man band. The brothers dance and sing about the impossible becoming possible when all three—Amar, Akbar, and Anthony—are together. Only by doing what seemed impossible—joining together as a family unit—can the brothers bring the film to its happily-ever-after ending. Because the brothers represent three different religious traditions—Hinduism, Islam, and Christianity—the film also suggests that only by doing what seems impossible—joining together as a national unit—will India's multiple religious communities arrive at a similar happily-ever-after conclusion. In this way, Sai Baba functions in this film not only as the patron saint of the nuclear family but also of the national family.

Complementing *Amar Akbar Anthony*'s pluralist message is its populist message. The hardships faced by each family member focus attention on class issues in modern Indian society, and the film suggests that Sai Baba can not only unite citizens across religious divides but also secure a better future for the working classes through faith in him. This film's populist mobilizing aesthetic is more obvious at first glance than that found in *Shirdi Ke Sai Baba*, for *Amar Akbar Anthony* features the "angry young man" Amitabh Bachchan. His character, Anthony, is not quite as angry as in *Zanjeer, Deewar*, and *Sholay*, but *Amar Akbar Anthony* nonetheless capitalizes on this persona by portraying Anthony as a likeable rabble rouser and petty underground liquor dealer, quick to jump into fisticuffs while also declaring Jesus to be his "partner" in crime—he gives half of his earnings to the Catholic Church. Anthony shares screen time with his brothers: Akbar, a *qawwali* singer and tailor, and Amar, an honest and hard-working police officer. Together, the three brothers represent not only three religions but also the working classes—those in the formal and informal sectors, those in the trades and the arts, those simply trying to eke out a day-to-day living in urban India without falling prey to criminal bosses, profit-driven employers, or the corrupt system. The brothers also represent the dispossessed who have been orphaned in society: after their father, Kishanlal, is wrongfully imprisoned and their mother, Bharati, plans to commit suicide because she cannot afford treatment for her tuberculosis, the brothers are shown abandoned under an apotropaic statue of Mahatma Gandhi on August 15 (India's Independence Day). But what the bronze statue of Gandhi is unable to accomplish, the marble statue of Shirdi Sai Baba can: helping the destitute and uniting the family/nation.

In the song sequence "Shirdiwale Sai Baba," as the empty-handed and blinded Bharati crawls forward to Sai Baba, the visuals make clear (as discussed above) that Sai Baba is available to Hindus and Muslims. But the lyrics of the qawwali-bhajan emphasize a class dimension as well, stressing that Sai Baba is available to the rich and the poor, the big people and the small; indeed, he is hailed as the savior of those who have been abandoned by all others, one who can rescue them from their dark nights. Repeatedly in *Amar Akbar Anthony* it is the poor, the working classes, and the abandoned who are shown to suffer at the hands of the wealthy and the greedy. This central song sequence is the turning point in the film, holding out the promise that Sai Baba can act as the balm that soothes these marginalized groups—just as he soothed Bharati and came to her aid—by bringing light and love into their lives after they turn to him in devotion.

Bringing Sai Baba to the Masses

Amar Akbar Anthony was the most popular film of 1977 and ranks among the top twenty all-time earners in Indian cinema. In their book-length study of this film, William Elison, Christian Novetzke, and Andy Rotman (2016, 8–9) argue that *Amar Akbar Anthony* was the quintessential Bollywood masala film, and as such many Indian film critics initially panned it, dismissing it as unrealistic, "escapist fare for the masses," and even "outright hokum." Yet unlike the elite English-speaking film reviewers, the Hindi-speaking audience embraced it. The film was the first to earn a silver jubilee (awarded when a film shows continuously in one cinema for twenty-five weeks), and it was screened in an unprecedented nine theaters in Bombay; it went on to earn golden (fifty weeks) and platinum (seventy-five weeks) jubilees as well (7–8). In 1977, it was nominated for seven Filmfare Awards and took home three: best actor (Amitabh Bachchan), best music (Laxmikant-Pyarelal), and best editing (Karkhanis). The film is now famous not just within India but worldwide among the ever-growing Hindi-film-viewing public; in 1980, it became the first Bollywood film to be shown on British television.[24] Elison and colleagues write that Indian film critics generally considered the film's target audience to be the "lumpen masses" in India:

> Some sense of *Amar Akbar Anthony*'s appeal to the so-called masses can be discerned from a curious newspaper article that recounts the findings of a team of middle-class student researchers who, at the prompting of their professor of mass communications in Bombay, interviewed "peons" and other representatives of the subordinate classes to gain the "experience of talking to people [that they would not normally encounter] about issues they don't know." The professor does not tell us why he or she sent those students out to ask about *Amar Akbar Anthony*, but the previously cited reviews give some notion that *Amar Akbar Anthony* was the film that the masses massed around that year. When asked if the "scenarios" of the film were "unrealistic," the subjects would almost unanimously dissent. "It wasn't at all unrealistic that such things could happen. They were God-fearing people, they said, and God could do anything." (Elison, Novetzke, and Rotman 2016, 8–9)

If the critics found the plot or the characters unrealistic, the "masses" apparently did not.

Filmmaker Manmohan Desai stated in an interview that his characters in *Amar Akbar Anthony* are realistic, even if his plot is not, for they are based on salt-of-the-earth people he knew as a child growing up in working-class Bombay: "You see, all my characters are from the lower middle class, characters who are down-to-earth, who have seen life in the raw. If I had been born an aristocrat, I could never have made it [the film]" (Haham 2006, 115). Elison and colleagues argue that contrary to the critics' claims that Desai's films are simply about entertainment and totally lacking in realistic social messages, his films "do have a 'social message,' even if he isn't calling for revolution, and this message is political":

> [They offer] a generalized politics of "escape" from poverty, from oppressive governments, and from the drudgery of reality, but also from the constraints of cinematic form itself. Although Desai's films offer a dizzying recycling of clichés and parody upon parody, his films are invariably morality plays. And this orientation provides the compass for differentiating heroes from villains, reality from fantasy, justice from injustice, and drama from melodrama. More-over, these idealized morality plays allow the audience to enter a kind of lim-inal fantasy world, more equitable and joyous than our own, and to leave with a new vision—of an idyllic world somehow closer at hand. (Elison, Novetzke, and Rotman 2016, 24–25)

For the film's viewers—the "lumpen masses"—part of the pleasure of view-ing *Amar Akbar Anthony* is the happy-ever-after vision of the three brothers ultimately reunited as a family and freed from the abandonment and desti-tution of their youth. It is this vision that brought viewers back again and again. After seeing *Amar Akbar Anthony* for the first time, many returned for repeat viewings; they bought the music cassette and listened to it at home, in the car, even at work; and they memorized the dialogues—especially Amitabh Bachchan's lines.[25]

Though the target audience was the "lumpen masses," and especially the young men among them, it is important to note that *Amar Akbar Anthony*'s happy-ever-after vision had crossover appeal beyond this target demo-graphic. In spite of the critics' assumptions, the film appealed not just to the working poor but to the middle classes as well, especially in the character of Anthony Gonsalves as played by Amitabh Bachchan. Vijay Mishra writes that in the history of Bollywood, "no actor has achieved the status of Amitabh Bachchan" (2002, 127). Bachchan became famous for playing sub-altern heroes, angry young men like Anthony, a poor orphan who toils to become a petty street boss. However, Bachchan himself comes from privi-lege, and the actor's superstar status is due to the fact that he is greatly admired by Indians from across class backgrounds. Thus, Mishra writes of Bachchan, "It is ironic that someone with impeccable middle-class roots (poet father, socialite mother, connections with the Nehru/Gandhi dynasty) begins to espouse the dreams of Bombay shanty dwellers and speaks for them" (128). Elison and colleagues elaborate on this point:

> Whereas the masses could see reflected in *Amar Akbar Anthony* their own yearnings for insurgent release, the middle class—poised for their tasty first bite of the Maharaja Mac in the dawn of economic liberalization fifteen years in the future—could consume the film as a comedy about the incipient demise of the poor and powerless, the dethronement of the "people" as the central concern of the Indian state. Through Anthony, Bachchan emerged as a social polyglot, and has now ascended to the status of something like India's cultural pope. It is as if the Anthony-Bachchan sandwich had been designed as part of a government Five-Year Plan in anticipation of the move to a neoliberal model of development: a figure who in life represented the aspirations of bourgeois India to realize the full measure of what market ideology had to offer, and who in film could cathect the experiences of disenfranchised "heroes" on the street hoping to catch a break. At least through the 1980s, Bachchan and his many subsequent characters provide the missing link in Indian public culture between the toiling masses and the prosperous "classes." (Elison, Novetzke, and Rotman 2016, 121–22)

Bachchan may deserve the credit for bridging the class divide, but it is Shirdi Sai Baba who must be credited (diegetically speaking) with bringing about this happy-ever-after vision that had such appeal for the so-called masses and even the middle and upper classes. Why was Sai Baba chosen for this exalted role in *Amar Akbar Anthony*? Elison and colleagues explain: "One reason for the attention the film lavishes on Sai Baba—visually, narratively, musically—over other divine personalities like Jesus, Mary, and Santoshi Maa is undoubtedly the personal devotion of Manmohan Desai's wife, Jeevanprabha (who also received a story credit for the film). Desai imbibed some of her enthusiasm and, years later, would go on pilgrimage to Shirdi to mark the date of her death" (2016, 105).[26]

Although *Amar Akbar Anthony* is not a mythological film, the great popularity of its hit song "Shirdiwale Sai Baba" and accompanying visual sequence have contributed to spreading Sai Baba's name to audiences throughout India (and beyond) that were previously unfamiliar with him.

Furthermore, this song has become incorporated into the devotional practices of many Sai Baba devotees. While I was in Shirdi in 2010, standing in line waiting to enter the Samadhi Mandir for darshan with Sai Baba, the refrain from this song was among the devotional bhajans sung by the crowd. In fact, if popularity can be measured by the volume of the crowd's singing, then this was perhaps the most popular song sung that day. I have also encountered versions of "Shirdiwale Sai Baba" sung at temple bhajan sessions in Mumbai and New Delhi, and I have seen it remixed on various Sai Baba devotional albums.

"THERE SHALL BE NO WANT IN THE HOUSE OF MY DEVOTEES"

Together, these two films of 1977 raised awareness of Shirdi Sai Baba, presenting him as both a pluralist and populist hero. In the mythological *Shirdi Ke Sai Baba*, Sai Baba is a heroic, this-worldly savior able to cure sick children, infertility, blindness, leprosy, and plague; he can cure what even medical doctors, including the father of young Deepak featured in the framing narrative, cannot. But with the interspersing of social commentary throughout the miraculous scenes of the core narrative, Sai Baba becomes a healer not only of physical ailments but of the ailing nation of India itself, which is fractured and wounded by communal, caste, and class strife. The "good guys" in this film (beyond Sai Baba as the lead hero, of course) are the lowly in caste status, the poor, the sick, and women. These downtrodden villagers are the ones with sincere faith in Sai Baba, as opposed to the "bad guys" who doubt that Sai Baba is the genuine thing: the elite Brahmin priests in Shirdi and the colonial Indian officers who visit the village. In the end, however, even these skeptics are converted into believers, bringing about the happy-ever-after conclusion of Shirdi—and, by allegorical extension, the nation at large—united across lines of creed and class. In the masala *Amar Akbar Anthony*, Sai Baba appears in a pivotal scene to bring about the reunion of three long-lost brothers with one another and their mother, Bharati. The "good guys" in the film are the three working-class brothers, each adopted into a different religious tradition. The "bad guys" are the underworld boss Robert and his henchmen, greedy criminals obsessed with profits and power. In the end, however, Robert is defeated when the brothers band together, bringing about the happy-ever-after conclusion of a family—and, by allegorical extension, the nation at large—united across lines of creed and class.

And yet, looking beyond such happy-ever-after endings, one can question how far both films take their pluralist messages. Several scholars have pointed out the limitations of this message in *Amar Akbar Anthony*, commenting that even as the film presents a vision of a pluralist family/nation united in its diversity, it simultaneously affirms the centrality of Hinduism above and beyond other religions within the family/nation. Philip Lutgendorf (2014) notes that because all three brothers are born into a Hindu family, they are still "reassuringly Hindu inside," despite the outer appearances of Akbar and Anthony. This is reinforced, Lutgendorf points out, during the blood transfusion scene, when the voice-over lyrics proclaim, "Khoon khoon hotaa hai paani nahin [Blood is always blood, not water]."[27] Blood being thicker than water underlines the strength of the family bond. However, such lyrics can also suggest that deep within, it is Hindu blood that flows through the veins of all three brothers. Viewed on the level of the nation, this can in turn imply that Indian members of other religions—such as Islam and Christianity—nonetheless still have Hindu blood in their veins, despite their outer appearances. Given the fraught history of the politics of conversion in colonial and postcolonial India, the implication that all Indians are Hindu at their core can be very troubling indeed to the country's Muslims and Christians.[28]

Similarly, in their book on *Amar Akbar Anthony*, Elison and colleagues note the film's ambivalent message, writing at the outset: "While *Amar Akbar Anthony* is conventionally read in India as a film about national integration—and we don't altogether controvert this position—our argument will make room for the opposite reading as well" (Elison, Novetzke, and Rotman 2016, 4). They note that in the film as a whole, and in the final "Amar Akbar Anthony" song sequence in particular, fraternity does not imply equality, for Christianity and Islam are placed within the domain of an unmarked Hinduism, embodied by Amar. Nonetheless, these authors also point out that even though Anthony, like Akbar, ultimately learns of his "true" origin, he does not reconvert to Hinduism. Rather, he marries a Christian girl and drives of into the sunset with her. Thus, they write, "The film rejects the political narrative that casts Christians (and Muslims) as wayward, misled Hindus, even while it appears to support the idea that all Indians have some essential 'secular Hinduism' at the core of their being" (Elison, Novetzke, and Rotman 2016, 140).[29]

Likewise, the film *Shirdi Ke Sai Baba* can also be seen as "reassuringly Hindu," for despite its proclamations about the benefits of pluralism and the composite nature of Sai Baba, a Hindu normativity permeates the film and its interpretation of Sai Baba. For instance, the framing story that draws us into the film and transports us to Shirdi features a Hindu family; the priest in the framing story uses Hindu terminology in explaining that although Sai Baba has left his mortal body, "avatars" come and go; and Sai Baba is repeatedly equated with Hindu gods, especially in the song sequences "Dam Dam Dam Damroo," "Sai Bhola Bhandari," and "O Dukhiyon Ke Data," even as he is simultaneously praised as a composite saint in the songs "Sumer Manva," "Sai Baba Bolo," and "Tuhi Fakir." These narrative choices presume a predominantly Hindu viewership and can contribute to the interpretation of Sai Baba as a Hindu god incarnate, albeit a very inclusive one.

Beyond the film's narrative, its very form also suggests an overall Hindu normativity. As part of the mythological or mythodevotional genre, *Shirdi Ke Sai Baba* emphasizes the Hindu ritual of darshan. Viewers are not only informed about Sai Baba and entertained by the narration of the many lilas associated with him; they are also encouraged to participate in ritual behavior in the form of sacred gazing that arises out of Hindu tradition. The entire film is marked as sacred space and time through a darshanic framing device—a frame that bookends the film's framing narrative, which in turn bookends the core narrative. In this darshanic frame, the viewer is invited to take part in the ritualized viewing of the marble statue of Sai Baba in Shirdi that is presented frontally for a prolonged exchange of glances between devotee and deity at the beginning and end of the film, and thus to ideally maintain this devotional mind-set while watching the entire film. This presumes a predominantly Hindu viewership (though the viewership of the mythological genre of Indian films is by no means exclusive to Hindus, just as darshan is not exclusive to Hindus), and such ritualized viewing can encourage an interpretation of Sai Baba as a Hindu god incarnate.

But what of the populist message in these films? As noted at the outset of this chapter, M. Madhava Prasad argues that in response to the nation's political turmoil in the 1970s, a new mode of address arose in Bollywood cinema: a subaltern hero, the best example of which is the working-class "angry young man" persona of Amitabh Bachchan, as portrayed in the hit films *Zanjeer, Deewar,* and *Sholay.* In these films, Bachchan's character acts as an agent of national reconciliation and social reform by violently enacting a transition from feudal to populist power (Prasad 1998, 138–59). *Zanjeer,* for example, is a story of vengeance, wherein the character Vijay Khanna (Bachchan) takes the law into his own hands, killing the gang leader Teja

(Ajit Khan), who had murdered Vijay's parents when he was just a boy and continued to plague society for the next twenty years. *Zanjeer* was Bachchan's thirteenth film but his first superhit, and thus this was the film that catapulted him into his career as an angry young man seeking revenge outside of the justice system. If measured against the standard set by *Zanjeer*, *Deewar*, and *Sholay*, then *Amar Akbar Anthony* would perhaps appear to be populist mobilization "lite." After all, revenge is not the sole driving force behind the story. Love—both romantic and familial (and national, when the family is read as an allegory of the nation)—is also central to the characters' motivations and the film's narrative.

Take, for example, the final song sequence and finale of *Amar Akbar Anthony*, in which Anthony (Bachchan) collaborates with his brothers, Amar and Akbar, to rise up against the criminal boss Robert and his henchmen, defeating them in a scene that is as much a violent take down of the reigning power as it is a comical song and dance filled with slapstick hijinks. After Robert receives a powerful punch from each brother, he lands in jail, along with his cronies. In jail next to him is Kishanlal, the birth father of the three brothers. As the brothers appear, along with their mother, Bharati, the whole family embraces. Following the family hug, the three brothers are shown riding off into the sunset, with their three brides in the backseat behind them. This fantasy was part of the film's appeal to the so-called masses.

Writing of Amitabh Bachchan's popularity, Vijay Mishra says that he often played revenge-seeking antiheroes on the opposite side of the law but importantly also came out better for it in the end. This "rebelliousness thus synthesized reflected the disenchantment, the oppression, the hopelessness of the slum dweller who saw in Bachchan's acts of 'antiheroism' a symbol of his or her own aspirations. The rags-to-riches theme that always paralleled the narrative of personal revenge in Bachchan's films was the imaginary fulfillment of the slum dweller's own fantasies" (Mishra 2002, 128). It is this two-pronged approach that we see at play in *Amar Akbar Anthony*: the appeal of the rebellious antihero paired with the appeal of the escapist resolution. *Amar Akbar Anthony* is less angry, violent, and vengeful than the other films that Bachchan starred in during the 1970s—but anger, violence, and vengefulness, combined with love, comedy, and a happy ending, are together part of the masala that made this film such a success with its target audience.

If *Amar Akbar Anthony* is populist mobilization "lite" in terms of its emphasis on outlaw vengeance and violent revolution, then how much more so is *Shirdi Ke Sai Baba*. As previously noted, this film depicts two types of villains: the Brahmin priests who seek to protect their orthodox hold on the village and the indigenous officers employed by the British Raj who seek to protect the colonial hold on the nation. A third, but disembodied, villain is also present: British colonial rule. With this villain, violence is not completely foresworn in this film; after all, Sai Baba is shown endorsing the efforts of the bloodied freedom fighters who arrive seeking his blessing, and he says they are working to uproot the British Raj. Sai Baba also endorses Tilak's interpretation of the Bhagavad Gita and his call to action—including armed insurrection—against the British. All the same, violence is not advocated against either the indigenous officers or the village Brahmins. Instead of vengeance, Sai Baba seeks to convert these figures to his side. And, of course, by the film's end he is successful: Das Ganu and Chandorkar have foresworn the colonial service, and Kulkarni and his sidekick have foresworn their orthodox casteism.

Conversion, rather than revenge, is what *Shirdi Ke Sai Baba*'s "hero" is all about. Like *Amar Akbar Anthony*, this film ends on a happy-ever-after note. Sins have been redeemed, physical illnesses have been cured, animosities have been reconciled, social wrongs have been righted, and skepticism about Sai Baba's saving grace has been lifted (for all in the core narrative, for the doctor in the framing narrative, and perhaps also for some viewers). Philip Lutgendorf argues that the 1975 mythological film *Jai Santoshi Maa* represents "part of a larger picture of non-elite assertiveness and agency" (2002, 35), and the same can be said of *Shirdi Ke Sai Baba*. But whereas *Jai Santoshi Maa* sought to appeal to lower-middle-class women in particular, *Shirdi Ke Sai Baba* aimed at the downtrodden more broadly, including in its ranks of "good guys" the lowly in caste status, the poor, the sick, and women. It is their adversities that the film focuses on, and their aspirations, which are fulfilled in the end through their faith in Sai Baba.

The last of Sai Baba's 11 Sayings is "There shall be no want in the house of my devotees." Both *Amar Akbar Anthony* and *Shirdi Ke Sai Baba* present visual theologies of this assurance, suggesting that all of the needs of the faithful will be fulfilled by Sai Baba. Importantly, this includes not just spiritual needs but also very worldly needs. Together, these two films illustrate that through faith in Sai Baba, long-lost loved ones will be reunited, good guys will be rewarded, sinners will be redeemed, and society at large will be unified. But also, through faith in Sai Baba, the poor will be fed, the blind and sick will be cured, the destitute will be cared for. The films suggest that just like such characters, the aspiring classes watching the films can also attain their own happy-ever-after ending through faith in Sai Baba. An additional measure of the widespread and lasting appeal of this message—as well as its Hindu normativity—can be seen in the outpouring of devotional spin-offs these films have inspired in both Bollywood television and film during the past decade or two, including Deepak Balraj Vij's films *Shirdi Sai Baba* (2001) and *Maalik Ek* (2010) and Ramanand Sagar's television series *Sai Baba* (which began airing in 2005).

CHAPTER 5

Shirdi Is for Humanity

MANY GURUS AND THEIR PLEAS TO THE WORLD

Ritual doesn't matter. In fact, religion doesn't matter. Baba never asked anyone to change their religion. Religion is not even the shape of our discussion.

MUKUND RAJ, FOUNDING MEMBER,
SHIRDI SAI TEMPLE OF CHICAGO AND SUBURBS

There is a shift in society now. Hindu rituals, they are very complicated. Not everyone now is interested in that kind of religion. Baba said the rituals were fine, if you want to do them, do them. But they don't really matter.

CRAIG SASTRY EDWARDS, CO-FOUNDER,
SRI SHIRDI SAI BABA TEMPLE OF AUSTIN

IN one of the few photographs of Shirdi Sai Baba, he stands, leaning against the outer wall of a house, looking at the camera. He is elderly, perhaps even frail, as suggested by the care with which his attendants hold onto each of his arms. Bracing Sai Baba's right arm is Nana Saheb Nimonkar; behind Sai Baba is Bhagoji Shinde (holding the umbrella); bracing Sai Baba's left arm is Bapu Saheb Buty, and next to him is Nana Chopdar (with a walking staff). For devotees of Sai Baba, this photograph is important because it is one source of *darshan*, a way of visually engaging with Sai Baba's presence even after his physical demise, as well as proof of his former embodied existence. I have seen many devotees worship this photo, and I have attended one devotional lecture about its deeper mystical meaning.

For my purposes, however, this photograph is important because it provides visual evidence of some of the ritual worship of Sai Baba that was conducted in the latter years of his life. Notice the large *chhatra*, or umbrella, held by Bhagoji Shinde. Shinde was a social outcaste in Shirdi, a leper who was ostracized because of his illness. But Sai Baba accepted him with open arms, and for this reason Shinde was his loyal devotee and servant. Chapter 7 of Govind Rao Dabholkar's *Shri Sai Satcharita* records that Shinde was rewarded for his devotion by being given intimate access to Sai Baba as well as privileged chores. One of these chores was holding the chhatra over Sai Baba's head as he walked to the Lendi Garden each morning: "As a result of the great sins of his past births, Bhagoji was afflicted with leprosy. But great indeed was his good fortune that he had the privilege of Sai's company. As Baba set out on his daily round to the Lendi, Bhagoji would be his umbrella-bearer. His body was full of bleeding sores, yet he was the foremost among the attendants" (Dabholkar 2007, 112). The umbrella is not intended to merely provide shade on a hot summer day; rather, in India the umbrella is a visual sign of royalty and/or divinity. Stylized chhatras are typically carved into the statues or drawn into the paintings of sacred figures in classical Indian devotional traditions (including Hinduism, but also Buddhism and Jainism), and in Hindu temples today they are often placed over the *murti*, or statue, that is at the heart of ritual worship. As Sai Baba entered public space to walk to the Lendi Garden, then, his loyal attendant Bhagoji Shinde followed him with the umbrella to publicly signify his exalted status.[1]

An even more elaborate procession took place on the evenings when Sai Baba walked to the *chavadi*, the village record office, where he spent alternate nights for the final decade of his life (he continued his long-standing tradition of sleeping in the Dwarkamai mosque on the other nights). His Hindu followers gathered together outside of the mosque, waiting to accompany him to the chavadi. They did so in the manner of the Varkari pilgrimage to Pandharpur, singing devotional songs and playing music as they walked. Chapter 37 of the *Shri Sai Satcharita* dates the origin of such ritual worship of Sai Baba to December 10, 1909, and describes it in detail:

FIGURE 5.1. Shirdi Sai Baba standing under an umbrella, prior to 1918. Photo: Anonymous.

While Tatyasaheb held Baba's left hand, Mhalsapati held the right. Babusaheb
Jog held the large and lofty umbrella over his head. And so proceeded Baba to
the Chavadi. In front walked the fine, copper-coloured heavily ornamented
horse, named Shamkarna, the bells on his feet jingling as he walked. The staff-
bearers, walking in front, loudly proclaimed Baba's name from time to time. . . .
Alongside walked men and women, all steeped in the spirit of joy and love the
bhajans generated, and pronounced *Sainaam* loudly which seemed to fill the
air. As the sky above resounded with the music, the heart of the spectators
swelled with joy" (Dabholkar 2007, 617–18)

Sai Baba's feet were then washed, and he was seated within the chavadi
under a white umbrella and adorned with flower garlands and other finery.
Dabholkar goes on to describe in some detail the formal ritual worship of
Sai Baba that then took place.

The umbrella in the photo is visual testimony to these formal Hindu
ritual practices as they began to be undertaken in Sai Baba's final decade of
life. In his own daily routine Sai Baba continued his composite practices,
such as offering lights and incense in the Hindu manner, saying *namaz*
(prayer) in the Muslim manner, and keeping a perpetual fire burning in a
clay hearth, or *dhuni*, as some ascetics do, such as the Nathpanthi Order.[2]
But he also acquiesced to being worshiped in the manner of a deity by his
Hindu followers—or, as Dabholkar puts it, he "indulged his loving devotees
by allowing them these little acts of devotion" (2007, 621). Today, the chavadi
procession is re-created on Thursday and Saturday evenings in Shirdi. It is
also re-created at many Shirdi Sai Baba temples around the world, usually
on Thursday evenings (it is often referred to as *palkhi seva*). In these ceremonies, it is not the marble statue of Sai Baba that resides within the temple
that is paraded in the procession, but a smaller image, typically a framed
picture of Sai Baba. This is similar to the public procession of Hindu temple
gods during festivals, in which the smaller, portable images of the gods are
brought out of the temple and, like royalty, they travel by chariot or palanquin through the streets of town (Eck 1998, 57).

To give a sense of the ritual involved in such chavadi processions, I
include an excerpt here from my field notes, written after attending the
procession at the Sai Ka Angan Temple in Gurgaon, Haryana, one Thursday
evening in late May 2010. In this suburb of New Delhi, an elaborate replica
of Shirdi as it was in Sai Baba's day had been re-created for the devotees of
Sai Baba living in this area, complete with the Dwarkamai mosque, the

chavadi, and the Maruti (Hanuman) Temple. I had come early in the day to conduct interviews with temple officials and attendees, and I had been invited to stay for the evening ceremony. My guide was a woman affectionately known as Mausiji, "Aunty," who was instrumental in the founding and maintenance of the temple and who warmly welcomed me to take part in the procession:

> First we lined up in Dwarkamai outside the chamber in which the *palkhi* (palanquin) is stored. Over one hundred people were present, and most of them were on one side of a velvet banister partition, crowding toward the front for a view. A select group of devotees was on the other side of the partition, and I had been invited to join them. Men stood to one side and women on the other. The men wore white kurta-pajamas and had been given white caps with a small image of Sai Baba on them, as well as a gold-colored sash, to wear for the ceremony. These were the men who would carry the palkhi for the procession. There were also two men dressed in full uniform from Sai Baba's day: red pants and shirt and a Marathi-style turban. They served as the gatekeepers who opened the doors to the chamber and who led the procession. The women were dressed in nice saris and had been given baskets of flower petals—roses and marigolds— to spread along the path of the palanquin. The women also had the role of leading the large group in singing hymns.
>
> As the doors of the chamber opened, Mausiji went inside. The whole room was singing as she and a priest retrieved the framed photo of Sai Baba, touching first his feet with a loving gesture. Then the palkhi was brought out, and Mausiji followed, carrying the photo snug to her chest. She then placed it in the palanquin in the view of all. There the first *puja* (ritual worship entailing offerings presented to the deity) was conducted: candles, incense, sandalwood paste, flowers, a coconut, and an apple. Then the procession moved out of Dwarkamai, slowly progressing toward the chavadi. Devotees continued to sing *bhajans* (hymns) along the way, and handfuls of flower petals were thrown along the way by those devotees who were close enough to reach into one of the baskets carried by the women.
>
> Reaching the chavadi, men moved to one side and women to the other as the palkhi stopped. Then Mausiji carefully removed the framed image of Sai Baba, again clasped it to her chest, and handed it over to a priest. The priest placed the photo in the chavadi, next to a golden murti of Sai Baba that resides permanently within the chavadi, and propped it up to face the crowd of devotees. Another priest placed a cloth-covered copy of the *Shri Sai Satcharita* before

the statue and then stood in position to pull the cord of the cloth fan in order
to provide Sai Baba with a cool breeze throughout the ceremony. Yet another
priest began the puja ceremony of the framed image of Sai Baba, taking each
item off the tray that had been placed in the palkhi and offering it to the image.

One thing that stood out to me was the offering of the *chillum*, an earthen
tobacco pipe. The priest lit it and took several puffs on it himself to get it going,
and then offered it to Sai Baba's mouth in the photo for several seconds. While
highly unorthodox from the standpoint of Hindu temple ritual, this is in keeping with the description of the chavadi ceremony as set forth in chapter 37
of the *Shri Sai Satcharita* (verses 196–201). During this puja, the crowd of
devotees continued to sing bhajans, and we in the front sat down on the ground
so that those behind us could also take darshan with Sai Baba. After the puja
was over, the priest again handed the framed photo to Mausiji, who placed
it back in the palanquin. Again we women threw handfuls of flowers before
the palanquin as the men carried it back to the storeroom in Dwarkamai.
Along the way, one elderly woman held my hand and whispered in my ear
that Shirdi times are replicated here, and Baba is himself present here, just
as he was then.

I have since then attended similar processions at many other temples
dedicated to Shirdi Sai Baba, both in India and abroad. Yet repeatedly, I have
been matter-of-factly informed by Hindu devotees of Sai Baba that ritual is
not important, even as they simultaneously took part in rituals such as the
chavadi procession. Even Kishore More, the executive officer of the Shri
Saibaba Sansthan Trust who is in charge of the day-to-day operations at
Shirdi, stated that one of the primary reasons for the exploding numbers
of pilgrims to Shirdi is that there is "no ritual. There is no compulsion for
customs or rituals." Yet, as noted in chapter 1, he also said that the Hindu
temple priests who engaged in the formal worship of the murti of Sai Baba
in the inner sanctum of the Samadhi Mandir adhered precisely to the same
rituals that started during Baba's lifetime: "Whatever he accepted is what
we do." And he added that the Trust was creating a standard operating
manual, with the goal of ensuring that all Shirdi Sai Baba temples around
the world would adhere to these same rituals.[3]

At a Shirdi Sai Baba temple in Austin, Texas, one devotee similarly
claimed that Sai Baba devotion was spreading "because there is no ritual. It
is not about chanting, bathing, puja. It is ritual free. It is just about devotion. Devotion and service. That is what the appeal is. So it self-proliferates.

People are looking for this, for something beyond traditional rituals."[4] And yet, immediately after our conversation, this young man lined up to take part in the *abhishekam* (ritual bathing) of the primary murti of Sai Baba within the Austin temple, followed by darshan with the chavadi procession of the movable image of Sai Baba around the temple courtyard that takes place every Thursday night. Repeatedly, Hindu temple founders and attendees felt the need to include such disclaimers in my conversations with them: "Faith and service are what matter, not ritual"; or, "There is no ritual for Shirdi Sai Baba." And yet, this did not preclude them from engaging in ritual worship. I call this the "paradox of ritual." This chapter argues that this paradox of ritual draws our attention to an important ambivalence about not only the role of Hindu ritual in Sai Baba temples but also the much larger question of what it means to be Hindu today.

A TALE OF TWO GOD-MEN:
MEHER BABA AND SATHYA SAI BABA

The previous chapters have demonstrated how devotion to Shirdi Sai Baba spread rapidly throughout India during the twentieth century: radiating outward from the village of Shirdi in western India and spreading throughout the Bombay Presidency (modern-day Maharashtra state) through the hymns of Das Ganu Maharaj, then spreading throughout southern India due to the proselytizing efforts of B. V. Narasimhaswami, and eventually infusing popular pan-Indian culture in the form of films like *Amar Akbar Anthony*. In addition to the rapid circulation of Shirdi Sai Baba devotional media and messages because of our increasingly interconnected global society, the international spread of devotion to Sai Baba in the latter half of the twentieth century can be traced to two primary factors: First, to the spate of Indian gurus and "god-men" who have taken devotion to Sai Baba to new national and international heights through their own charisma and transnational followings. Second, to the increasing number of Indians who have migrated to other countries, bringing their devotion to Sai Baba with them. With regard to the former, two god-men stand out as especially influential for claiming a spiritual lineage to Shirdi Sai Baba and in so doing spreading awareness of and devotion to him among their respective transnational flocks: Meher Baba (1894–1969) and Sathya Sai Baba (1926–2011). Given that a substantial body of literature already exists on both figures, my concern here is to draw out their unique interpretations of Shirdi Sai Baba, to think about their influence on the global growth of Sai Baba devotion, and to examine the ways that ritual is understood in these devotional circles.

Meher Baba was born Merwan Sheriar Irani to Zoroastrian (Parsi) parents of Persian descent in Pune, western India (Bombay Presidency). At a young age, he was drawn to mystical experiences. When he was nineteen and a student at Deccan College in Pune, he cycled past the elderly female *fakir* (holy person) Hazrat Babajan. She beckoned to him, and he began to spend time with her. One day, she kissed young Merwan on the forehead, which enabled him to receive her spiritual grace and enraptured him in a state of God-consciousness. Merwan then began to travel throughout western India in search of spiritual wisdom and transformation. He spent time with four other spiritual figures: Hazrat Tajuddin Baba, Narayan Maharaj, Sai Baba in Shirdi, and Upasni Maharaj. He spent the longest time with Upasni Maharaj, living with him in Sakori for seven years before leaving to establish his own spiritual following. In 1921, his first followers gathered around him and gave him the name Meher Baba, "Compassionate Father" (Meher Baba 2011, xiii–xiv).

In 1923, Meher Baba established an ashram in Ahmednagar District (in modern-day Maharashtra), which he called Meherabad. It was there in 1925 that he took a vow of silence, which he maintained until his death in 1969. During these forty-four years, he communicated his teachings to his disciples either by using a small alphabet board or through a unique sign language that was understood by a few of his closest disciples. He personally composed some writings in the 1920s before he gave up writing in 1927.[5] His best-known books, *Discourses* and *God Speaks*, were dictated to his close disciples before he gave up use of the alphabet board in 1954. Other works attributed to him were recorded by his close followers based on his teachings, such as *Listen, Humanity*.

In the 1920s, Meher Baba also traveled throughout India, present-day Pakistan, and Iran, gaining additional disciples. During the 1930s, he began to travel to Europe and the United States, gaining disciples in these places as well. In the 1950s, he again traveled broadly, with many trips to the United States, Europe, and also Australia. He allowed select groups of these Westerners to visit him in Meherabad in the 1950s.[6] He also inaugurated two international centers: the Meher Spiritual Center in Myrtle Beach, South Carolina, in 1952; and Avatar's Abode in Woombye, Queensland, in 1958. In November 1962, Meher Baba held "The East-West Gathering" in Pune, wherein he invited thousands of his international followers to join his

Indian disciples for a week of joint devotional activities. Through such travels and activities, Meher Baba gained a substantial global following, in addition to his Indian following, prior to his death in 1969.

These followers were drawn to his charismatic presence and his teachings about eliminating the selfish ego and realizing God within themselves.
Meher Baba stressed that his mission was not to set forth any new philosophy or religion; rather, it was to awaken humanity to an age-old message
that had been presented many times before. In his teachings, he drew upon
his background in Islamic (especially Sufi), Hindu, Christian, and Zoroastrian concepts to advance a theory of "involution," the inward journey across
seven planes of consciousness that the individual self (*atman*) must travel
toward the divine Self (*param Atman*) within, before attaining Self- or God-
realization (Meher Baba 1973). Meher Baba described ultimate reality as a
nondual state that could ultimately only be experienced to truly be known:
"The state of God-realization cannot be described. It can only be known to
those who achieve that supreme experience of the conscious state of God. It
is beyond the domain of the mind, which persists only through the sixth
plane of spiritual consciousness. At that stage God is seen through the mind
as being everywhere, all the time. But that is not the supreme experience, as
the 'seer' and the 'seen' still remain two" (Meher Baba and Stevens 1998, 61).
Ultimately, in the seventh plane, the "seer" and the "seen"—self and Self—
are united as one. Here, the Self-conscious person is aware of him- or herself
as God and experiences infinite power, knowledge, and bliss (Meher Baba
1973, 51–54). Here, the Self-conscious person also realizes that God is infinite and eternal Love (Meher Baba 2011, 399–403).

At all times, Meher Baba taught, there are fifty-six God-realized souls
in human form on earth. All of these fifty-six are Perfect Ones who have
completed the process of involution and attained the seventh plan of consciousness (Meher Baba 1973, 150–51). Among these fifty-six Perfect Ones,
there are always five Perfect Masters, or Sadgurus (which he also called
Qutubs, using the Sufi term). It is nearly impossible for a person to advance
to the sixth plane of consciousness, let alone the seventh, through their own
efforts. The role of the Perfect Masters is to aid humanity on this journey.
These Perfect Masters are "five persons of their age who not only become
God but, after achieving God-realization, also come down to the ordinary
normal consciousness of man" (Meher Baba and Stevens 1998, 61). As God-
realized individuals who simultaneously possess both individual human
consciousness and God-consciousness, who can therefore span the seven

planes of consciousness, they are able to use their advanced spiritual perception and powers to aid the advancement of others.

In addition to the five Perfect Masters, there is also the Avatar. The Avatar is the original or Supreme Perfect Master, who undergoes incarnation again and again, through the pull of the Perfect Masters, to help humanity on its path toward God-realization. Meher Baba describes the Avataric period, when the Avatar is present, as the springtide of creation, bringing "a new release of power, a new awakening of consciousness, a new experience of life—not merely for a few, but for all. . . . Life, as a whole, is stepped up to a higher level of consciousness, is geared to a new rate of energy. The transition from sensation to reason was one such step; the transition from reason to intuition will be another" (Meher Baba 2011, 268). The Avatar arrives when times are desperate, when immorality, exploitation, greed, and anger prevail, and brings with him the potential for liberation for those who are ready, and the potential for greater spiritual awakening for humanity at large.[7] The Avatar, Meher Baba taught, has appeared in different forms, under different names—including Zoroaster, Rama, Krishna, Buddha, Jesus, and Muhammad—but he is always One and the same, because God is always One and the same (Meher Baba 1973, 152–53).

The difference between the divine status of a Perfect Master and the Avatar of the Age is that a Perfect Master must first go through the whole process of cosmic evolution and spiritual involution before entering into and living the life of God as a "Man-God," while the Avatar does not have to go through the process because he is already God, who then becomes man and lives on earth as the "God-Man" (Meher Baba 1973, 149). Meher Baba identified the five Perfect Masters living in his lifetime as the five spiritual adepts he had visited in his youth: Hazrat Babajan of Pune, Hazrat Tajuddin Baba of Nagpur, Narayan Maharaj of Khedgaon, Upasni Maharaj of Sakori, and Sai Baba of Shirdi. Furthermore, Meher Baba claimed to be the Avatar of the current age, stating: "All the five *Sadgurus* (Perfect Masters) put together mean [Meher] Baba. I have come so that you can escape from the cage of *maya* [illusion], and experience (know) me in your lifetime. Since the very beginning of the illusion of creation, *maya*, which makes illusion appear as reality, has been hanging around my neck in all of you. That is why I must come (as the Avatar) again and again" (Meher Baba and Stevens 1998, 62).

For Meher Baba, then, Shirdi Sai Baba was one of the fifty-six Perfect Ones of the age. He was a person who had navigated the process of involu-

tion to attain the seventh plane of consciousness, and therein he had realized his innate identity as God. He was also one of five Perfect Masters of
the age, a "Man-God" who not only attained God-consciousness but who
actively helped other people on the path to God-realization out of his love
for them. These Perfect Masters are able to help an aspirant in several ways:
through darshan with the Perfect Master, which can help the person experience momentary bliss and contentment; through falling at the feet of the
Perfect Master, which can help the person unburden his or her past karmic
impressions; through mental contact with the Perfect Master when not in
his or her physical presence, which can help the person receive grace and
love each time his or her thoughts turn to him; and through following the
instructions given by the Perfect Master, who may direct an aspirant to
undertake particular spiritual practices or instruct an aspirant to associate
with certain adepts, providing unique instructions to different aspirants
according to their individual natures and stages on the journey (Meher Baba
2011, 186–92).

Meher Baba therefore emphasized devotion to and meditation upon the
Avatar and the Perfect Masters in his teachings. He taught that the best way
to understand the nondual ultimate reality—the unity of spiritual self and
divine Self—was through the heart, not the mind, for the mind constantly
discriminates and is trapped in a dualistic worldview (Meher Baba 2011, 94–
98). Devotion to and meditation upon the Avatar and the Perfect Masters—
including Sai Baba—can help aspirants minimize their own mind and ego
by focusing with intense love upon God as realized in these human forms.
Various types and stages of meditation are then prescribed to help the aspirant to go beyond the dualistic limitations of the mind, progressing through
the seven planes of consciousness toward God-realization and the experience of infinite love.[8]

Sathya Sai Baba claimed a very different spiritual lineage to Shirdi Sai
Baba than Meher Baba. Sathya Sai Baba was born Sathya Narayana Raju to
Hindu parents in Puttaparthi in southern India (Madras Presidency, now
part of the state of Andhra Pradesh). Hagiographies recount that miracles
at his birth and during his childhood testified to his special nature.[9] In 1940,
at the age of thirteen or fourteen, he lost consciousness after being stung by
a scorpion and awakened a changed person. He claimed to be the reincarnation of Shirdi Sai Baba, stating: "I am Sai Baba. I belong to Apastamba Sutra,
the school of sage Apastam and am of the spiritual lineage of Bharadwaja; I

am Sai Baba, I have come to ward off all your troubles, keep your houses clean and pure."[10] After this revelation, young Sathya Narayana began to be known as Sathya Sai Baba. He also purportedly began to materialize holy ash and other objects (including flowers and jewelry). In the years that followed, as his reputation for performing a range of miracles (material, psychic, and healing) grew, increasingly large numbers of visitors began to arrive in Puttaparthi. In 1950, his ashram Prasanthi Nilayam was built to accommodate these pilgrims (Babb 1986, 162–64).[11] In 1963, after recovering from an illness that involved a seizure (the doctor diagnosed it as tubular meningitis), he stated that he had experienced the illness in order to save a devotee from it. He then disclosed that the first Sai Baba of Shirdi had been an *avatar*, or incarnation, of Shakti, the consort of the Hindu god Shiva, while he was an avatar of both Shiva and Shakti. He further predicted that after living a long life, he would reincarnate again as a third Sai Baba, called Prem Sai Baba (or Prema Sai Baba), who would be the incarnation of Shiva alone (Babb 1986, 165–66).

Between 1963 and 1965, Sathya Sai Baba's fame spread throughout India as he toured various pilgrimage centers. Tulasi Srinivas (2010, 63) writes that at this time he established himself as a national guru-avatar who merged various Hindu traditions and teachings, including the Upanishads, the Bhagavad Gita, Vedic sacrifice, yoga, and various schools of Hindu philosophy. Sathya Sai Baba's outlook then grew more international. Thus, in the first World Conference of Sai Organizations held in 1968 in Bombay, Sathya Sai Baba expanded his focus to all of humanity and proclaimed himself to be a world divinity, saying: "Continue your worship of your chosen God along the lines already familiar to you. Then you will find you are coming nearer and nearer to Me for all the names are Mine and all the forms are Mine. . . . I will succeed in warding off a crisis that has come upon humanity" (Srinivas 2010, 69–70).[12] Though Sathya Sai Baba engaged in very limited international travel in his lifetime—making just one trip to Kenya and Uganda in 1968—he gained a wide following, with millions of followers in India and overseas. By 2001, there were about nine thousand official Sathya Sai Baba centers of devotion in India and about two thousand in over 130 countries outside of India (Srinivas 2008, 1).[13]

During the jointly held Third World Conference of Sai Organizations and Ninth All-India Conference in 1980–81, a permanent charter was granted by Sathya Sai Baba, which briefly spells out his primary teachings. "The charter states that the organization is a spiritual one founded for the establishment of Sanatana Dharma (eternal religion)," summarizes Smriti Srinivas, "and does not recognize any separateness based on religion, caste, color, or creed":

> It has three principal objectives: 1) to help the individual to become aware of one's inherent divinity and to conduct oneself accordingly; 2) to ensure that all human relations are governed by the principles of truth, right conduct, love, peace, and non-violence; and 3) to make devotees of various religions more sincere and dedicated in the practice of their respective religions. These objectives are to be attained by observing the principles laid by Sathya Sai Baba: there is only one religion, the religion of love; there is only one language, the language of the heart; there is only one caste, the caste of humanity; and there is only one God, who is omnipresent. (Srinivas 2008, 140)

In her rich study of the Sathya Sai Baba movement, Smriti Srinivas describes Sathya Sai Baba's teachings in terms of a "bio-civic ethics." The Sathya Sai Organization has undertaken three primary areas of programming— healing, education, and service (*seva*)—in the belief that only by addressing the societal problems of suffering, ignorance, and injustice can devotees locate the divinity inherent within humanity. Thus, Sathya Sai Baba devotion is "a sensory moral praxis that establishes a meaningful and transformative relationship between the body-self and civic space—a sphere of embodied citizenship" (Srinivas 2008, 112).

Nonetheless, when it comes to Sathya Sai Baba's teachings, Lawrence Babb (1986, 174) astutely observes that devotees care less about what Sathya Sai Baba has to say than that *he* is the one saying it: "His devotees long to see him, to hear him, to be near him, to have private audiences with him, to touch him (especially his feet), and to receive and consume, or use in other ways, substances and objects that have been touched by him or that originate from him. But above all, what one hears about are the miracles."[14] As both Smriti Srinivas and Tulasi Srinivas have documented in sensitive detail, the primary rituals of this devotional community are therefore focused on being in or invoking the presence of Sathya Sai Baba. Prasanthi Nilayam serves as the primary pilgrimage center of the movement, and before Sathya Sai Baba's death in 2011, it regularly hosted five thousand daily visitors (as many as twenty thousand on festival days), who came from around the world for darshan (Srinivas 2010, 157). This darshan experience not only entailed seeing and being seen by Sathya Sai Baba but was in fact a much larger sensory experience involving all of the senses, as devotees reached out to touch him, smelled and tasted the *vibhuti* (sacred ash) he produced, and listened to bhajans (see Srinivas 2008, 76–110; Srinivas 2010, 156–72).

D. A. Swallow describes in detail the celebration of the annual Mahashi-varatri festival at Prasanthi Nilayam. For this festival celebrating Shiva, Sathya Sai Baba would allegedly perform two "miracles." The first occurred as he ascended onto a platform in front of the crowd of devotees. On the platform was an image of Shirdi Sai Baba, and Sathya Sai Baba would upend a tub of sacred ash over this image. When the tub was empty, he then raised his arm into the container, stirred it round, and churned out more ash. He did this again and again, until the whole image of Shirdi Sai Baba was covered with ash. The sacred ash was then distributed to all the devotees present, who either consumed it or placed it on their bodies. The second "miracle" occurred when Sathya Sai Baba would regurgitate a small *lingam*, an aniconic symbol of Shiva, which was then worshiped by the assembled crowd. Swallow (1982, 146–52) writes that in performing these two acts together, Sathya Sai Baba reminded his devotees of his identity as both the reincarnation of Shirdi Sai Baba and the incarnation of Shiva-Shakti.[15]

When not in the physical presence of Sathya Sai Baba, members are encouraged to invoke his presence through various media. In fact, the permanent charter of 1980–81 wrote this into its nine-point code of conduct for members, which includes daily meditation; devotional singing with one's family at least once a week; children's education in approved programs; devotional singing in public with the Sai community at least once a month; participation in community service (seva); regular study of Sai literature; speaking softly and lovingly with everyone; not talking ill of others; and minimizing waste of time, food, and resources in order to better serve humanity (Srinivas 2008, 140–41). Devotees, thus, are enjoined to regularly meditate upon Sathya Sai Baba, to repeat his name, to sing about him, and to study stories of him. Sathya Sai Baba's presence is also invoked through the substances and objects that he produced. For instance, Smriti Srinivas writes that the ash and lingams he manifested for devotees must be understood in a "metaphysics of presence": "Even if ash and *lingam* emerge from Baba's body, they do not signify his body. Instead they are signs of his powers, have curative properties, indicate his subtle or energetic presence, and are symbols of correspondence between the material and formal world and non-material and spiritual reality" (2008, 96). Similarly, of course, many new and visual media are used to invoke Sathya Sai Baba's presence, as is common throughout much of Hindu tradition.[16]

Despite a shared emphasis on universal humanism and divine love, Meher Baba and Sathya Sai Baba advanced very different philosophies and teachings. They also articulated very different claims about their personal connections to Shirdi Sai Baba: Sathya Sai Baba claimed to be Shirdi Sai Baba's reincarnation and simultaneously an incarnation of Shiva and Shakti; Meher Baba, in contrast, claimed that Shirdi Sai Baba was one of the five Perfect Masters working alongside Meher Baba, who was himself the Avatar of the Age. Nonetheless, both of these charismatic god-men spread their message throughout India and far beyond, acquiring a substantial international following comprised of members from both within and without the South Asian ethnic fold. And as they did so, both contributed to the spread of Shirdi Sai Baba's name within India and beyond. Both encouraged their domestic and international followers to claim Shirdi as one of their sacred sites, in addition to Puttaparthi for Sathya Sai Baba and Meherabad for Meher Baba. Both also encouraged their domestic and international followers to incorporate Shirdi Sai Baba into their devotional routine. And in this regard, both contributed to a devotional context that deemphasized orthodox Hindu temple ritual, favoring instead an emphasis on god-man- or guru-focused darshanic meditation.

A TALE OF TWO TEMPLES: CHICAGO AND AUSTIN

The second factor that has contributed to the global spread of devotion to Shirdi Sai Baba in the latter half of the twentieth century is the increasing number of Indians who have migrated to other countries, bringing their devotion to Sai Baba with them. In the remainder of this chapter, I turn to the United States as a case study, examining the transnational afterlife of Shirdi Sai Baba in the context of two recently constructed temples: the Shirdi Sai Temple of Chicago and Suburbs in Illinois (founded 2004) and the Sri Shirdi Sai Baba Temple of Austin, Texas (founded 2010). The past several decades have witnessed a proliferation of "mini gurus," each setting forth their own eclectic interpretation of Shirdi Sai Baba and attracting a following of devotees who view them as the living conduit to Sai Baba.[17] Some of these gurus have been successful in raising funds for the construction of new temples, and in recent years these temple-building efforts have gone international. The Chicago and Austin temples were established by two different founders, each following a different guru lineage and thus articulating different understandings of Shirdi Sai Baba's identity and teachings. In addition to examining the founding history and guru lineage of these temples, this chapter also examines their liturgical programs, seeking to understand the paradox of ritual in Shirdi Sai Baba devotion.

The first Shirdi Sai Baba temple established in North America was located in the Monroeville suburb of Pittsburgh, Pennsylvania. It was founded by Panduranga Rao Malyala, who accepted Shirdi Sai Baba as his guru after experiencing two miraculous visions of him while working as a young professional in Hyderabad, India, in 1970 and 1973. In the second of these encounters, Shirdi Sai Baba stated that he would send Malyala to the United States to do his divine service there. In 1976 Malyala arrived in Pennsylvania, and in 1979 he founded the Sri Shirdi Sai Baba Temple in Monroeville. At that time, the temple was just a temporary abode for Shirdi Sai Baba, but by 1982 a permanent temple was established when a permanent murti of Shirdi Sai Baba was installed within its inner sanctum. Today, the temple maintains a full-time Hindu priest who performs liturgical services from 9:00 A.M. until 7:30 P.M., including four daily *aaratis*, or sessions of ritual worship, of the murti of Sai Baba. The Monroeville temple is modest in scale, just a simple blue house set into the wooded hillside, transformed into a temple through a room addition. Jutting out of one side of the house is a small square sanctum (*garbha griha*), which is topped by a pointed tower (*shikhara*) that is painted saffron and capped with a round metal pot (*kalasha*) that identifies it as a sacred Hindu space.[18] Inside, the temple is intimate, with a casual but welcoming feel as visitors slip off their shoes and enter through the back door, passing by the bookcase and administrative counter as they make their way to the small central room for collective worship in front of the murti (there is space to seat perhaps twenty people on the floor).

Just five miles to the west of the Sri Shirdi Sai Baba Temple, located in the Penn Hills suburb, is the Sri Venkateswara Temple of Pittsburgh. This temple was consecrated in November 1976, the same year that Malyala moved to Pittsburgh, and has received much acclaim as one of the earliest temples built in North America in the form of an authentic Hindu temple. Diana Eck (2001, 125) reports that for most of the 1980s, more than twenty thousand people a year visited this temple from throughout the United States and Canada. It is modeled on one of the most popular early medieval temples in India, the Tirumala Venkateswara Temple in Tirupati, Andhra Pradesh, which is dedicated to a form of the god Vishnu known as Venkateswara. The Penn Hills temple is a majestic structure, with a gleaming white multistory gateway and towers that rise above the tree line on the hillside, so that the temple can easily be seen by passersby commuting on Interstate 376. One of the temple leaders described it in these regal words: "The backdrop of the green trees behind the white temple makes it like a gem studded in the emerald hills of Pennsylvania" (Eck 2001, 125). This temple, like its founding temple in India, belongs to the Srivaishnava sect of Hinduism, and as Vasudha Narayanan notes, in addition to its authentic form the temple has also received acclaim for its emphasis on authentic rituals: "This temple has been successful in attracting large numbers of devotees from all over the eastern seaboard; until similar temples were built in other parts of the country, it attracted pilgrims from all over the United States and Canada. It is still seen as the trendsetting south Indian temple in its celebration of expensive, time consuming and intricate rituals; many other younger temples want to be like the one in Penn Hills when they grow up" (2006, 232).

Hindu temples began to be built in the United States in the 1970s because of a demographic shift. Under the Immigration Act of 1924, Indians were categorized as "non-white Asians" and accordingly prohibited from immigrating to the United States. However, the Immigration and Nationality Services (INS) Act of 1965 abolished the earlier national origins quota system and replaced it with a preference system focused on immigrants' professional skills. Thus, Indians who had previously been barred from immigration and naturalization on the basis of race were now eligible, particularly those with professional training. This resulted in a wave of immigrants from South Asia in the late 1960s and early 1970s. Diana Eck describes these new immigrants as professional engineers and doctors, metallurgists and biochemists who came during their student years and then took jobs and settled in: "They all intended to return to India, eventually. Then they began to have children, and before long their children were in grade school. By now, these young families were putting down deeper roots in America and beginning to look toward a future here. They realized that their children would have no cultural or religious identity as Hindus at all unless they themselves began to do something about it" (Eck 2001, 88). So, these professionals also became temple patrons.

Pittsburgh was one of the earliest cities to see the rise of multiple Hindu temples, including the first ones dedicated to Venkateswara and Shirdi Sai Baba in the United States. In the decades since the founding of these two temples, this pattern has been repeated in many cities throughout North

America. Sri Venkateswara temples now exist in Malibu (Los Angeles), California; Casselberry (Orlando), Florida; Aurora (Chicago), Illinois; Novi (Detroit), Michigan; Bridgewater, New Jersey; Cary, North Carolina; and Memphis, Tennessee. And many more are currently under construction or in the planning stages. Part of the appeal of these Sri Venkateswara temples is the duplication of sacred geography, the making of a *tirtha*, or crossing place of the divine—in this case, the popular hilltop temple of Tirupati where Venkateswara dwells—which is then available to devotees living far from India (Eck 2001, 124–25). Another part of the appeal is the emphasis on orthodox ritual worship—in this case, Srivaishnava ritual modeled on the parent temple in Tirupati—and the need to retain such ritual traditions in the diaspora and transmit them to the next generation of Hindu devotees and nonresident Indians (Narayanan 2006, 234–38).

Similarly, temples dedicated to Shirdi Sai Baba now exist in many cities, including Montebello (Los Angeles) and Sunnyvale (Bay Area), California; Centennial (Denver), Colorado; Inverness, Florida; Suwanee (Atlanta), Georgia; Hampshire (Chicago), Illinois; Minneapolis, Minnesota; Cedar Park (Austin) and Plano (Dallas), Texas; and Dulles (DC), Virginia. And, as with the Sri Venkateswara temples, many more are under construction or being planned. What accounts for the appeal of these Shirdi Sai Baba temples? The Shirdi Sai Temple of Chicago and Suburbs and the Sri Shirdi Sai Baba Temple of Austin were established in cities where prominent Hindu temples already existed. Frequently in my conversations with temple attendees and founders, they stressed that their Sai Baba temple provided an alternative to Sri Venkateswara and other orthodox Hindu temples. This claim was made most vociferously with regard to ritual, even as orthodox ritual traditions were upheld in the temples and partaken of by attendees. This paradox of ritual suggests a degree of ambivalence about how much those attending these new Shirdi Sai Baba temples do or do not want their temples to become like the Sri Venkateswara one in Penn Hills.

The Shirdi Sai Temple of Chicago and Suburbs

In the greater Chicago area, the South Asian population was between 50,000 and 75,000 by 1985, with half of those being immigrants from India who arrived between 1975 and 1980 (Williams 1988, 226). In the 1980s, several prominent Hindu temples were constructed to meet the religious needs of this growing South Asian population: the Sri Venkateswara Temple, located in Aurora (established in 1986); the Hindu Temple of Greater Chicago, located in Lemont and dedicated to the god Rama (established in 1985); and the Akshar Purushottam Swaminarayan Temple, located in Glen Ellyn (established in 1984). Beyond these large temple organizations, a number of smaller groups met for regular prayer sessions, usually focused on regional languages (singing devotional bhajans in Tamil, Malayalam, or Hindi), on a particular scripture (such as the Gita Mandal, dedicated to the study of the Bhagavad Gita), or on a particular deity or saint not already represented in one of the larger temples (Williams 1988, 226–39). The Shirdi Sai Temple of Chicago and Suburbs grew out of one such small prayer circle, which was initiated in the early 1990s by Hindu devotees of Shirdi Sai Baba who had emigrated from India to America. Most of these devotees were professionals who worked in the information and technology industry, including Mukund Raj, a computer programmer and founding member of the prayer circle. By the late 1990s, the prayer circle had grown and members began to think about establishing a temple.

Mukund Raj contacted C. B. Satpathy in India for guidance in establishing a temple to Shirdi Sai Baba. As noted in chapter 4, Satpathy was living in New Delhi in the 1980s, working as an officer in the Indian Police Service, when on a whim he rented the film *Shirdi Ke Sai Baba*. Watching this film transformed him, to the extent that he felt called to Shirdi. The next morning, he packed and left for Shirdi, where he accepted Sai Baba as his guru and undertook a vow to build 108 temples to him. To accomplish this, he founded the Shri Shirdi Sai Heritage Foundation Trust. Based in New Delhi, the mission of this nonprofit organization is to "spread Sai philosophy and His teachings among the devotees who are living all over the world and for charitable activities with the purpose of giving something back to the society" (McLain 2012, 191). In 2006, Satpathy retired as the director general of police in Uttar Pradesh and dedicated himself to spreading "Sai philosophy" full-time. When the 108th temple was completed, Satpathy decided that there were still more temples to build, both in India and beyond. Today, working through the Shri Shirdi Sai Heritage Foundation Trust, Satpathy has helped to establish over two hundred temples in India and has been instrumental in the globalization of devotion to Shirdi Sai Baba through the founding of temples in Australia, Canada, Malaysia, New Zealand, Singapore, and the United States.

By the time Mukund Raj reached out to Satpathy in the late 1990s, Satpathy was well known in India among devotees of Shirdi Sai Baba for his ability to bring together potential donors and set the wheels in motion for the creation of temples. He was also increasingly known as a guru in his own right, someone who acted as a spiritual teacher and conduit to Sai Baba through his teachings and devotional writings, poems, and music. Thus, Raj invited Satpathy to Chicago to be the keynote speaker for a celebration of Sai Baba, or Sai Utsav, that was held on Thanksgiving weekend in 2000. This festival was the first official step that the Chicago prayer circle took toward building a larger community of devotees and patrons in order to establish a temple, and funds were expressly solicited in order to create a lending library for the devotional community. The festival featured an array of activities, including communal singing of devotional hymns, public readings from the *Shri Sai Satcharita*, a pictorial exhibit of Shirdi, and ritual puja of a small statue of Shirdi Sai Baba. In addition to Satpathy, the other featured guest was the Indian actor Sudhir Dalvi, who had played Shirdi Sai Baba in the 1977 film *Shirdi Ke Sai Baba*. At the festival, Dalvi performed a dramatization of Sai Baba's 11 Sayings, the assurances he is said to have made to his devotees.[19]

To continue their efforts, Mukund Raj and C. B. Satpathy organized a *chitra yatra*, an image pilgrimage, in 2002 in an effort to raise what they term "Sai-consciousness," or awareness of and devotion to Shirdi Sai Baba, in the United States. In an interview, Raj described the chitra yatra and its results:

> By this time we had established an Internet bulletin board and we had a list
> of some Baba devotees living in the US. So we contacted them and asked them
> to serve as anchor homes for the chitra yatra. Then we sent each anchor home
> a picture. These were pictures of Baba seated on the rock and pictures of him
> under the umbrella. We had four hundred of these pictures printed in Shirdi,
> did puja of the pictures there in the temple, then brought them back to Chi-
> cago. Then we mailed each picture to the anchor home with vibhuti from Shirdi,
> told them they needed to frame the photo, and do the full program at their
> home and invite people to it—family, neighbors, friends. The program was
> singing bhajans, reading the *Satcharita*, doing aarati. Then, each anchor home
> should pass it to another home to continue the program. In this way the pic-
> tures moved through every major city in the US. As they did, some prayer
> groups formed. Some fizzled out, but some matured into organizations, that
> then began to think about building temples. The Bay Area, Dallas, Minneap-
> olis, Atlanta—all of these Sai Baba temples started from this chitra yatra.[20]

The goal of the chitra yatra was to raise not only "Sai-consciousness" but also funding for temple construction in Chicago and other North American

FIGURE 5.2. Shirdi Sai Temple of Chicago and Suburbs. Photo: Karline McLain.

cities. It succeeded. In 2003, an old church was purchased in the Hampshire suburb of Chicago, which was formally inaugurated as a Shirdi Sai Baba temple on August 30, 2004.

From a distance, the Shirdi Sai Temple of Chicago and Suburbs could easily be dismissed as one of the many small, white, nondescript nineteenth-century Christian churches that dot the landscape of the rural American Midwest. However, upon closer inspection, one might notice that instead of a cross at the top of the steeple, there is a round kalasha; and a saffron flag flies atop the sign. Within the temple, much of the original architectural features remain, including the stained-glass windows featuring images of Jesus and Mary. The pews have been removed, however, to make room for devotees to sit on the floor. And at the center of the rear wall, instead of a pulpit, there is a large murti of Shirdi Sai Baba. Mukund Raj, who now serves as the temple manager, stated that he and the other temple founders felt it was an auspicious sign when the church went up for sale just as they were looking for a property to buy. "Sai Baba didn't care where he lived, because all religions were the same to him. He went to a temple in Shirdi, but when he was turned away he lived in a mosque. So why not let him live in a church here in the US.?"[21] This comment highlights one difference in the appeal of Shirdi Sai Baba temples compared to the appeal of Sri Venkateswara temples. The Sri Venkateswara temples in the United States are usually constructed according to orthodox and time-honored conventions, designed to look like their parent temple in Tirupati. American Shirdi Sai Baba temples, on the other hand, take a wide variety of forms, ranging from room add-ons to houses or other existing structures, to converted churches, to new temple construction. However, the Shirdi Sai Baba temples do share in common with other Hindu temples the emphasis on reduplication of the sacred, in the form of the presence of the divine—in this case, Shirdi Sai Baba—through the installation of his murti.

The establishment of a Hindu temple entails the formal installation of a murti through the ritual establishment ceremony (*pratishtha*) according to orthodox Hindu tradition, whereby ritual labor transforms the inert statue into a living icon infused with divine presence. As previous scholars of diaspora Hinduism have pointed out, building a temple and establishing the divine presence in this way entails "a deeper and more serious level of religious commitment" than the informal worship of images in homes or temporary shrines (Eck 1998, 80), for deities established within a temple require the daily attention of a priest, or *pujari*, to perform all the rites of hospitality and praise. As Diana Eck explains:

The *murtis* and polychrome pictures worshipped on a temporary altar in the Knights of Columbus hall can be carefully packed up in a box and put in storage for a week or two, but the images established in a temple have become permanent dwelling places of the Divine. They must be attended daily: awakened in the morning; provided with food, water, and clothing; honored with incense, oil lamps, and hymns of praise. The decision to bring this kind of permanent divine embodiment to life in an American temple cannot be entered into lightly. It requires the full-time employment of at least one priest, and perhaps several. And it requires the commitment of the community for many generations. (Eck 1998, 80–81)

One full-time priest is employed at the Chicago temple, to ensure that Shirdi Sai Baba receives the appropriate daily ritual attention according to orthodox Hindu tradition. However, on my first visit to the temple, when I asked about the daily ritual schedule, Mukund Raj insisted that it was not important for me to observe or attend the aaratis (though I did); instead, he said, it was more important for me to understand the meaning of Sai Baba:

> Ritual doesn't matter. In fact, religion doesn't matter. Baba never asked anyone to change their religion. Religion is not even the shape of our discussion. Religion has no purpose beyond channeling the mind to God. This is the point of ritual, of idol worship. To entice the mind to channel itself to the Super Energy. To develop Sai consciousness. Beyond that there is no purpose to religion, to ritual. But people get hung up on which religion, they debate, they even fight. In history, every religion is oppressive at some time. But God's purpose now is to align humanity and bring them together. It is an era of globalization, the world is coming together as one. Scientific knowledge will be shared by all. To do this, to become one, we need to share in love of God, love of neighbors, and love of all creatures. This is the future. This is what Baba taught.[22]

In my interviews with C. B. Satpathy, who serves as a personal guru to Mukund Raj and to many other Shirdi Sai Baba devotees at the temples with which he is affiliated, he similarly insisted that Hindu ritual no longer matters:

> The Sai Baba movement is growing today because Baba was about assimilation, not contradiction. Religions die out when there is contradiction, they wage war and one wins and one loses. But the winner will eventually become a loser in this system of contradiction. Sai Baba was about assimilation. About humanism. He even emphasized kindness to animals, so he went beyond humanism. This is the appeal of Baba. People want a clearer path today. Killing by religious war isn't acceptable today. Not acceptable. Also, people want to revert out of idol worship. They don't want the ritual. They don't want to fight over the ritual any more.[23]

When pressed as to why he had founded so many temples, if it is basic humanism that Sai Baba was teaching and not Hinduism or any other religion, Satpathy explained further:

That is a good question. Yes, I have built many temples to Sai Baba—217, in fact. But not for the ritual, that you must understand. People need a focus point. There needs to be a way to lead people on a different path. There are many awful religious leaders in the world today, many who incite violence. Why do people follow them? Because there is no other model, no other path to follow. So, we provide another model this way. And you have to start with what people want. What do they want? They want a temple. It is like the demand-supply theory of economics. So, we give them a temple. But in the temple you can change patterns, change ways of thinking, introduce a new path. You can do this in small ways, like dress. Why should people have to dress up to go to the temple? Why should you look down on someone who doesn't? You should look at all people the same, no matter what they wear. That is just surface. So also you can change patterns in big ways. Why should it matter how someone prays? That too is just surface. Why should it matter if someone prays like a Hindu and another person prays like a Muslim? They are both praying, after all, that is what matters. What is in their heart as they pray is what matters, not the form of their prayer.[24]

The Chicago temple, like the others in North America affiliated with Satpathy, adheres to his interpretation of Shirdi Sai Baba as the Param Sadguru, or Supreme Perfect Master. In a modified take on Meher Baba's theory, Satpathy views Shirdi Sai Baba not just as one of the five Perfect Masters but as the Supreme Perfect Master, whose mission is to help humanity evolve physically, culturally, and spiritually. He frames this discussion in explicitly global terms in his book *Shirdi Sai Baba and Other Perfect Masters*:

Today, when India and the whole world is torn asunder with religious conflicts, communal strife and armed clashes, the stream of compassion of the great humanist Shri Sai is yet flowing unabatedly. Today Shirdi is being visited by around 30 thousand people every day on an average for paying homage to the Shrine of Baba, and their number is increasing everyday. . . . The growing multitude of Sai devotees signals that the historic Sai movement would establish in the coming century, "peace and amity" in India and abroad. Shri Sai is the incarnation of the age and therefore faith in Him is bound to spread with far-reaching consequences in the future. Only time will prove this. (Satpathy 2001, 20)

Satpathy understands Shirdi Sai Baba as the latest in a long line of Sadgurus from across the world's religions who formerly lived in India and around the world: "Even in ancient times the *Sadgurus* came on this earth as the Hindu *rishis* [sages] like Kapila, Vasistha, Suka, Vishwamitra, Bharadwaj and Dattatreya. In other countries they came as Herrnes [*sic*], Enoch, Orpheus and others. They reincarnated as Abraham, Zoroaster, Moses, Buddha, Christ, Prophet Mohammad, Adi Shankara and many others in different countries and at different times" (Satpathy 2001, 11). Five such Sadgurus are said to operate in the world at any given time, assisted by a number of spiritually evolved figures who transcend the categories of religion, race, gender, and caste and who work on both physical and metaphysical planes. Of these five Sadgurus, one is the Param Sadguru, the Supreme Perfect Master. Whereas Meher Baba had claimed to personally be such a figure, using the term "Avatar," here Satpathy asserts that it is Shirdi Sai Baba who was that figure, the Supreme Perfect Master of our age (18–19). According to Satpathy, this Param Sadguru initially takes on an embodied form and then after death remains the Supreme Perfect Master for the next seven hundred years. Sai Baba's death in 1918 therefore marks not the end of an era, but the beginning of seven centuries of growing Sai consciousness under his metaphysical guidance.

The work of these Sadgurus is to "advance evolution" (Satpathy 2001, 5). Satpathy seeks to blend science and religion, arguing that natural evolution has a divine purpose. He writes of the Sadgurus: "Their job is to bring perfection to anything and everything coming in contact with them, whether living or non-living, cutting across all reference of time, distance and space. Anyone coming into contact with them is bound to evolve whether he likes it or does not like it, whether it is to happen immediately or within a certain period of time. They are upholders of the ultimate laws of nature and the divine principles" (6). At the individual level, the soul begins to evolve after coming into contact with the Sadguru, developing or enhancing the qualities of "love, sacrifice and forbearance" (7). These qualities enable the individual to evolve spiritually by gradually eliminating the negative karma that binds a person's soul to its current body and to the cycle of rebirth and redeath, resulting ultimately in freeing the soul to merge "with God, the Over-soul from which it came" (72). In *Baba: May I Answer*, Satpathy elaborates further on the process of the soul's evolution, suggesting that the biological evolution of the human species has a divine purpose behind it: "Every soul in the process of its evolution, life after life, tries to understand God slowly. In fact, this understanding of God, more and more, is the real purpose of evolution of souls. If man is better equipped with cerebral capacity than a monkey, it is for understanding God at the first stage and then realising God at the ultimate stage" (2009, 35–36).

At the societal level, civilization begins to evolve after coming into contact with a Sadguru. Citing as past examples the Sumerian, Egyptian, Roman, Aztec, Harappan, Aryan, and Chinese civilizations, Satpathy argues that the developments made in each of these ancient cultures was due to the presence of a Sadguru: "These sons of God the Almighty, born in groups in different parts of human society, taught the human race at its infant state its primary lessons in science and arts and gave a thrust to the progress of human civilisation" (2001, 11). As a result of the succession of Sadgurus throughout history, human knowledge has continued to advance. And yet, human civilization today is still in need of further evolution. Satpathy writes: "The world today is going through a process of 'intellect explosion' in all fields of knowledge. Yet the lack of moral values to properly utilise the fruits of the intellect for the greatest good of the greatest number on this earth is the biggest limitation. It is these Masters who will redefine religious codes and re-establish moral values on earth" (12).[25]

As the Param Sadguru, the incarnation of the Supreme Perfect Master for the current age, Shirdi Sai Baba is actively working from beyond the grave to evolve our individual souls and our human civilization, so that we may all eventually realize Godhood by merging our individual souls with the Over-soul. During my first interview with Satpathy at the Sai Ka Angan Temple in Gurgaon, one of the many temples he has helped found in India, he explained that given this emphasis on the evolution of the entire human species, the Shirdi Sai Baba movement is not technically a Hindu movement, even though the Shirdi Sai Baba temples are officially classified as Hindu. Instead, he insisted that it is better understood as a spiritual movement, not a religious one:

> Religion divides, but spirituality is universal. This is why Baba doesn't care what your religion is—he doesn't care if you are Hindu or Muslim, Sikh or Christian. He cares what is in your heart. . . . Many Hindus come to Sai Baba. But anyone can come to this temple. You have already met Hindu and Sikh people here today. Muslims and Christians also come. This is because this temple is not about Hinduism, not about any religion. It is about spirituality. It is about love of God and service to humans—not even service just to humans, love and service to the world. . . . Baba's message is love. Love of God, love of self, love of neighbor. In this time, we need this message. There are many diffi-

culties here today because of religion. Not just in India, in the whole world, in the US too. But spirituality is above all of this, beyond all of this.[26]

Thus, according to Satpathy, Sai Baba devotion cannot be classified as either Hindu or Muslim. Like Mukund Raj, he prefers to speak of this devotional movement as a spiritual rather than religious movement, for he feels that religious traditions are too often exclusive and divisive while spiritual ones are all-inclusive and unifying.

With the emphasis placed on the need for a temple to house a permanent image of Shirdi Sai Baba in Chicago, and the role of image worship in establishing and promoting devotion to Sai Baba, how are we to make sense of the disclaimers made by Mukund Raj and C. B. Satpathy that "ritual doesn't matter"? First, although the Chicago temple clearly makes great use of darshan and other elements of Brahminical Hindu temple ritual, Raj and Satpathy can claim that ritual does not matter because it is a personal choice, not a mandatory requirement for worship of Shirdi Sai Baba. In an interview with Satpathy in the Gurgaon temple, he firmly insisted that one could approach Shirdi Sai Baba in whatever way one was most comfortable. For Hindus, he stated while pointing at a framed painting of Sai Baba in the temple office, images and idols are important because Hindus practice darshan: "You look at this image, you sit and meditate on it, and you will feel a connection with Baba. You need not even come to the temple for this. You can do this at home, anywhere. But you should try to do this daily, try to cultivate this. After some time, Baba will come to you without the image, from inside of you." The goal of such image worship, Satpathy continued, is to realize Sai Baba's all-pervasiveness, to "realize Baba is everywhere, to see him in yourself and in everything. The goal is to find internal darshan of Baba, and to always be in that state, constantly, to develop Sai-consciousness." But those who do not practice image worship can develop Sai-consciousness in other ways, such as reading the *Shri Sai Satcharita* and meditating upon its words. "Paths are many, but goal is one," Satpathy concluded.[27]

Second, Raj and Satpathy can claim that ritual does not matter because what they advocate is the development of a higher spiritual and moral consciousness. Viewing darshan and image worship as forms of meditative practice that result in a greater humanism removes these practices from the realm of Hindu liturgy, priestly orthodoxy, and exclusivism. Despite the disclaimer—indeed, because of it—ritual in the form of darshan and image worship can be the central mode of interacting with Sai Baba. Thus, Mukund Raj can claim:

> Baba teaches that in the future to come, all of society will walk together, bound by universal love. Only when we walk together can we develop as a society and reach our fulfillment. We must pursue practices of equality and justice. Sai Baba leads us on this path. But we must each experience God individually. By our own free will we must go to God. This is why Shirdi Sai Baba speaks only about faith and patience, *shraddha* and *saburi*. Not ritual. In these modern times we don't have long periods for temple rituals, or for renunciation. In our daily lives, all we must do is look at Baba, have darshan of him, and have faith and patience that he will respond to us.[28]

The Sri Shirdi Sai Baba Temple of Austin

The Sri Shirdi Sai Baba Temple of Austin was founded in 2010 by Craig Sastry Edwards and Jill Yogini Edwards, a husband and wife team who converted to Hinduism. After retiring from their property management business in Hawaii in 2006, the couple chose Austin, Texas, as the site for their "second career" as temple founders and managers. They sought to establish a Shirdi Sai Baba temple in an area where a ready-made community of devotees already existed, thanks to the growing population of South Asian workers employed in Austin's burgeoning high-technology industry. Census data shows that between 1990 and 2010, in Austin alone (not including the suburbs), the Asian population grew from 15,366 to 49,560 (3.3% and 6.3% of the population, respectively), with Asian Indians being the largest group of Asians (Castillo 2011). In 2008, the Edwardses opened a temporary Shirdi Sai Baba temple in a strip mall called the Railyard Shopping Center in the northern Cedar Park suburb of Austin. In just a few months, they rented a larger space in the same complex, and a few months later an additional room a few doors down. Reflecting on the temple origins, Craig said: "It was a very exciting time. So many people of good will came forward to support the Temple. After eight months of operation, the Temple hired its first priest" (Edwards 2014a).

On March 19–21, 2010, the *kumbhabhishekam*, or grand inauguration, of the permanent temple took place. The temple is built to look like a Hindu temple in that it has a large tower (shikhara) over the inner sanctum (garbha griha), complete with a kalasha on top. The temple complex is quite large, encompassing nearly eight thousand square feet. It features a small Ganapati shrine at the outside entrance, a large main hall with the inner sanctum at its far end, a community room, a meditation space, a small room with the constantly burning fire (dhuni) and a shelf for lighting candles, a room with a *homa kunda* (fire pit) for Vedic fire rituals (*havans* or *yagnas*), a kitchen, and an office and bookstore. The temple grounds are carefully landscaped and manicured and feature a playground for children and a pond stocked with koi fish. The grand inauguration was publicized in area newspapers as an event open to people of all faiths, and it was well attended—five thousand visitors came over the course of the weekend (Sanders 2010). A second full-time priest was hired at this time, and an additional ten priests were brought from elsewhere in the United States and India to help officiate during the inauguration.

During the kumbhabhishekam of the temple, a five foot, five inch marble statue of Shirdi Sai Baba was ritually installed in the main hall in an elaborate ceremony. (The smaller marble murti of Sai Baba that had been worshiped in the temporary temple now resides in the meditation hall.) This ritual establishment ceremony was conducted according to orthodox Hindu tradition, in which ritual labor transforms the inert statue into a living icon infused with divine presence. The marble statue was carved in India and shipped to Austin, where it arrived at the temple blindfolded and carefully packaged in a large wooden crate. Upon opening the crate, the priests greeted it with recitations of Vedic mantras and offerings of flowers, incense, and candles. The statue was then moved into the inner sanctum of the main hall, where it underwent a series of ritual immersions, or *adhivasams*, intended to induce divine energy in the murti: immersion in water, milk, rice, and finally flowers. Throughout this entire process, the priests recited Vedic mantras and made offerings into a ritual fire. As Richard Davis explains, the "idea behind the repetitive, cumulative procedures of affusion is to concentrate within the body of the subject all the auspicious substances of the world" (1997, 36).

Next, it was time for the eye-opening ceremony. The murti was placed in its upright position on a pedestal in the center of the sanctum, where the priest then rubbed the eyes with a mixture of ghee, honey, and sandalwood paste. A curtain was then closed around the statue, and a mirror was placed in front of it, so that the first thing the newly awakened statue would see was the auspicious sight of itself as the priest carefully washed away the paste mixture. The curtain was then opened, allowing the congregants to engage

FIGURE 5.3. Sri Shirdi Sai Baba Temple of Austin. Photo: Karline McLain.

in darshan with Sai Baba, now understood to be fully awakened and present in the statue. As this first darshan took place, priests continued to chant Vedic mantras while performing the *kalashabhishekam*, in which one thousand small vessels, or *kalashas*, that have been filled with sanctified water are used to ritually bathe the image. The priests had previously invoked divine power into each of these vessels by reciting mantras over them. Again, I cite Richard Davis, who explains the significance of this element of the ritual of establishment with regard to medieval Shaivism in particular: "The priest worships each pot, since each is in itself now divine, and then pours the contents of each one over the image. As the water washes over it, the divinities and powers embodied in the pots infuse the image, until it becomes a 'divine body' (*divyadeha*) composed of the cumulative mantra-energies of all the pots. The ritual of establishment transfigures the material form of the image not simply as an animate being, but as a divine body of mantra powers, so that Shiva himself will see fit to inhabit and act through it" (1997, 37). In the Austin context, of course, it was the image of Shirdi Sai Baba (not Shiva) that became animated with the divine presence and infused with divine powers through this ritual.

Once permanently established in this manner, a Hindu image requires daily ritual worship. The Sri Shirdi Sai Baba Temple of Austin follows a program of four daily aaratis: morning (*kakad aarati*), midday (*madhyam aarati*), evening (*dhoop aarati*), and night (*shej aarati*). These are the same four prayer sessions offered in Shirdi, although as is common in US Hindu temples, the times have been adjusted for the American schedule (thus, for instance, the morning worship takes place at 7:30 A.M. in Austin versus 5:15 A.M. in Shirdi, and the evening worship takes place at 8:00 P.M. in Austin versus 10:00 P.M. in Shirdi). In the temporary temple, Sai Baba's image had received ritual worship on a daily basis, but not four times each day. In recognition of this increased ritual work, a second full-time priest was hired at the time of the temple's grand inauguration. Today, the temple employs four full-time priests, who share the work of performing the four daily aaratis as well as the supplemental rituals requested by devotees or performed for various calendrical and festival occasions.

In my first interview with Craig Edwards, I asked what he thought accounted for the rising popularity of Shirdi Sai Baba. He immediately disclaimed the centrality of ritual, stressing the importance of service and unity over liturgical action: "There is a shift in society now. Hindu rituals, they are very complicated. Not everyone now is interested in that kind of religion. Baba said the rituals were fine, if you want to do them, do them. But they don't really matter. Also, it is a more and more cosmopolitan world. Baba's message of love all, serve all has genuine appeal in this world, and is also genuinely needed."[29] During my visits to the Austin temple I met many devotees for whom the primary appeal of Sai Baba was the emphasis on seva. For instance, every Sunday morning a "sandwich seva" session is held in the temple kitchen, where volunteers make 200–250 lunches that are then delivered to the Salvation Army to feed the homeless in downtown Austin.

In my conversation with one regular participant in the sandwich seva, nicknamed "the Bread Man" because of his weekly donation of dozens of loaves of bread, he told me that he was just "not a ritual kind of guy." He said he was not very interested in the temple, until one day five or so years ago when his wife was in India and he took her place in the kitchen as a favor to her. As the men and women and children made row after row of peanut butter and jelly sandwiches, they also checked in with one another, asking how their week had been, following up on earlier conversations about family, work, and other matters. Not only were they doing something good for the larger Austin community, but these families had formed their own support community. The Bread Man stressed that this community included native Hindi and Telugu speakers, which brought him and his family into contact with other Indian families that would not otherwise be in their social network, given the regional and linguistic divisional patterns of Indian immigrants. "Some people focus on the puja," he said. "Some people focus on Baba's major *lilas* [miracles]. But it is not the rituals, not the lilas that matter to me. For me, Baba is about small changes for the better in my everyday life," said the Bread Man.[30]

And yet, that very Sunday morning I spoke with the Bread Man was Guru Poornima, the full moon festival day celebrating the guru. In addition to the usual four daily aaratis to Shirdi Sai Baba, a special series of pujas was also planned at the temple, including a Sai Satya Vrat Puja from 3:00 to 5:30 P.M. (a participatory puja guided by temple priests and modeled on Satyanarayan Puja); a participatory abhishekam and bhajan session at 7:00 P.M., prior to the palkhi seva; and a Sahasranama Archana session reciting the 1,000 names of Shirdi Sai Baba at 8:00 P.M. As I observed the evening rituals, I noticed the Bread Man and his family taking part among the approximately 300–350 participants. Such festival and calendrical rituals, of course, are the big turnouts at this temple, as at other Hindu temples.

Beyond such festival and calendrical rituals, the Austin temple also engages in supererogatory rituals in the form of fire sacrifices. To the left of the temple's main hall is a homa kunda room for Vedic fire rituals, not a standard feature in Shirdi Sai Baba temples or Hindu temples more generally. When I asked Craig Edwards about this architectural feature, I learned just how important fire rituals, called havans or yagnas, are to him. Craig explained: "My teacher, Panduranga, he's very into the fire sacrifices. So that is where I got the training, and my original interest was only in the yagnas. I wasn't interested in Shirdi Sai Baba or Sathya Sai Baba, whom he also worships."[31] The Edwardses are disciples of the guru Sri Panduranga Rao Malyala, who founded the Shri Shirdi Sai Baba Temple near Pittsburgh. Malyala places a strong emphasis on the importance of Vedic ritual sacrifice. In such yagnas, various oblations are traditionally offered into one or more sacrificial fires, with the idea that the Vedic fire deity, Agni, will convey the offerings to the other deities, who will in turn confer their blessings to the sacrificer.

Malyala teaches that the Vedas contain fundamental truths of the universe that have been passed down in an unbroken tradition from one generation to the next. In the fire sacrifice, the energy of the smoke from the *homa* fire mixes with the vibrations from the Sanskrit mantras, allowing one to not only tap into the fundamental truths of the universe but to bring about change, transforming disorder into order. Malyala insists that this is "scientific," that this is knowledge that has been repeatedly tested and proven true, not religious superstition (Malyala 2006). Furthermore, he insists that the Vedas are not strictly associated with Hinduism or with India, as is generally thought, but are about the fundamental truths of the universe that are beyond caste and creed. Thus, knowledge of "Vedic science" can be applied to global problems, such as drought, war, and environmental devastation. Likewise, knowledge of "Vedic science" can be taught to anyone willing to learn Sanskrit mantras and rituals, regardless of caste, gender, ethnicity, or religion.

As Craig's interest in Hinduism grew while he was living in Hawaii, he first became aware of Malyala from advertisements about the Pittsburgh temple in the *Hinduism Today* magazine. Craig recalled: "When I had extra money I would send some money [to the Pittsburgh temple] and have them do a yagna for me. And then I would sometimes write some questions, you know, what's this mantra, what's that mantra. And then I just invited the fellow I was corresponding with to come visit us in Hawaii." That fellow was Panduranga Malyala, with whom Craig struck up a lasting friendship. Malyala accepted the invitation to visit Hawaii, as Craig recounted:

> So when Panduranga came to Hawaii, he said, "Okay, what do you want?" I guess we [Craig and his wife, Jill] were in our thirties then and just trying to make something of our lives. We had started a business and had maybe ten to fifteen employees. We were doing okay but wanting to do better. So I said, we'll do Ganapati and Mahalakshmi Havan, because we want that [i.e., prosperity]. So we built a homa kunda in our backyard, a fire pit. Then we did the havan, and that night I got a call from one of my competitors, who said, "I know you want this one account I have, and I'm quitting, so I set up a meeting tomorrow morning for you with them." I didn't really want to do it because I had this houseguest. But I woke up at 4:00 A.M. anyway, being an alert businessman, and got all my presentations ready . . . I didn't even think about it while it was happening, but later I did—how often does a competitor call you up to give you an account?[32]

Craig's interest in ritual fire sacrifices grew as the tangible benefits mounted, and it was only later that he began to pay attention to Sai Baba. In his words: "What happened was we had a lot of miracles happen when we did the homas, and so my first thought was this is like Las Vegas where you always win. You put the money in and you get ten times more out. So, at first it was sort of a greed thing, and then after so many years of studying Sai Baba I realized it's not all about fulfilling my own needs, it's about helping society, so that is what I do now."[33]

Like Malyala, Craig accepts Sathya Sai Baba as the incarnation of Shirdi Sai Baba.[34] He recounted the incident that first caused him to start thinking seriously about Sathya Sai Baba. One summer a number of years ago, he was traveling with Malyala and some of Malyala's relatives on a visit to Niagara Falls, and they stopped on the drive back to Pittsburgh to meet with a Caucasian woman who had become a devotee of Sathya Sai Baba. Edwards was skeptical but listened politely as she told her conversion story. One of the miracles she claimed to have experienced involved a Polaroid photo that she had taken of her poster of Sathya Sai Baba, which she then showed to Craig, telling him to look closely at it and compare it with the poster. "So I looked and looked," Craig told me:

> And finally I saw that in the photograph, in the folds of Sathya Sai Baba's robes, there is a small image of Shirdi Sai Baba, one that wasn't there in the poster. And so when I saw this, even though it was 90 degrees out and humid and I was hot, all the chills went up and down my spine. So then driving back, I started to think, how could that happen? I thought, well maybe the lady could be faking it. But she seemed sincere, she wasn't after our money or anything, and you couldn't manipulate Polaroid photos then the way you can digital photos now. And Sathya Sai Baba wasn't anywhere near. You know they always say that he's just a magician, he's just doing hand tricks. But he wasn't there, so how did it happen? So I thought, well maybe he is God. So that started changing my psychology where I got more interested in Shirdi Sai Baba and Sathya Sai Baba, whereas before that I was just interested in the yagnas.[35]

This story demonstrates Craig's journey from skeptic to devotee of Sai Baba and the importance of miraculous intervention in that transition. It is possible to manipulate Polaroid photographs, of course. However, here we see what Maya Warrier (2003) has described as the "active process of miracle construction," whereby devotees are constantly on the lookout for instances in their lives that can be interpreted as miraculous experiences of the guru's grace. Warrier describes this as an iterative process in which devotees' interpretations of even mundane events as miracles reinforce their faith in the guru:

Every fortuitous event in their lives comes to be interpreted as a miracle worked
by the guru and a sign of his or her graces. It is thus up to the devotees to be
able to see the guru's divine love behind the most ordinary, the most mundane
incidents in their everyday lives, and to see every chance happening as a miracle worked by him or her. Devotees' "experiences" then are not merely a sign of
the guru's love for them. Equally, they are devotees' expressions of their absolute faith in their guru. The onus of making miracles happen rests not on the
guru but on each individual devotee (Warrier 2003, 46)

For Craig, then, the more he and his business prospered, the more his faith
in Sai Baba as his guru and in the efficacy of the fire sacrifices grew. Thus,
in the Austin temple, ritual worship of Sai Baba is combined with the ritual
performance of fire sacrifices.[36] With regard to the ritual worship of Sai
Baba, it is Shirdi Sai Baba who receives pride of place—it is his murti in the
inner sanctum, and he is the focus of devotional attention—although one
large poster of Sathya Sai Baba hangs on the wall to the right side of the
sanctum in the Austin temple.

Concerning the fire sacrifices, Craig and Jill Edwards have provided
financial assistance to Malyala and his wife, Mahalakshmi, to enable them
to found four Vedic schools in India with the intention of reviving and pre-
serving Vedic ritual, which they fear is rampantly being lost as knowledge
of Sanskrit diminishes in contemporary India. In the Austin temple, Craig
regularly performs Vedic fire sacrifices in the homa kunda room. During my
visit in July 2013, Craig was two months into a yearlong Ganapati-Mahalakshmi Havan. He had vowed to perform a havan at 6:00 A.M. every day for
one year, with the aim of raising funds for the temple. Like Malyala, Craig
similarly invites all interested temple members and attendees to participate
in such rituals, regardless of their caste, gender, ethnicity, or religion, and as
I attended the Ganapati-Mahalakshmi Havan one early morning three other
people were present in addition to Craig and Jill: one young man of Indian
heritage and two Caucasian women. Other havans are undertaken for less
material goals, such as a Varuna Yagna that was conducted in February 2014
with the goal of bringing rain to drought-stricken Texas and California.
After rain began to fall in California, the temple newsletter proclaimed success, attributing the rain to "Vedic science" and Sai Baba:

How is it possible for priests performing a ceremony near Austin, Texas to
change the weather in California? It may seem impossible! This is the gift of

the Vedic teachings, brought out by the sages and rishis and passed down for
countless generations. Remember, many things that once seemed impossible
or ridiculous, such as speaking over long distances through the telephone,
travelling to the moon, seeing a man thousands of miles away in a box television, etc. are now considered normal. Having this technology of the Vedic
yagnas, we should use them for the benefit of mankind. Furthermore, we should
bow down again and again to Sai Baba and all the saints, through which these
great mysteries continue to be revealed. (Edwards 2014b)

Ultimately, according to Craig, Shirdi Sai Baba's message is a universal
one. This, he said, was Sai Baba's point on the occasion (as related in the *Shri
Sai Satcharita*) two years before his death when he dramatically stripped off
his head wrap, robe, and loincloth, threw them into the fire, and revealed
his naked body to the Hindus and Muslims gathered around him in Shirdi.
As he stood there, exposed, he demanded of them angrily, "Today, see
clearly, whether I am a Hindu or a Muslim!" (Dabholkar 2007, 692).[37] "His
point," Craig explained, "was that God doesn't have anything to do with
Hinduism or Islam or religion. . . . The big lesson of Shirdi Sai Baba is to see
God in everyone. And the problem with all religions—not even between two
religions, or between two temples, but within one temple—is that sometimes people just don't like each other. So it seems like it is almost impossible to find that divine love. But that is the purpose of the temple. To give
people some taste of that." Craig then pointed to the lintel above the front
door of the temple, where a series of symbols representing the major world
religions had been painted as a visual statement about the temple's inclusiveness, welcoming members of all of the world's religions to enter into the
presence of Shirdi Sai Baba in keeping with Sai Baba's own practice and
teaching that "all religions are good. They're all going in the same path, but
are designed for different types of people."[38]

Given the emphasis placed on ritual in general, and Vedic fire sacrifices
in particular, at the Austin temple, how are we to make sense of Craig
Edwards's disclaimer that rituals "don't really matter"? First, although the
Austin temple clearly makes great use of Hindu ritual, Craig can claim—like
C. B. Satpathy and Mukund Raj in Chicago—that ritual does not matter
because it is a personal choice, not a mandatory requirement for worship of
Shirdi Sai Baba. Craig explains: "So my belief is that certain people have an
affinity towards a certain type of worship, for whatever reason. And so some
people like Panduranga [Malyala] and myself, we have an affinity for the

havan. We like it a lot. Other people get lost in happiness with bhajans or they do hatha yoga or pranayama, or they read books and they get knowledge that way. All those are legitimate things. One of the remarkable things about Hinduism is there are just so many thousands of practices."[39]

Second, Craig can claim that ritual does not matter because what he employs in the Austin temple is "Vedic science" or "technology." Viewing the fire ritual as scientific, universal, and equitable removes it from the realm of Hindu liturgy, orthopraxy, and exclusivism. Despite the disclaimer—indeed, because of it—ritual in the form of Vedic yagnas can be the central mode of interacting with Shirdi Sai Baba. Thus, Craig can claim that "Hinduism can be a very conservative, ritual based tradition. For many Hindus that is the religion they know. But it also has a much more liberal strand, that is not so grounded in ritual. This liberal side, it is the side I am more comfortable with, the side of Hinduism that I had in mind when founding this temple. Because the rituals do matter to some Hindus, we include them too."[40]

THE PARADOX OF RITUAL

The two scholars who have studied Shirdi Sai Baba in-depth, Antonio Rigopoulos and Marianne Warren, both lament the increasing "Hinduization" of Shirdi Sai Baba by his followers since the latter years of his life, as can be seen in the use of Hindu rituals to worship him, the use of Hindu architectural elements in new temple construction, the use of Hindu symbols in devotional pictures of him, and the use of Hindu terminology to describe him. Warren writes that in the years since his death, Shirdi Sai Baba "has been slowly transformed from that of an obscure ascetic Muslim *faqir* into that of a popular Hindu saint worshipped with full traditional pomp, grandeur, rituals, *abhisekam*, garlands, *puja* and *arati*, in a manner usually reserved for Hindu deities" (2004, 338). My research in Chicago and Austin demonstrates that Shirdi Sai Baba is in fact worshiped in the manner of a Hindu deity in these new temples, just as he is in Shirdi. However, my interviews with temple founders, managers, and attendees also demonstrate an important ambivalence about the role of Hindu ritual in these Sai Baba temples. These temple founders, managers, and attendees make great use of Hindu ritual while at the same time claiming that ritual is not important.

The larger implications of this paradox of ritual are twofold. First, I argue that it is a mistake to interpret the worship of Shirdi Sai Baba in temples as part of an activist effort to reclaim a syncretic or Muslim figure as originally and authentically Hindu. Far from such a conservative Hindu agenda, my field research at the Chicago and Austin Sai Baba temples, as well as at temples in India, has demonstrated that those who establish and patronize such temples instead align with a more ecumenical agenda. Describing modern Hinduism in practice, Nancy Falk writes that there is a "massive Hindu revival in today's India." She classifies this revival into two broad categories: the "cluster of movements promoting Hindu nationalist senti-ments" on the one hand and the "spate of new 'spiritual' movements" on the other hand that emphasize self-transformation, service to others, and the need to work for the good of all (Falk 2006, 236–37). As the previous chap-ters have shown, many Hindus who choose to turn to Shirdi Sai Baba fall into this latter category. They are aware that premodern Hindu scriptures have prescribed caste- and gender-based practices of inclusion and exclu-sion in temples and other ritual settings, and they seek to promote a form of Hinduism that is inclusive, no matter one's caste, class, or gender. They are aware that Hindu nationalists have promoted antagonism toward other religious groups, and they seek to promote a form of Hinduism that is unify-ing and concerned with the common good.

Joanne Punzo Waghorne (2009) has demonstrated that these two broad categories—Hinduism as an ethnic and caste-based bounded religion versus Hinduism as a universal and pluralistic religion—have also played out in the context of the South Asian diaspora in America since the arrival of Swami Vivekananda (1863–1902), who famously electrified the attendees at the 1897 World's Parliament of Religions in Chicago with his speech about Hindu-ism. However, when examining Hindu temples in the United States in par-ticular, it quickly becomes apparent that historically there have been far fewer options for Hindus who seek to forge a liberal and inclusive form of Hinduism. Hindu temples in the diaspora rarely operate as unifying forces for all Hindus, even when they set out to do so. Instead, they usually affirm regional, linguistic, and/or sectarian ties. This was the case for the Hindu Temple of Greater Chicago in Lemont, which originally intended to encom-pass all the sectarian and linguistic groups present in the greater Chicago area and become a unifying force for all Hindus. Enshrined within this temple are Rama, Venkateswara, and Radha-Krishna, in an effort to appeal to Hindus from Vaishnava and Shaiva sects and from northern and south-ern India. Yet, the temple's leadership and attendees come primarily from southern India, and even among these southern Indians a faction defected in the early 1980s to build a separate Sri Venkateswara temple in nearby Aurora. Raymond Brady Williams comments, "The difficulties encountered in developing the plans and in raising the funds for the temple indicate how hard it is to unite people from the various regions and sects in support of one project" (1988, 229)

Sri Venkateswara temples in particular, while well known for their orthodoxy in terms of their re-creation of authentic architectural features and adherence to traditional Srivaishnava liturgy, are not especially known for their inclusiveness. Discussing the Sri Venkateswara temple in Pittsburgh, Vasudha Narayanan writes: "While syncretism extends as far as some Telugu and Kannada practices, the temple has not actively sought to fulfill the needs of Hindus from many other regions. . . . Just a few miles from Sri Venkateswara temple is another beautiful place of worship, known simply as the Hindu-Jain temple. The architecture, the deities, and rituals here are principally 'north-Indian,' and the two temples serve the Pan-Indian Hindu community in tandem" (2006, 242).

When the founders of the Chicago and the Austin Shirdi Sai Baba temples set out to establish their temples, they did so not in a vacuum of other Hindu temples in these cities, for several prominent Hindu temples already existed in each location. Rather, they did so in what they perceived as a vacuum of inclusive Hindu spaces that emphasized the common good and were open to all—Hindus from various sectarian, regional, and linguistic backgrounds, as well as non-Hindus. In their view, far from setting out to "Hinduize" the once syncretic or Muslim figure of Shirdi Sai Baba, as Rigopoulos and Warren would have it, these temple founders have instead set out to liberalize Hinduism through the worship of Shirdi Sai Baba.

The second implication of the paradox of ritual is that it points to the larger challenges of defining Hinduism in the context of globalization. Given how closely tied traditional religions are to particular cultures, Peter Beyer (1994) notes in his study of religion and globalization that there are two basic possibilities for the survival of traditional religions in the modern global context: One is a conservative or even "fundamentalist" response that seeks to minimize changes. The other is a liberal response that entails reorienting a religious tradition toward the global whole and away from the particular culture with which that tradition identified itself in the past. He writes: "Such a liberal direction is not a move toward a new 'meta' or world religion so much as an attempt to reformulate the old in the absence of particularity. That, of course, is in its own way paradoxical" (10).

The founders of the Chicago and Austin Sai Baba temples have actively worked to reorient Hinduism toward the global whole, as is apparent in their interpretations of Shirdi Sai Baba as a figure who preached a humanitarian message centered on universal love and service. It is also apparent in their vociferous insistence that ritual does not matter. And yet, as we have seen, ritual does in fact matter very much—and this ritual is steeped in the particularity of traditional Hindu liturgy. This lingering particularity offers one explanation for why Shirdi Sai Baba temples in North America typically have not been successful in attracting many devotees who are not ethnically South Asian, in spite of their inclusive theology and rhetoric. A contrast can be drawn in this regard with other Indian gurus such as Sathya Sai Baba or Mata Amritanandamayi. Such so-called hypergurus have succeeded in drawing a large following of what Amanda Lucia has termed "adopter" devotees, who are not ethnically South Asian, in addition to a large following of "inheritor" devotees. Lucia writes: "In the global economy of the variety of gurus who compete for audiences' attention, gurus must brand their messages and modalities in order to render them distinct from other religious leaders. The guru as a charismatic leader fundamentally differs from the priest who upholds and maintains tradition through the reenactment and reinforcement of ritual structures" (Lucia 2014a, 241).[41]

In the Indian context, Shirdi Sai Baba's "brand" is frequently interpreted in terms of his Hindu-Muslim syncretism; but in the US context, this distinction does not have the same appeal to potential adopter devotees, given the very different demographic makeup of the two countries. Furthermore, the ritualized activities within Shirdi Sai Baba temples in the United States may appeal to inheritor devotees who can perceive the subtle differences in the way these rituals are performed—signaling inclusion rather than exclusion along lines of caste and gender by inviting devotees to be active participants in the ritual rather than passive observers of Brahminical priestly liturgy; but for potential adopter devotees, these rituals may fail to adequately differentiate between charismatic guru and temple priest. As adopter devotees of Shirdi Sai Baba, then, Craig and Jill Edwards are exceptions, not the norm.

In concluding this chapter, I offer a further example of the paradox of ritual: Craig and Jill Edwards have recently completed construction on a new Sri Venkateswara temple on the grounds of the Sri Shirdi Sai Baba Temple of Austin. During my last visit to the Austin temple in the summer of 2013, twenty-one *shilpis* (temple artisans) had just arrived from India to start sculpting components of the new temple. The Austin Sri Venkateswara temple held its grand inauguration during the week of June 18, 2014, when the primary murti of Venkateswara was installed. Discussing the decision to build a second temple in a recent newsletter, Craig wrote: "Sometimes people ask 'Why are you starting a second temple?' If Sai Baba is equivalent to all gods, why build another temple? This is like asking an ice cream vendor 'Why do you sell all these flavors? Isn't vanilla enough?' Of course, vanilla is good, but many people like different flavors. Should we deny them because we prefer vanilla only?" (Edwards 2014c) The Shirdi Sai Baba temple in Austin may not want to be like the Penn Hills Sri Venkateswara temple when it grows up, but it does want to have a Sri Venkateswara temple as its younger sibling.

In my interview with Craig, I questioned him further about the reason for building a Sri Venkateswara temple, given his desire to forge a liberal and inclusive form of Hinduism. He acknowledged the tension in choosing to build a Sri Venkateswara temple, stating that it could attract a different type of devotee than those who come to the Shirdi Sai Baba temple:

> This temple to Baba is not just for Hindus, although we do Hindu things
> and we have Hindu priests. But that one [Sri Venkateswara] will be more of
> a Hindu temple. So it will probably attract more fundamentalist type people.
> There is one [Sri Venkateswara] temple in Memphis similar to the one we're
> building, and they make the men, if they're not wearing a *kurta-pajama* [tra-
> ditional Indian men's long shirt and pants], they make them put on a *dhoti*
> [traditional South Indian men's wrap] or something. There is always that ten-
> sion. Even in this temple [Sai Baba], there are some who say you should not let
> anyone talk when they're in here. But then no one would come if we adhered to
> these formalities.[42]

As a businessman who has retired from his Hawaii-based property management business to undertake another sort of property management endeavor with the Austin temple, Craig also recognized the financial benefits to be derived from building a temple to Sri Venkateswara. "See, Sri Venkateswara is the richest temple in the world," he told me. "And we do a lot of charity. So I thought, well, if it generates a lot of money, then that is good. . . . The plan is, right now we're up to our necks in debt here at the temple. But hopefully in ten or fifteen years we'll pay that off and then we'll be able to give $10,000, $20,000, $30,000, even $40,000 a month to whatever charity we want in India or here or whatnot."[43] The decision to build a Sri Venkateswara temple, then, is understandable from an economic standpoint, given the famous wealth of the parent Sri Venkateswara temple in India and the generous donations frequently made by pilgrims visiting it or its offspring temples around the world. Making use of his business acumen, Craig decided that building a Sri Venkateswara temple was the best way for him to put Shirdi Sai Baba's message to "love all, serve all" into direct action, because the new temple would allow him to finance the charitable work that he seeks to accomplish as a devotee of Shirdi Sai Baba. However, this decision is less understandable from the standpoint of reformulating Hinduism as a more inclusive religion, for it appears to be a retrenchment to the particular versus the global, to orthodox liturgical exclusion versus spiritual communion, to conservative versus liberal Hinduism.

Conclusion

After bowing in prostration at the feet of Sai,
I will narrate how Sai came to Shirdi and other events.
Who his mother was, who his father was—no one knows this,
Where Sai was born, where he first lived, these questions remain
  unanswered.
Some say he is from Ayodhya, that he is Lord Ramachandra,
Others say Sai Baba is Hanuman, son of the wind god.
Some say Sai is the auspicious Lord Ganesha,
Others say Sai is the beautiful boy of Gokul, Devaki's son Krishna.
Some devotees consider him Shiva, and worship Baba as such,
Others say Sai is the incarnation of Dattatreya and offer him puja.
You can consider him whomever you'd like, but know that Sai is
  truly God.
He has given the wealth of life to countless people, and shown great
  mercy to the wretched.

AUTHOR UNKNOWN, *SHRI SAI CHALISA*

O N one visit to Shirdi, I purchased a souvenir penny-pamphlet called
the *Shri Sai Chalisa*. A *chalisa* is a popular genre of Hindu devotional
poem that consists of 40 verses in praise of a particular god or goddess. The
Hanuman Chalisa, attributed to the sixteenth-century poet-saint Tulsidas

and dedicated to the Hindu monkey-god Hanuman, is an especially popular example of such praise-poems.[1] Though called a chalisa, the *Shri Sai Chalisa* features 101 Hindi verses (editions are also available in Marathi and Telugu). Its opening verses, given in the chapter epigraph, praise Sai Baba's religious ambiguity. These verses proclaim that Sai Baba's birth place and upbringing are a mystery and that his devotees conceive of him in many ways, worshiping him variously as Rama, Hanuman, Ganesha, Krishna, Shiva, or Dattatreya. "You can consider him whomever you'd like," the chalisa informs us, and then insists that no matter how you understand him, Sai Baba is truly God, using the Sanskrit-derived term *Bhagwan*.[2]

This phrase, "You can consider him whomever you'd like," attests to the malleability of Shirdi Sai Baba. There is no overriding interpretation of this figure or his teachings. In this way, Shirdi Sai Baba stands apart from other Indian gurus and god-people. Shirdi Sai Baba's popularity has skyrocketed dramatically in his afterlife, and although his devotees insist that he is still present and accessible from beyond the grave, there is no living central figure to control his message. Similarly, there is no single organization that was founded by him to control his image or legacy, though numerous groups have stepped into this void, including the Shri Saibaba Sansthan Trust in Shirdi, the All India Sai Samaj founded by B. V. Narasimhaswami in Madras (now Chennai), and the Shri Shirdi Sai Heritage Foundation Trust founded by C. B. Satpathy in New Delhi. Finally, there is no single scriptural authority to turn to for his teachings, as he wrote nothing down himself, though most devotees now regard Govind Rao Dabholkar's hagiography, the *Shri Sai Satcharita*, as the primary authoritative scripture whose writing was guided by Sai Baba himself in his afterlife.

In this book, I have not sought to uncover the "real" Shirdi Sai Baba or his teachings. Rather, I have focused on the interpretations of him set forth in a variety of forms and media by his most active and influential interlocutors in the century since his death in 1918. These have included the Shri Saibaba Sansthan Trust, whose trustees manage Shirdi as a pilgrimage destination; Govind Rao Dabholkar, who composed the *Shri Sai Satcharita*; the Marathi poet and performer Das Ganu Maharaj; the freedom-fighter-turned-renouncer and prolific proselytizer B. V. Narasimhaswami; the directors who created the Bollywood films *Shirdi Ke Sai Baba* and *Amar Akbar Anthony*; and founders of temples dedicated to Shirdi Sai Baba in India and now throughout the global South Asian diaspora.

By decentering Shirdi Sai Baba and focusing instead on these multiple afterlife interpretations, I have investigated how Hindu devotees have themselves not only actively interpreted Shirdi Sai Baba but also sought to reinterpret Hinduism as a modern and increasingly global religion through their faith in Sai Baba. All of these Hindu interlocutors share three things in common. First, they all turned to Shirdi Sai Baba for spiritual succor, believing the claim set forth in the 11 Sayings attributed to Sai Baba that if only they looked to him with faith, he would in turn look to them, for he is "ever active and vigorous, even after leaving this earthly body."[3] Second, they all turned to the religiously ambiguous figure of Shirdi Sai Baba in their quest for freedom from aspects of traditional Hinduism that they found undesirable. As discussed throughout this book, in turning to the religiously ambiguous figure of Shirdi Sai Baba, these Hindu devotees sought to reform Hindu religion and society in varying ways: they have tendered critiques of the caste hierarchy; promoted peaceful interaction between Hindus and non-Hindus; envisioned a pluralistic nation-state as opposed to an exclusively Hindu India; provided charitable service to the working poor, the sick, and the disenfranchised; and opened up Hindu temples and sacred pilgrimage spaces to devotees from multiple religious and caste backgrounds. Third, Sai Baba's Hindu interlocutors all utilized and advocated ritual liturgies and technologies (including not only temple rituals in Shirdi and elsewhere but also oral devotional performances and printed and moving images), which have transformed the religiously ambiguous figure of Shirdi Sai Baba into a Hindu deity. You can consider him whomever you would like, after all, "but know that Sai is truly Bhagwan" and should be worshiped as such.

This same trifold emphasis is also found in the anonymously authored *Shri Sai Chalisa*. First, its 101 verses emphasize the afterlife presence of Shirdi Sai Baba, stressing that auspicious sight of Sai Baba's *murti* (statue) in the Samadhi Mandir in Shirdi can bring countless blessings: the birth of children to childless couples; food, clothing, and other forms of nourishment to the destitute; relief from illness and other forms of physical suffering; and respite from other sorrows. Second, the *Shri Sai Chalisa* also emphasizes Sai Baba as a unifying figure, one who in Shirdi drew into his presence Indians from a variety of upbringings and traditions. For instance, in verses 55–57, he is described as a "priest [*pujari*] of humanity," ministering not just to Hindus as a typical Brahmin temple pujari would, but to Indians from all religious backgrounds:

Sai was a priest of humanity, rising above their differences,

He loved Sikhs and Christians just as much as he loved Hindus and Muslims.

Baba shattered the discriminations between Hinduism and Islam,

Ram and Rahim were his, as were Krishna, Karim, and Allahtala.

In every corner of his mosque, where the ringing of bells echoed,

There Hindus and Muslims met together, their mutual love growing day by day.

Third, while the verses of the chalisa praise Sai Baba's religious ambiguity and inclusivism, hailing him as a figure worshiped by Hindus of all sects and a figure who equally loved Hindus and non-Hindus, the poem simultaneously pleads for its listeners or reciters to recognize Sai Baba as Bhagwan and to worship him through Hindu ritual means. In popular Hindu practice, chalisas are intended to facilitate the ritual worship of a deity. These praise-poems are often memorized and chanted aloud during a *puja* (worship) session, either in private at one's home altar or in an informal communal gathering (*satsang*) of devotees at a home, shrine, or community center. For those who have not yet memorized the chalisa, penny-pamphlets act as memory aids to help the new devotee through the ritual procedure. In my own experiences observing Shirdi Sai Baba satsangs at devotees' homes and at temples in India and the United States, I have frequently seen newcomers handed a printed copy of the *Shri Sai Chalisa* at the start of the worship, and I have watched as more long-term devotees chanted the verses by rote. At these satsangs, the chanting of the chalisa takes place with the participants seated before an image of Sai Baba, in front of which have been placed copies of the *Shri Sai Satcharita* scripture and various offerings such as flowers and fruits.

Further evidence that the *Shri Sai Chalisa* pamphlet is intended to facilitate exactly this sort of ritual worship of Shirdi Sai Baba, in keeping with Hindu ritual practice, is found in the booklet's cover image and additional materials at the end of the praise-poem. The cover depicts Sai Baba, seated and peacefully gazing at the viewer. He is garlanded with flowers, and a tray is placed before him in the bottom frame, containing items of offering traditionally used in puja—lit candles, incense, flower petals, and a coconut. Through this incorporation of puja details, the image visually illustrates how a devout person should approach his or her own image of Sai Baba for *darshan* (the auspicious exchange of glances with the divine persona in Hinduism, whether in the form of a framed poster, photograph, or small statue). In the pamphlet, several shorter pieces follow the praise-poem (all in Hindi in this edition of the chalisa), including two of the hymns composed by Das Ganu that are used in temple worship and the 11 Sayings attributed to Sai Baba.[4] In this way, the chalisa is framed with a visual call to puja at the beginning and with supplemental liturgical hymns that can be incorporated into puja at the end of reciting the praise-poem.

I suggest that this paradoxical relationship between embracing the religiously ambiguous figure of Shirdi Sai Baba and promoting an approach to his worship that is thoroughly grounded in Hindu ritual arises from the tension between globalization and religion. Scholars of globalization have noted that in the twenty-first century, we live in an increasingly global social reality, wherein a wide array of technology and social media makes it possible to communicate rapidly with people around the world, and wherein we are increasingly encompassed within a transnational and homogenizing socioeconomic system. A number of scholars have asked what role or roles religion will have in this era of globalization. Initially, theorists of globalization viewed religion as a natural opponent of the homogenizing force.[5] However, more recent scholarship on religion and globalization has pointed to the ambivalence of religion in global society. For instance, Mark Juergensmeyer writes: "It is true that some religious activists have tried to blow things up. But others have tried to smooth things over. Religion plays diverse roles in today's globalized society, just as it has in local communities and transcultural interactions throughout the centuries. The violent religious rebels are just one part of the news" (2005, 4). Similarly, Peter Berger writes: "Globalization means that everyone is in a position to address everyone else, and religion is an important ingredient of this universal conversation. The tones of the conversation vary. Some are indeed civil, promoting peace, tolerance, and democratic values. Others are strident, aggressive, even homicidal. It is disingenuous to look at only one sort" (2005, 16). Nonetheless, Berger voices caution about the ability of religion to contribute to shaping a global civil society, concluding: "There are cases where religion polarizes societies and makes them less civil—probably the majority of cases. There are cases where religion has served to 'civilize,' or at least tried to do so" (19).

In the context of modern India, Hindu nationalism has arguably been a polarizing force. In the early twentieth century, as Indian independence loomed ever larger on the horizon, the decision to establish India as a pluralist democracy was far from unanimous, and a vocal Hindu nationalist contingent argued that independent India should be a Hindu nation. A foundational definition of Hindutva, or Hinduness, was set forth in 1923 by

V. D. Savarkar, who argued that a Hindu was anyone who regarded India as both motherland and holy land. Thus, adherents of indigenous Indian religions, such as Hinduism, Sikhism, Jainism, and Buddhism, can be considered Hindus according to this definition, but not Indian Muslims and Christians. For even if the same blood runs through their veins, Indian Muslims and Christians regard places outside of India (such as Mecca or Jerusalem) as their holy lands. Furthermore, according to Savarkar, India should be recognized as a Hindu land and governed according to Hindu custom and legal code (Savarkar 1923). Throughout the twentieth century, a handful of powerful Hindu nationalist groups arose, collectively known as the Sangh Parivar (Family of Associations). Prominent among these are the Hindu Mahasabha, founded in 1915; the Rashtriya Swayamsevak Sangh (RSS), founded in 1925; and the Vishva Hindu Parishad (VHP), founded in 1964. In 1980, the Bharatiya Janata Party (BJP) was formed as a Hindu nationalist political party to oppose the prosecular Congress Party, which had dominated Indian politics since independence in 1947. The BJP has gained a substantial following among the Indian middle classes. It won the majority of seats in national elections in 1996, 1998, 1999, and again in 2014 (as the BJP-led coalition known as the National Democratic Alliance, or NDA).[6]

The Hindus featured throughout this book who have actively promoted devotion to Shirdi Sai Baba have done so in the interest of civilizing, rather than polarizing, society. All of these figures—devotional authors and performers, film directors, and temple managers and founders—share the positive interpretation of Sai Baba as a hybrid figure and the desire for an inclusive society, one united in its diversity as variously construed. These figures are by no means seeking to enact a Hindu nationalist vision for society, nor are they bringing Hindutva ideology to bear upon their interpretations of Sai Baba. Rather, they come from the more left-leaning end of the social, religious, and political spectrum. In the face of vocal right-wing Hindu nationalist groups operating in India throughout the twentieth century and into the present, these Hindus have utilized Shirdi Sai Baba and the discourse of composite culture to express their desire for a diverse society and a religiously plural nation-state. And increasingly, in the face of vocal proclamations against religion writ large in the context of globalization, these Hindus have also utilized Shirdi Sai Baba and the discourse of spirituality to express their desire for a religiously inclusive and humane global civil society.

From one perspective, one could view the surge of Hindu devotion to Shirdi Sai Baba over the past century as entailing the "Hinduization" of a once syncretic (or Muslim) figure. This has been the approach of previous studies of Shirdi Sai Baba, for instance by Antonio Rigopoulos and Marianne Warren, who have lamented what they perceive as a trajectory of increasing Hinduization. However, this stance aligns with other scholarship on syncretism that views religious mixing as destined for failure. In their review of the various models of syncretism found in scholarship today, Tony Stewart and Carl Ernst (2003) have termed the most common model "alchemical." In this model, two substances mix together; however, this combination is typically not understood to create a new, sustainable entity. Rather, the "result is a temporary mixture that will invariably separate over time, because the component parts are unalterable and must remain forever distinct and apart. . . . What remains, as in all models of syncretism, are the original component parts that have been mixed against what was intended by nature; in this model, religious or cultural essence triumphs over history." A similar model is the "biological," whereby two contributing parents produce offspring "through a mysterious miscegenation" process, with the implication that "like all hybrids, the result is sterile or does not 'breed true,' but disaggregates in the next generation rather than reproducing itself, thereby ending the lineage or species" (587). Viewed this way, Shirdi Sai Baba personally represented a synthesis of Hinduism and Islam, but this synthetic blend was not viable for the long term.[7]

From another perspective, one could view the surge of Hindu devotion to Shirdi Sai Baba over the past century as a thriving example of composite culture, particularly in the face of at times vocal calls to "revive" and "purify" Hinduism.[8] In the context of South Asia, composite culture generally refers to the mixing of Hindu and Islamic religion and culture. Thus, Javed Alam writes that composite culture refers to the argument that Hindus and Muslims are not two completely separate communities; rather, "the unique genius of India worked to evolve, over the centuries since the coming of Muslims into the Indian subcontinent, modes of thinking and living which are a subtle intermixing or synthesis of the world-views and living habits of Muslims and Hindus (1999, 29). However, this approach aligns with other scholarship on religious pluralism in South Asia that often uncritically celebrates religious mixing in the sharing of sacred spaces or mutual adaptation of religious figures, vocabulary, and rituals as evidence of religious tolerance. Viewed this way, Shirdi Sai Baba personally represented a successful mixture of Hinduism and Islam, one that is part of a much longer history of such composite blending and interreligious tolerance.[9]

My approach has been to use both of these perspectives: viewing the surge of devotion to Shirdi Sai Baba as a vibrant example of the desire to promote a South Asian composite culture, while simultaneously acknowledging the ongoing Hindu ritualization of Shirdi Sai Baba as a striking example of the imbalanced relationship between Hinduism and Islam in this purportedly synthetic admixture. Throughout my examinations of each interpretation of Shirdi Sai Baba, therefore, I have sought to consider both the ideal and the reality of religious hybridity, both the utopian promises of these interpretations and their majoritarian pitfalls.

Thus, I draw out how the Marathi poet and performer Das Ganu Maharaj praised Sai Baba as the divine figure who could bring Brahmins and non-Brahmins together in mutual amity, comparing Sai Baba with the god Vithoba who is at the center of the Varkari pilgrimage tradition, and comparing Shirdi with Vithoba's residence in Pandharpur as a place where all castes come together in shared devotion. Yet even as Das Ganu articulated a staunch reformist critique of caste hierarchy in the first decades of the twentieth century, and called upon Brahmins to respect the contributions made by members of all castes, he simultaneously maintained Brahminical status. In his writings and proselytizing efforts, B. V. Narasimhaswami conceived of Sai Baba as the guru who would unite Hinduism and Islam, allowing Hindus and Muslims to experience the monistic loving bliss of God-realization that would bring spiritual liberation as well as an end to the communal antagonism of the mid-twentieth century. Nonetheless, the theology and ritual that Narasimhaswami promoted as necessary for understanding and undergoing this experience of God-realization are grounded in Hindu orthodoxy. In the production of two 1977 Bollywood films, Manmohan Desai's *Amar Akbar Anthony* and Ashok Bhushan's *Shirdi Ke Sai Baba*, Sai Baba was promoted as both a pluralist and populist hero, able to unite people across religious boundaries and help the working poor and the disenfranchised attain a happy-ever-after ending. Yet in different ways, through both their narrative and form, these films also affirmed the centrality of Hindus and Hinduism in the Indian context. Finally, the transnational spread of devotion to Sai Baba has resulted in the recent establishment of new temples in the United States and in many other countries around the world. These temples have opened their doors to devotees from all religious backgrounds, and their founders have characterized devotion to Sai Baba as "spiritual" rather than religious, stressing that ritual does not matter—even as the temples follow a liturgical program based in Hindu orthopraxy and conducted by Brahmin priests.

Each of these interlocutors looks up to Shirdi Sai Baba as an idealized figure, praising his religious ambiguity or hybridity and associating said hybridity with a more inclusive, just, and equitable society. Yet each interlocutor's interpretation of Sai Baba also affirms and remains grounded within the majoritarian Hindu fold in substantive ways. Some might argue that this is inevitable, for the complete erasure of religious boundaries is an utopian ideal that can never be completely attained. For instance, Michael Pye writes that religious ambiguity "stems from man's very nature in the sense that each man is a limited being unable to grasp the revelation of the divine or the ultimate truth except in so far as this or these are refracted in terms of his own situation" (1971, 91). Similarly, Eliza Kent uses metaphor to at once describe religious boundaries' permeability and the near impossibility of transcending them entirely: "Just as lines in water are drawn only to be eventually blurred or effaced, so are bodies of water rarely so still that no lines appear on their surfaces" (2013, 26).

I view this inability to completely transcend religious boundaries as central to the ambivalent relationship between religion and globalization. As Mark Juergensmeyer writes, "The tension between the parochialism of religion and its potentially global reach is at the heart of religion's ambivalence toward globalization" (2005, 9). The insistence in the *Shri Sai Chalisa* that each person can consider Shirdi Sai Baba "whomever you'd like" is evidence of the potentially global reach of Shirdi Sai Baba devotion, but the persistence in approaching Shirdi Sai Baba as Bhagwan through orthodox Hindu liturgy is evidence of this devotion's parochialism. Today, Shirdi receives millions of pilgrims each year, the vast majority of whom are Hindus. They come to pay homage to Sai Baba in the place where his afterlife presence is most potent, and they return home with religious souvenirs like the *Shri Sai Chalisa*, framed posters of Sai Baba, and little packets of sacred ash (*udi* or *vibhuti*) for their home altars. It is due to the efforts of the figures featured in this book—members of the Shri Saibaba Sansthan Trust in Shirdi; devotional authors, performers, and filmmakers; and temple managers and founders—that Sai Baba's popularity has grown so significantly over the past century, particularly among Hindus in India and throughout the global Hindu diaspora. The ambiguous religious identity of Shirdi Sai Baba is as central to his appeal to these devotees as is the explicitly Hindu ritualized approach to his afterlife presence.

FILMOGRAPHY

Amar Akbar Anthony. 1977. Dir. Manmohan Desai.

Coolie. 1983. Dir. Manmohan Desai.

Deewar. 1975. Dir. Yash Chopra.

Dharam Veer. 1977. Dir. Manmohan Desai.

Jai Santoshi Maa. 1975. Dir. Vijay Sharma.

Jhanak Jhanak Payal Baje. 1955. Dir. Rajkamal Kalamandir.

Maalik Ek. 2010. Dir. Deepak Balraj Vij.

Mumbai Meri Jaan. 2008. Dir. Nishikanth Kamath.

Pather Panchali. 1955. Dir. Satyajit Ray.

Raja Harischandra. 1913. Dir. D. G. Phalke.

Shirdiche Sai Baba. 1955. Dir. Kumarsen Samarth.

Shirdi Ke Sai Baba. 1977. Dir. Ashok Bhushan.

Shirdi Sai Baba. 2001. Dir. Deepak Balraj Vij.

Sholay. 1975. Dir. Ramesh Sippy.

Zanjeer. 1973. Dir. Prakash Mehra.

NOTES

1   Interview in Shirdi, Maharashtra, May 20, 2010. In their study of Shirdi, Shinde and Pinkney state that a conservative estimate is eight million pilgrims annually, based on the numbers of pilgrims served in the official dining hall run by the Shri Saibaba Sansthan Trust, writing that "in 2008, around eight million meals were served, which corresponds to an average of 22,545 daily diners. Given that a substantial numbers [*sic*] of visitors visit the site, but not the dining hall, a minimum weekday estimate of at least 25,000 daily visitors seems appropriate" (2013, 563, quotation p. 563n39).

2   Aside from Shirdi Sai Baba's death in 1918, all dates associated with Sai Baba are approximate, for they are based on his followers' recollections of key events and there is no consensus on the exact dates of much of the chronology. I have used the dates given in the *Shri Sai Satcharita* (Dabholkar 2007).

3   See, for instance, Aymard 2014, Hallstrom 2008, Lucia 2014b, Pechilis 2004, Srinivas 2008, Srinivas 2010, and Warrier 2005.

4   Also see Rigopoulos, who writes: "The majority of Shirdi Sai Baba's *bhaktas* have not shifted their devotion to the present Satya Sai. Many of them ignore him or are critical of him: when I was doing research at Shirdi, people preferred to avoid the issue altogether" (1993, 249).

5   Narasimhaswami does not mention Sathya Sai Baba by name, but he writes: "It is not necessary to discuss the claims of X, Y or Z, who occasionally put forward the claim that he is the successor of Sai Baba. A few such claims have been put forward. But they were all pooh-poohed. . . . Invariably, on investigation, it has been noted that any person, claiming to be Sai Baba, does not show even a very small fraction of Baba's nature. Mere power to read thought, mere clairvoyance, mere production of articles from empty box or hands and mere devotion to Sai or God, will not constitute one into an Avatar of Sai. So, we might conclude this chapter by saying that Sai left no successor to his seat, that there was no seat to succeed to (as God's seat can never be vacant) and that there is no person living who can be

recognised by all as having the entire Sai spirit or Soul in his body, that is, who can be regarded as the Avatar of Sai" (1983, 346–47).

6   For more on composite culture in South Asia, see Alam 1999 and Asher and Talbot 2006; for an overview of modern Indian responses to religious pluralism, see Coward 1987.

7   For additional discussion about how composite culture may encode a Hindu majoritarian point of view, see van der Veer 1994b and Mondal 2005.

1. SHIRDI IS FOR EVERYONE

1   This photograph and a handful of other photos of Sai Baba are now housed in the Dixit Wada Museum at the Shirdi pilgrimage complex run by the Shri Saibaba Sansthan Trust. However, much is unknown about the extant photographs of Sai Baba, including their provenance and even their authenticity (in the case of some photos), that is, whether it is actually Sai Baba who is depicted or another holy man, such as his similarly attired disciple Abdul Baba. The Dixit Wada Museum also contains drawings, paintings, and composite images of Sai Baba, as well as photographs. In my visit there in 2010, my guide referred to all of these images as "original photos," a slippage common in India with regard to printed images but that further complicates the question of identifying authentic photographs of Sai Baba.

2   For more on Hindu devotional prints see Davis 2012, Jain 2007, Neumayer and Schelberger 2003, Pinney 2004, and Ramaswamy 2010. For more on devotional posters of Shirdi Sai Baba—and images of the particular posters of Sai Baba presented as a Hindu, Muslim, and as a composite figure discussed here—see McLain 2011.

3   For an important study of baraka in the context of images of a Sufi saint in Senegal named Amadou Bamba, see Roberts and Roberts 2003.

4   Narasimhaswami dates Abdul Baba's arrival in Shirdi to 1889, but if Abdul was twenty years old, the date would have been closer to 1891. Note that Nanded is situated on the banks of the Godavari River, not the Tapti River. Narasimhaswami came from the south, so perhaps this confusion arises from his lack of familiarity with the geography of western India.

5   Marianne Warren notes that birds are often used in Sufi poetry for their symbolic imagery, with different species evoking different qualities. She states that the crow is often used "as a token for the mundane things of this material existence" and that Sai Baba "summoned Abdul in order to take care of the more mundane aspects of his daily life in Shirdi" (Warren 2004, 262).

6   However, I would caution that limiting one's diet and spending extended periods in meditation are preliminary steps for many Indian ascetic paths; these elements are not unique to Sufism.

7   To make darshan with Sai Baba available to devotees who cannot make the pilgrimage to Shirdi in person, the Shri Saibaba Sansthan Trust maintains a website that features a page for live darshan viewing during the hours that the Samadhi Mandir is open: www.shrisaibabasansthan.org/darshan.html.

8   Interview in Shirdi, Maharashtra, May 20, 2010.

9   Such government oversight of prominent temples is a common practice in India today, with most states having government departments that manage prominent Hindu temples through appointed boards, including these temples' rituals and festivals, their personnel, their security measures, and their accounts and assets. State government oversight of these prominent temples is also a contested practice. When reading Indian newspapers, it is not infrequent to see coverage of the politics at play behind the membership of the Shri Saibaba Sansthan Trust, such as stories in national newspapers—including the *Times of India* and the *Hindu*—about the Bombay High Court's rulings concerning legal challenges to Trust membership.

10   The vernacular-language translations of the *Shri Sai Satcharita* include Bengali, Gujarati, Hindi, Kannada, Konkani, Nepali, Oriya, Punjabi, Sindhi, Tamil, and Telugu. The English translation of the *Shri Sai Satcharita* published by the Shri Saibaba Sansthan Trust is an abridged edition translated by Nagesh Vasudev Gunaji. However, Gunaji's translation is not a literal one. It omits some sections of Dabholkar's text and expands on others. Indira Kher's 1999 translation is far more accurate and is therefore the version I cite throughout this book. For a detailed discussion of Gunaji's adaptation, and the ways in which it enhances a Hindu interpretation of Shirdi Sai Baba, see Warren 2004, 5–8.

11   Interview in Shirdi, Maharashtra, May 20, 2010.

12   Ibid.

13   On the importance of "giving away, using up, spending money" as a virtue of Hindu pilgrimage, see Gold 1988, 262–98.

14   Interview in Shirdi, Maharashtra, May 20, 2010.

15   Kiran Shinde and Andrea Pinkney (2013, 568) note that as more and more pilgrims arrive in Shirdi, long-time local residents are less inclined to visit the Sai Baba temple in order to avoid the crowds, as well as the staff of the Shri Saibaba Sansthan Trust, who informally discourage them from entering the temple during rush hours. Local Muslims may opt to leave roses at the gate simply to avoid the crowds. However, one elderly Muslim man with whom I spoke explicitly said that he preferred to "look to Baba" in his heart, rather than enter "the Hindu temple" (the Samadhi Mandir) and look at Brahmins (interview in Shirdi, Maharashtra, May 19, 2010).

16   Interview in Shirdi, Maharashtra, May 20, 2010.

17   Beyond the pilgrimage complex maintained by the Trust, the entire town of Shirdi is all-vegetarian and all-sober, in keeping with the traditional practice of more established Hindu pilgrimage centers. Thus, on the roads outside of town, a preponderance of *dhaba* stands (roadside food stands) cater to those desiring a fix of non-vegetarian food immediately before or after their visit to Shirdi.

18   Shinde and Pinkney (2013) note that most pilgrims to Shirdi are middle-class urbanites. But on my visits to Shirdi I have encountered many middle-class pilgrims and also many working poor, though the former come from cities located throughout India while the latter tend to come primarily from nearby locations in Maharashtra or else from the state of Andhra Pradesh, which provides free bus service to Shirdi.

19   Beyond the accommodations provided the Trust, there are many independently operated hotels, restaurants, and other businesses in Shirdi that cater to the pilgrims. For discussion of some of these, and especially the influx of business migrants from Andhra Pradesh, see Shinde and Pinkney 2013.

20   Interviews in Shirdi, Maharashtra, May 21, 2010.

21   Interview in Shirdi, Maharashtra, May 22, 2010.

22   India's 1991 census counted 15,129 people in Shirdi. By the time of the 2011 census, the population had more than doubled, to 36,004.

23   Interviews in Shirdi, Maharashtra, May 20, 2010.

24   On the concept of dargah in South Asia, see Bellamy 2011, Currim and Mitchell 2004, and Troll 1989.

25   On the concept of tirtha, see Eck 2012, 7–11; and Eck 1981.

2. SHIRDI IS MY PANDHARPUR

1   Hymn nos. 1 and 2 are included in the morning prayer session (*kakad aarati*), and Hymn no. 3 is included in both the noon (*madhyam aarati*) and evening (*dhup aarati*) prayer sessions.

2   Das Ganu's kirtans have also been included in many popular Indian films and television serials featuring Shirdi Sai Baba. As a result, they are often familiar to many Indians who do not regularly attend Shirdi Sai Baba temples but who have encountered them through popular media.

3   In the hymn given in this chapter's epigraph, Das Ganu explicitly refers to Sai Baba as "Mother." This is modeled on the preexisting Maharashtrian tradition of worshiping Lord Vitthal as Mother; for more on this, see Dhere and Feldhaus 2011, chapter 12.

4   All three hymns presented here are translated from the Marathi and Hindi originals in Das Ganu 1967.

5   Narasimhaswami dates this incident to 1912 in *Life of Sai Baba* (1983, 143) and 1916 in *Sri Sai Baba's Charters and Sayings* (1954, 37–38).

6   In India, caste is not unique to Hinduism but also exists in practice among Jains, Buddhists, Sikhs, Christians, and Muslims. Each of these religious communities usually has a wide variety of castes and subcastes. However, as minority communities themselves, they are not infrequently lumped together as one caste, particularly by Hindu authors and public figures. Thus, Muslims may be thought of as both a religious community and a caste group by Hindu Brahmins, as Narasimhaswami does here. A similar conflation of caste and creed with regard to Indian Muslims can be seen in the writings discussed throughout this chapter.

7   Das Ganu's multivolume *Samagra Vanmaya* (Collected works) has not been translated from Marathi into any other languages. His primary writings about Shirdi Sai Baba have been translated into Hindi and English by Rabinder Nath Kakarya (see Das Ganu 2007); however, it is not a scholarly translation. For my criticism of the accuracy of this translation, see note 28 below.

8   On the Varkari pilgrimage to Pandharpur, see Deleury 1960, Karve 1962, and Mokashi 1987. For more on Vithoba, see Novetzke 2005 and Dhere and Feldhaus 2011.

9   For a discussion of biography writing as embodied devotion, see Prentiss 1999, 7; for more on the genre of hagiography and its conventions in the context of modern Hinduism see Rinehart 1999, 1–16.

10   On the Maratha Empire, see Gordon 1993.

11   This date is approximate; Athavale (1955, 54) dates Das Ganu's first visit to Shirdi to "around 1896," while Narasimhaswami (1983, 135) dates it to "1890 or 1892."

12   W. C. Rand was chairman of the Special Plague Committee that was formed to deal with the plague epidemic. The antiplague emergency measures employed under Rand's command were widely regarded as brutal, as Athavale describes. Seeking revenge for these brutalities, the Chapekar brothers shot Rand and his military escort, Lieutenant Ayers, on June 22, 1897. Both colonial officers died, and the Chapekar brothers were tried, sentenced to death, and executed by hanging. On the significance of the Chapekar brothers in Marathi nationalist kirtans, see Schultz 2013, 52–56.

13   On rashtriya kirtan in Maharashtra, see Schultz 2013.

14   On Tilak and the Ganapati festival, see Kaur 2000; Barnouw 1954; and Cashman 1975, 75–97. On Tilak as an advocate of Marathi kirtan, see Schultz 2013, 21–49. On Shivaji, see Cashman 1975, 98–122; Laine 2003; and McLain 2009, 114–40.

15   Also see Athavale 1955, 54–58.

16   Though Narasimhaswami writes here that Das Ganu "made no collections" at his kirtan performances, it is not that Das Ganu did not accept donations voluntarily made by those in attendance, for that was in fact how he made his living; rather, he seems not to have actively solicited his audience for donations, as most kirtankars did.

17   On literacy and the medieval Marathi kirtankars, see Novetzke 2008, 75–80.

18   On Jotirao Phule, see O'Hanlon 1985 and Omvedt 1976.

19   On Dalit politics in nineteenth- and twentieth-century western India, see Rao 2009.

20   On Ambedkar, see Jaffrelot 2005 and Zelliot 1996.

21   Taraporevala dates the *Santakathamrita* to 1903, the *Bhaktalilamrita* to 1906, and the *Bhaktasaramrita* to 1925 (Das Ganu 1987, viii). Athavale does not provide specific dates for them in his compilation of Das Ganu's *Samagra Vanmaya* but includes the *Bhaktalilamrita* in volume 5 (Das Ganu 1965a), the *Santakathamrita* in volume 6 (Das Ganu 1965b), and the *Bhaktasaramrita* in volume 7 (Das Ganu 1966). If this ordering is chronological, it suggests that the *Bhaktalilamrita* was composed before the *Santakathamrita*. Narasimhaswami (1983, 149) dates the *Bhaktalilamrita* to 1906 but does not provide specific dates for the other works. Both the *Bhaktalilamrita* and the *Santakathamrita* were composed while Sai Baba was living, thus between 1903 and 1918; the *Bhaktasaramrita* was composed after Sai Baba's death in 1918.

22   All translations of Das Ganu's *Bhaktasaramrita* in this chapter are from the original Marathi in Das Ganu 1966.

23   This vision of a Muslim drinking the milk flowing miraculously from a cow is significant in light of the Cow Protection Movement that began in the late nineteenth century, led by the Arya Samaj, and continued through the first half of the twentieth century. On the Cow Protection Movement and the Arya Samaj, see Adcock 2010. In his discussion of popular images associated with this movement, Pinney (2004, 105–44) notes that some images depicted the Cow Mother as an allegory for the nation, one in which members of multiple religious communities accepted milk under the slogan "drink milk and protect the cow," thereby including only those within the space of the nation who agreed to protect the cow, rather than slaughter it. Remains of this ideology linger in images of Sai Baba that still circulate today. In one popular poster (held in the author's personal collection), Sai Baba is dressed as a Muslim holy man, and a mosque (*dargah*) is depicted behind him. Also in the background are two white cows, suggesting that they too fall under Shirdi Sai Baba's protection. For this image, and further discussion of popular posters of Sai Baba, see McLain 2011.

24   For an overview of the differing accounts of Sai Baba's mysterious origins and background prior to his arrival in Shirdi, see Rigopoulos 1993, 3–43.

25   For instance, Narasimhaswami (1983, 2) writes that Mhalsapathy "first raised the orthodox objection to Baba's stepping into and residing at the Khandoba temple in his charge, but soon developed into the most zealous admirer and ardent worshipper of Baba."

26   Sontheimer also points out that another of Khandoba's five wives was Candai Bhagvanin, a Muslim woman, though she does not have much presence in folk songs.

27   On Chokhamela, see Zelliot 1995, 212–20; and Zelliot 1981, 136–56.

28   This list of anti-Brahmin insults is so expansive that Rabinder Nath Kakarya, who translated the Marathi work into Hindi and English, omits the verses for fear of offending readers. Kakarya writes, "Verses 126 to 183 refer to mutual abuse and mutual differences between the various sections of Hindu community and [are] therefore omitted" (Das Ganu 2007, 69).

29   Hindu scripture holds that the Ganges River was originally a divine river that descended from heaven to earth to bring salvation to its inhabitants. The Godavari River is often invoked in scripture from this region of western India to be symbolically the same river, also descended from heaven, and duplicated in a second geographical setting. For the mythological account of the Ganges's descent to earth, and its duplication, see Eck 2012, 19, 131–88.

30   Athavale includes a chapter on Das Ganu's social views in his biography, wherein he praises him for his reform work. Athavale (1955, 194–97) writes that rigid and orthodox Hindus might condemn some of Das Ganu's work, such as that with the Shraddhanand Mahilashram (Hindu Women's Welfare Society, founded in 1927 in Matunga), but that Das Ganu viewed such work against injustice as a form of worship.

31   On Gandhi and Ambedkar, also see Zelliot 1972.

3. SHIRDI IS THE FUTURE OF RELIGION IN INDIA

1 For a brief historical overview of colonial rule in India, the independence struggle, and partition and its aftermath, see Trautmann 2015, chapters 10–12; and Metcalf and Metcalf 2002.

2 On Shivamma Thayee, see Ruhela 1996.

3 Narasimhaswami's strongest critic is Kevin R. D. Shepherd, a controversial and self-published author who argues in *Gurus Rediscovered: Biographies of Sai Baba of Shirdi and Upasni Maharaj of Sakori* that Shirdi Sai Baba was a Sufi Muslim who has been recast as a Hindu god incarnate. Shepherd holds Narasimhaswami responsible for this Hindu casting, noting how popular his books were, especially with Hindus who were more interested in miracle workings and pilgrimage to Shirdi than in higher spiritual teachings: "Swami Narasimhaswami was indeed successful in that he himself became worshipped as a guru, but an objective evaluation of his contribution is in general long overdue. Though he did salvage some interesting material, his editing favoured reports that buttressed the image of the wonder-worker, and the biographical details of Sai Baba's life suffered accordingly" (Shepherd 1985, 4).

4 Also see Saipadananda 1973, 4. The Montague-Chelmsford reforms were introduced in 1918–19 by the British government in India with the intention of gradually introducing self-governing institutions.

5 On "extremist" and "moderate" politics within the Indian nationalist movement, see Wolpert 1962. On Tilak, see Cashman 1975.

6 On Gandhi's Noncooperation Movement, see Gandhi and Fischer 2002, esp. 133–41.

7 Sources agree that Narasimhaswami spent three years with Ramana Maharshi, but the dating of those three years is not precise. Vijayakumar (2009, 43) states that Narasimhaswami arrived in January 1926; Saipadananda (1973, 9) dates the stay from 1928 to 1930; Varadaraja Iyer (1974, 12) says that he left in 1932; and the publisher's note to Narasimhaswami's book *Self Realisation* (2010, iii) guestimates his arrival as "around 1929."

8 For more on Upasni Maharaj, see Upasani 1957, vols. 1–3.

9 In common usage, *satsang* often refers to the experience of being in the company of sadhus or saints, often in the form of regular devotional gatherings. As Robin Rinehart (1999, 13, 196) notes, such satsangs are commonly understood in the South Asian context to have "physical, emotional, intellectual, moral, and spiritual effects." Here, Narasimhaswami clearly views satsang as transformative in these many ways.

10 The sexuality of Indian gurus has a history of debate in modern India and beyond. See, for instance, Kripal 1995 and Urban 2015.

11 See also the Bhagavata Purana 7.5.23–24.

12 All translations of Narasimhaswami's verses in this chapter are from the original Sanskrit in Narasimhaswami, n.d.

13 In 1987, this poster was replaced by a marble *murti* of Shirdi Sai Baba, which remains the focus of devotion in the Mylapore temple today.

14   For more on Hindu-Muslim relations in India pre- and postindependence, see Ludden 2005, Mittal 2003, Pandey 2001, van der Veer 1994a, and Varshney 2002.

15   Marianne Warren (2004, 196–97, 391–402) argues that Sai Baba may have actually fought on the other side of this war, fighting for the British and not against them.

16   This designation is not without controversy, however. An example can be found in Kamath and Kher 2008, 297–303. In the chapter "Sai Baba Had No Apostles," the authors argue that neither Narasimhaswami nor Upasni Maharaj should be considered apostles, for Shirdi Sai Baba continues to speak for himself and therefore does not have any need for an apostle.

17   The popularity of Shirdi Sai Baba in the southern states is due not only to the work of Narasimhaswami but also to the popularity of Sathya Sai Baba, who claimed to be the reincarnation of Shirdi Sai Baba and is discussed in chapter 5. For a discussion of regional traffic to Shirdi, including the large proportion of pilgrims from Andhra Pradesh, see Shinde and Pinkney 2013.

18   For a similar discussion of the medieval poet-saint Kabir's hagiography and the increasing popularity of the assertion that Kabir was born to Hindu parents, not Muslim, and that he was initiated by a Brahmin guru, see Lorenzen 1991, 3–22.

4. SHIRDI IS FOR UNITY IN DIVERSITY AND ADVERSITY

1   Elison describes in fascinating detail several of these Mumbai street shrines to Shirdi Sai Baba, and he discusses their demolition by the Bombay Municipal Corporation in fall 2003 as part of a "traffic flow" improvement plan to remove illegal encroachments, as well as the nearly instantaneous rebuilding of these spaces and repopulation of them with miniature effigies of Sai Baba.

2   Hymn nos. 1 and 2 are included on the soundtrack; see chapter 2 for translations.

3   Also see Metcalf and Metcalf 2002, 252; and Wright 1977.

4   Also see Jain 2007, 340–53.

5   On D. G. Phalke, see Rajadhyaksha 1993 and Saklani 1998.

6   On defining the mythological genre, see Dwyer 2006, 15; and Lutgendorf 2002.

7   On frontality, see Kapur 1993.

8   For an alternate version of this story as told by Das Ganu Maharaj, see chapter 2.

9   G. S. Khaparde (1854–1938) was a lawyer, political activist, and close associate of Tilak's in the late nineteenth century. He was a devotee of both Shirdi Sai Baba and Gajanan Maharaj. For more on his visits to Shirdi, see his diary (Khaparde 2000).

10   On Tilak, see Cashman 1975 and Wolpert 1962.

11   For more on the 11 Sayings, see the introduction.

12   Kulkarni is not figured among the seventy-nine devotees featured in Narasimhaswami's *Devotees' Experiences of Sri Sai Baba*, the second textual source for the film, though Narasimhaswami does mention the *Gita Rahasya* in the second volume of his four-volume *Life of Sai Baba*. In his chapter on Khaparde in this work, he notes that although Sai Baba did once endorse Tilak's *Gita Rahasya*, he did not fully support Tilak's mission and methods; rather, Narasimhaswami suggests that during Tilak's visit to Shirdi in 1917, Sai Baba counseled Tilak to retire because he

believed that Mahatma Gandhi would better unite Hindus and Muslims in a non-violent struggle for independence. See Narasimhaswami 1983, 333–34.

13 Other examples of the film's difference from its textual sources, in accordance with Hindi cinematic convention, are the second Brahmin priest who accompanies Kulkarni and acts at times as a joker or clown character, and the item girl who performs the catchy song and dance number "Pyar Mein Tere."

14 Philip Lutgendorf (1995, 223) reports that conservative estimates of Doordarshan's daily viewership during the *Ramayan* serial ranged from forty million to sixty million, with the most popular episodes viewed by anywhere from eighty million to a hundred million people. For further audience statistics, see Rajagopal 2001, esp. 72–120, 326n48.

15 For a discussion of the ritualized viewing of the *Ramayan* serial, see Lutgendorf 1995, esp. 224–25.

16 Interview in New Delhi, September 25, 2008.

17 In addition to the discussion of C. B. Satpathy in chapter 5, also see McLain 2012.

18 Interview in Gurgaon, Haryana, May 29, 2010.

19 Ibid.

20 Interview in Bengaluru, Karnataka, August 13, 2008.

21 Interview in Mumbai, Maharashtra, July 30, 2008.

22 Interview in Mumbai, Maharashtra, May 18, 2010.

23 In this chapter, I summarize only those plot elements in *Amar Akbar Anthony* that are pertinent to the discussion of Shirdi Sai Baba. For a detailed synopsis of the entire film, see Elison, Novetzke, and Rotman 2016, 207–51.

24 However, Rosie Thomas notes that "the BBC not only programmed it early one Sunday morning, without even troubling to list it with other films on the *Radio Times* film preview page, but pruned it of all its songs and much narrative, including most of the first two reels, which are, not surprisingly, crucial to making any sense of the film" (2008, 22).

25 On the cassette revolution in India in the 1970s and 1980s, see Manuel 1993; on the life of Hindi film songs beyond their cinematic context, see Morcom 2007, esp. 207–38; on the wide appeal of Amitabh Bachchan's dialogue and songs in his many films see Mishra 2002, 147–54. As anecdotal testimony to the popularity of *Amar Akbar Anthony*'s songs—even extending beyond India—Bachchan once reported his surprise when, on a visit to London's Piccadilly Circus, a group of Kurds ran up to him and started singing songs from that film and another, *Muquaddar Ka Sikander* (Rajadhyaksha 2008, 21).

26 Also see Haham 2006, 39.

27 Rachel Dwyer (2005, 14) similarly points out the "underlying Hinduness of all Indians" in *Amar Akbar Anthony* in her *100 Bollywood Films*. For other discussions of the limitations of the film's intercommunal message, see Chakravarty 1993, 214; and Chadha and Kavoori 2008, 139.

28 On conversion in colonial and postcolonial India, see Viswanathan 1998.

29 Further, the depiction of Bharati as an inclusive Mother India figure who loves her three adult children no matter their religion—Hindu, Muslim, and Christian—can

also have a similarly "reassuringly Hindu" interpretation. On the multivalent significance of the national goddess Bharat Mata, see Ramaswamy 2010 and McKean 1996.

5. SHIRDI IS FOR HUMANITY

1   Shirdi Sai Baba walked to the Lendi Garden every morning. Some sources state
     that he went there to meditate, taking only Abdul Baba inside with him. Other
     sources say that this is where he took his morning constitutional.

2   For more on the Nathpanthis and their connections to Shirdi Sai Baba, see White
     1972.

3   Interview in Shirdi, Maharashtra, May 20, 2010.

4   Interview in Austin, Texas, July, 25, 2013.

5   See *Infinite Intelligence*, based on a body of manuscripts from the 1920s, that has
     now been published by the Sheriar Foundation (Meher Baba 2005).

6   For a detailed description of one *sahvas* program—a gathering of close Western
     devotees in the presence of Meher Baba for devotion, meditation, and spiritual
     instruction—that took place at Meherabad in November 1955 as described by one
     disciple, see Meher Baba and Stevens 1998, 3–90.

7   I use masculine pronouns for the Avatar intentionally, for Meher Baba proclaimed
     that the Avatar always descends in human male form (whereas Perfect Masters can
     be male or female). See Meher Baba 1973, 148–53.

8   For a detailed description of the types of meditation prescribed by Meher Baba,
     see Meher Baba 2011, 201–51.

9   The official biography of Sathya Sai Baba, written by his secretary and devotee, is
     Kasturi 1971.

10   As D. A. Swallow (1982, 125, 128n12) points out, this claim asserted that Sathya
     Narayana was not only Shirdi Sai Baba reincarnated but also of Brahmin status,
     in spite of Sathya Narayana's Raju (Kshatriya) birth caste. For an in-depth discus-
     sion of the significance of the Bharadwaja claim in terms of Shaiva mythology, see
     Swallow 1982, 136–45.

11   For more on Prasanthi Nilayam, see Srinivas 2008, 162–215; and Srinivas 2010,
     93–155.

12   But for an important counterpoint about the limits of Sathya Sai Baba's syncretism,
     see Swallow 1982, 157; and Babb 1986, 200–201. On the limits of Sathya Sai Baba's
     social positions regarding caste and gender, see Urban 2003.

13   For case studies of the global Sathya Sai Baba movement in Bengaluru, Nairobi,
     and Atlanta, see chapters 6 through 8 in Srinivas 2008.

14   For more on the miracles performed by Sathya Sai Baba, see Babb 1986, 176–201.
     For more on the consumption of sacred objects touched by Sathya Sai Baba, see
     Srinivas 2010, 282–322.

15   These and other acts have been accepted as miracles by devotees and denounced
     as tricks by others. Among the denouncers, some of the most vocal have been
     Indian rationalists such as Abraham Kavoor, who called Sathya Sai Baba a fake in
     his book *Begone Godmen!* (Kavoor 1976). For more on the skeptical reception of

Sathya Sai Baba, see Srinivas 2010, 232–81. For more on the rationalist movement in India, see Quack 2011.

16   For more on the use of new and visual media in Hinduism, see McLain 2015. On new and visual media in Sathya Sai Baba devotion specifically, see Srinivas 2008, 96–110; and Hawkins 1999.

17   I am indebted to Joanne Punzo Waghorne for the phrase "mini gurus," which arose during our co-organization of a panel on Shirdi Sai Baba that took place at the Association for Asian Studies conference in 2014.

18   On Hindu temple architecture and its symbolic significance, see Michell 1988.

19   For a list of the 11 Sayings, see the introduction.

20   Interview in Chicago, Illinois, March 28, 2010.

21   Ibid.

22   Ibid.

23   Interview in Gurgaon, Haryana, May 29, 2010.

24   Ibid.

25   Satpathy mysteriously states that the Sadgurus are working to evolve a more superior "fifth human race" that will have the capacity to "communicate through a mental process with each other" and will discover and make use of "newer energy fields" (2001, 10). However, he does not provide further information about this fifth human race or the previous four human races.

26   Interview in Gurgaon, Haryana, October 4, 2008.

27   Ibid.

28   Interview in Chicago, Illinois, March 28, 2010.

29   Interview in Austin, Texas, April 30, 2013.

30   Interview in Austin, Texas, July 21, 2013.

31   Interview in Austin, Texas, July 24, 2013.

32   Ibid.

33   Ibid.

34   Malyala maintains that God incarnates in human form whenever righteousness is in need of restoration. The Hindu god Shiva thus took the form of Shirdi Sai Baba for this purpose. When Shirdi Sai Baba was reaching the end of his lifetime, he told his disciple Abdul Baba that he would "appear again after eight years of his samadhi and that he would give darsan in the name of Satya to uphold the Truth. That was the advent of Sri Sathya Sai Baba" (Malyala 2012, 4).

35   Interview in Austin, Texas, July 24, 2013.

36   One could argue that Shirdi Sai Baba's image is imposed on the Vedic fire sacrifice, much in the way that Krishna's was imposed on the performance of the first Vedic soma sacrifice outside of South Asia when it was performed in London in 1996. On this, see Smith 2000. On Vedic fire sacrifices outside of South Asia, see also Bechler 2014.

37   Craig Edwards's interpretation of this incident is similar to B. V. Narasimhaswami's, whereas Govind Rao Dabholkar focuses not on the composite implications of Sai Baba's act but on Sai Baba's miraculous ability to select his time of death. For Dabholkar, the significance of this act is that it occurred on the Viajayadashami

holiday (Dasara), at which time Sai Baba would take his *mahasamadhi* (pass away) two years later, in 1918. See Narasimhaswami 1982, 100; and Dabholkar 2007, 690–704.

38   Interview in Austin, Texas, July 24, 2013.

39   Ibid.

40   Interview in Austin, Texas, April 30, 2013.

41   On "adopter" versus "inheritor" devotees, see Lucia 2014b, 149–52. Another reason, of course, that Shirdi Sai Baba temples have not attracted as many adopter devotees as other Indian gurus is that adopters are often drawn to the charisma of the living guru who is physically present to offer an unmediated experience of the divine.

42   On the rules of etiquette at the Sri Venkateswara temple in Memphis, Tennessee, see https://icctmemphis.org/icct/home/etiquette. These rules stress that devotees should wear "conservative and traditional clothing," that they must observe silence within the temple, and that "when occasion calls for it, devotees with traditional Indian dress only will be allowed into the antechambers of sanctums."

43   Interview in Austin, Texas, July 24, 2013.

CONCLUSION

1   On the *Hanuman Chalisa*, see Lutgendorf 2007, 397–99.

2   The chalisa verses in this chapter are translated from the Hindi original in *Shri Sai Chalisa*, n.d.

3   The 11 Sayings attributed to Shirdi Sai Baba are translated and discussed in further detail in the introduction.

4   The Das Ganu hymns are Hymn nos. 1 and 2, which are translated in chapter 2.

5   See, for instance, Barber 1995 and Huntington 1996.

6   For studies of Hindu nationalism, see Hansen 1999, Jaffrelot 1996 and 2007, and Ludden 2005.

7   On defining terms like "synthesis" and "syncretism," and considering their usefulness or lack thereof, see Baird 2004, Berner 2001, Leopold and Jensen 2004, and Pye 1994.

8   For instance, in June 2014, Swami Swaroopanand Saraswati, the Shankaracharya of the Dwaraka Peeth in Gujarat, India, announced that Shirdi Sai Baba was not a guru, saint, or god, and therefore called upon all Hindus to stop worshiping him (Pinglay-Plumber 2014).

9   For an overview of religious pluralism in South Asia, see Kent and Kassam 2013.

BIBLIOGRAPHY

Adcock, C. S. 2010. "Sacred Cows and Secular History: Cow Protection Debates in Colonial North India." *Comparative Studies of South Asia, Africa, and the Middle East* 30 (2): 291–311.

Alam, Javed. 1999. "The Composite Culture and Its Historiography." *South Asia* 22:29–37.

Anand, Swami Sai Sharan. 1991. *Shri Sai the Superman.* 5th ed. Shirdi: Shirdi Sansthan Publication.

Asher, Catherine B., and Cynthia Talbot. 2006. *India before Europe.* Cambridge: Cambridge University Press.

Athavale, Anant Damodar. 1955. *Santakavi Shridasaganumaharaja: Vyakti ani Vanmaya.* Pune: Aryabhushan Mudranalaya.

Aymard, Orianne. 2014. *When a Goddess Dies: Worshipping Ma Anandamayi after Her Death.* New York: Oxford University Press.

Babb, Lawrence A. 1986. *Redemptive Encounters: Three Modern Styles in the Hindu Tradition.* Berkeley: University of California Press.

Baird, Robert D. 2004. "Syncretism and the History of Religions." In *Syncretism in Religion: A Reader,* ed. Anita Maria Leopold and Jeppe Sinding Jensen, 48–58. New York: Routledge.

Barber, Benjamin. 1995. *Jihad vs. McWorld: How Globalism and Tribalism Are Reshaping the World.* New York: Random House.

Barnouw, Victor. 1954. "The Changing Character of a Hindu Festival." *American Anthropologist,* n.s. 56 (1) (Feb.): 74–86.

Bechler, Silke. 2014. "Globalized Religion: The Vedic Sacrifice (*Yajna*) in Transcultural Public Spheres." In *Experiencing Globalization: Religion in Contemporary Contexts,* ed. Derrick M. Nault, Bei Dawei, Evangelos Voulgarakis, Rab Paterson, and Cesar Andres-Miguel Suva, 59–76. London: Anthem Press.

Bellamy, Carla. 2011. *The Powerful Ephemeral: Everyday Healing in an Ambiguously Islamic Place*. Berkeley: University of California Press.

Berger, Peter. 2005. "Religion and Global Civil Society." In *Religion in Global Civil Society*, ed. Mark Juergensmeyer, 11–22. Oxford: Oxford University Press.

Berner, Ulrich. 2001. "The Notion of Syncretism in Historical and/or Empirical Research." *Historical Reflections / Reflexions Historiques* 27 (3): 499–509.

Beyer, Peter. 1994. *Globalization and Religion*. London: SAGE Publications.

Cashman, Richard. 1975. *Myth of the* Lokamanya: *Tilak and Mass Politics in Maharashtra*. Berkeley: University of California Press.

Castillo, Juan. 2011. "Asian Population Surges in Austin." *Austin-American Statesman*, May 6. Accessed Mar. 11, 2014. www.statesman.com.

Chadha, Kalyani, and Anandam P. Kavoori. 2008. "Exoticized, Marginalized, Demonized: The Muslim 'Other' in Indian Cinema." In *Global Bollywood*, ed. Anandam P. Kavoori and Aswin Punathambekar, 131–145. New York: New York University Press.

Chakravarty, Sumita S. 1993. *National Identity in Indian Popular Cinema, 1947–1987*. Austin: University of Texas Press.

Coward, Harold, ed. 1987. *Modern Indian Responses to Religious Pluralism*. Albany: State University of New York Press.

———. 2003. "Gandhi, Ambedkar, and Untouchability." In *Indian Critiques of Gandhi*, ed. Harold Coward, 41–66. Albany: State University of New York Press.

Currim, Mumtaz, and George Mitchell. 2004. *Dargahs: Abodes of the Saints*. Mumbai: Marg.

Dabholkar, Govind R. 2007. *Shri Sai Satcharita: The Life and Teachings of Shirdi Sai Baba*. Trans. Indira Kher. New Delhi: Sterling Publishers.

Das Ganu, Maharaj. 1960. *Samagra Vanmaya*. Vol. 1. Ed. Anant Damodar Athavale. Kolhapur: Shrijnaneshwar Printing Press.

———. 1961. *Samagra Vanmaya*. Vol. 2. Ed. Anant Damodar Athavale. Kolhapur: Shrijnaneshwar Printing Press.

———. 1962. *Samagra Vanmaya*. Vol. 3. Ed. Anant Damodar Athavale. Kolhapur: Shrijnaneshwar Printing Press.

———. 1964. *Samagra Vanmaya*. Vol. 4. Ed. Anant Damodar Athavale. Pune: Ayurvidya Mudranalaya.

———. 1965a. *Samagra Vanmaya*. Vol. 5. Ed. Anant Damodar Athavale. Pune: Ayurvidya Mudranalaya.

———. 1965b. *Samagra Vanmaya*. Vol. 6. Ed. Anant Damodar Athavale. Pune: Sangam Press.

———. 1966. *Samagra Vanmaya*. Vol. 7. Ed. Anant Damodar Athavale. Pune: Sangam Press.

———. 1967. *Samagra Vanmaya*. Suppl. vol. Ed. Anant Damodar Athavale. Pune: Sangam Press.

———. 1987. *A Humble Tribute of Praise to Shri Sainath: Marathi Text of Shri Sainath Stavanamanjari*. Trans. Zarine Taraporevala. Bombay: Sai Dhun Enterprises.

———. 2007. *Sai Hari Katha*. Trans. Rabinder Nath Kakarya. New Delhi: Sterling Publishers.

Davis, Richard H. 1997. *Lives of Indian Images*. Princeton, NJ: Princeton University Press.

———. 2010. "Temple in a Frame: God Posters for and of Worship." *Tasveer Ghar: A Digital Archive of South Asian Popular Visual Culture*. Accessed Sept. 25, 2014. www.tasveergharindia.net/cmsdesk/essay/97.

———. 2012. *Gods in Print: Masterpieces of India's Mythological Art: A Century of Sacred Art (1870–1970)*. San Rafael, CA: Mandala Publishing.

Deleury, G. A. 1960. *The Cult of Vithoba*. Poona: Deccan College Postgraduate and Research Institute.

Deshpande, Prachi. 2007. *Creative Pasts: Historical Memory and Identity in Western India, 1700–1960*. New York: Columbia University Press.

Dharap, B. V. 1983. "The Mythological or Taking Fatalism for Granted." In *Indian Cinema Superbazaar*, ed. Aruna Vasudev and Philippe Lenglet, 79–83. New Delhi: Vikas Publishing House.

Dhere, Ramacandra Cintamana, and Anne Feldhaus. 2011. *The Rise of a Folk God: Vitthal of Pandharpur*. New York: Oxford University Press.

Dwyer, Rachel. 2005. *100 Bollywood Films*. London: British Film Institute.

———. 2006. *Filming the Gods: Religion and Indian Cinema*. New York: Routledge.

Eck, Diana L. 1981. "India's *Tirthas*: Crossings in Sacred Geography." *History of Religions* 20 (4): 323–44.

———. 1998. *Darśan: Seeing the Divine Image in India*. 3rd ed. New York: Columbia University Press.

———. 2001. *A New Religious America: How a "Christian Country" Has Become the World's Most Religiously Diverse Nation*. New York: HarperCollins.

———. 2012. *India: A Sacred Geography*. New York: Three Rivers Press.

Edwards, Craig Sastry. 2014a. "Personal Reflections on the Temple's First Six Years." Newsletter of the Shri Shirdi Sai Baba Temple of Austin, Jan. 16.

———. 2014b. "Success of Rain Yagna!" Newsletter of the Sri Shirdi Sai Baba Temple of Austin, Feb. 27.

———. 2014c. "Temple Update." Newsletter of the Sri Shirdi Sai Baba Temple of Austin, April 24.

Elison, William. 2014. "Sai Baba of Bombay: A Saint, His Icon, and the Urban Geography of *Darshan.*" *History of Religions* 54 (2): 151–87.

Elison, William, Christian Lee Novetzke, and Andy Rotman. 2016. *Amar Akbar Anthony: Bollywood, Brotherhood, and the Nation.* Boston: Harvard University Press.

Ernst, Carl W., and Bruce B. Lawrence. 2002. *Sufi Martyrs of Love: The Chishti Order in South Asia and Beyond.* New York: Palgrave Macmillan.

Falk, Nancy Auer. 2006. *Living Hinduisms: An Explorer's Guide.* Belmont, CA: Thomson Wadsworth.

Flueckiger, Joyce Burkhalter. 2006. *In Amma's Healing Room: Gender and Vernacular Islam in South India.* Bloomington: Indiana University Press.

Forsthoefel, Thomas A. 2005. "Weaving the Inward Thread to Awakening: The Perennial Appeal of Ramana Maharshi." In *Gurus in America*, ed. Thomas A. Forsthoefel and Cynthia Ann Humes, 37–53. Albany: State University of New York Press.

Gandhi, Mahatma. 1999. "The Ideal Bhangi." In *The Collected Works of Mahatma Gandhi*, vol. 70, 126–28. New Delhi: Publications Division Government of India.

Gandhi, Mahatma, and Louis Fischer. 2002. *The Essential Gandhi: An Anthology of His Writings on His Life, Work, and Ideas.* New York: Vintage Spiritual Classics.

Ganti, Tejaswini. 2004. *Bollywood: A Guidebook to Popular Hindi Cinema.* New York: Routledge.

Gokulsing, K. Moti. 2004. *Soft-Soaping India: The World of Indian Televised Soap Operas.* Sterling, VA: Trentham Books.

Gold, Ann Grodzins. 1988. *Fruitful Journeys: The Ways of Rajasthani Pilgrims.* Long Grove, IL: Waveland Press.

Gordon, Stewart. 1993. *The Marathas, 1600–1818.* New York: Cambridge University Press.

Government of Maharashtra. 2004. "The Shree Sai Baba Sansthan Trust (Shirdi) Act, 2004." Mumbai: Director, Government Printing, Stationery and Publications, Maharashtra State.

Guha, Ramachandra. 2007. *India after Gandhi: The History of the World's Largest Democracy.* New York: HarperCollins.

Haham, Connie. 2006. *Enchantment of the Mind: Manmohan Desai's Films.* New Delhi: Roli Books.

Hallstrom, Lisa Lassell. 2008. *Mother of Bliss: Anandamayi Ma*. New York: Oxford University Press.

Hansen, Kathryn. 2010. "Who Wants to Be a Cosmopolitan?" *Indian Economic and Social History Review* 47 (3): 291–308.

Hansen, Thomas Blom. 1999. *The Saffron Wave: Democracy and Hindu Nationalism in Modern India*. Princeton, NJ: Princeton University Press.

Hawkins, Sophie. 1999. "Bordering Realism: The Aesthetics of Sai Baba's Mediated Universe." In *Image Journeys: Audio-Visual Media and Cultural Change in India*, ed. Christiane Brosius and Melissa Butcher, 139–62. New Delhi: Sage.

Hawley, John Stratton, and Mark Juergensmeyer. 1988. *Songs of the Saints of India*. New York: Oxford University Press.

Huntington, Samuel. 1996. *The Clash of Civilizations and the Remaking of World Order*. New York: Simon and Schuster.

India Cultural Center and Temple Inc. 2014. "Temple Etiquette for a Serene Experience." Accessed May 14, 2014. https://icctmemphis.org/icct/home/etiquette.

Jaffrelot, Christophe. 1996. *The Hindu Nationalist Movement in India*. New York: Columbia University Press.

———. 2005. *Dr. Ambedkar and Untouchability: Fighting the Indian Caste System*. New York: Columbia University Press.

———, ed. 2007. *Hindu Nationalism: A Reader*. Princeton, NJ: Princeton University Press.

Jain, Kajri. 2007. *Gods in the Bazaar: The Economies of Indian Calendar Art*. Durham, NC: Duke University Press.

Joshi, Priya, and Rajinder Dudrah. 2012. "The 1970s and Its Legacies in India's Cinemas." *South Asian Popular Culture* 10 (1): 1–5.

Juergensmeyer, Mark. 2005. "Introduction: Religious Ambivalence to Global Civil Society." In *Religion in Global Civil Society*, ed. Mark Juergensmeyer, 3–10. Oxford: Oxford University Press.

Kamath, M. V., and V. B. Kher. 2008. *Sai Baba of Shirdi: A Unique Saint*. New Delhi: Jaico Publishing House.

Kapur, Geeta. 1993. "Revelation and Doubt: *Sant Tukaram* and *Devi*." In *Interrogating Modernity: Culture and Colonialism in India*, ed. Tejaswini Niranjana, P. Sudhir, and Vivek Dhareshwar, 19–46. Calcutta: Seagull.

Karve, I. 1962. "On the Road: A Maharashtrian Pilgrimage." *Journal of Asian Studies* 22 (1): 13–29.

Kasbekar, Asha. 2006. *Pop Culture India! Media, Arts, and Lifestyle*. Santa Barbara, CA: ABC-CLIO.

Kasturi, N. 1971. *The Life of Bhagavan Sri Sathya Sai Baba*. 2nd ed. Tustin, CA: Sri Sathya Sai Baba Book Center of America.

Kaur, Raminder. 2000. "Rethinking the Public Sphere: The Ganapati Festival and Media Competitions in Mumbai." *Polygraph* 12: 137–58.

Kavoor, Abraham. 1976. *Begone Godmen! Encounters with Spiritual Frauds*. Bombay: Jaico Publishing House.

Khaparde, G. S. 2000. *Shirdi Diary of the Hon'ble Mr. G. S. Khaparde*. Mumbai: Shri Sai Baba Sansthan Trust.

Kent, Eliza F. 2013. Introduction to *Lines in Water: Religious Boundaries in South Asia*, ed. Eliza F. Kent and Tazim R. Kassam, 1–37. Syracuse, NY: Syracuse University Press.

Kent, Eliza F., and Tazim R. Kassam, eds. 2013. *Lines in Water: Religious Boundaries in South Asia*. Syracuse, NY: Syracuse University Press.

Kripal, Jeffrey. 1995. *Kali's Child: The Mystical and Erotic in the Life and Teachings of Ramakrishna*. Chicago: University of Chicago Press.

Laine, James W. 2003. *Shivaji: Hindu King in Islamic India*. New York: Oxford University Press.

Leopold, Anita Maria, and Jeppe Sinding Jensen, eds. 2004. *Syncretism in Religion: A Reader*. New York: Routledge.

Lorenzen, David. 1991. *Kabir Legends and Ananta-Das's "Kabir-Parachai."* Albany: State University of New York Press.

Lucia, Amanda. 2014a. "Innovative Gurus: Tradition and Change in Contemporary Hinduism." *International Journal of Hindu Studies* 18 (2): 221–63.

———. 2014b. *Reflections of Amma: Devotees in a Global Embrace*. Berkeley: University of California Press.

Ludden, David. 2005. *Making India Hindu: Religion, Community, and the Politics of Democracy in India*. Delhi: Oxford University Press.

Lutgendorf, Philip. 1995. "All in the (Raghu) Family: A Video Epic in Cultural Context." In *Media and the Transformation of Religion in South Asia*, ed. Lawrence Babb and Susan Wadley, 217–53. Philadelphia: University of Pennsylvania Press.

———. 2002. "A Superhit Goddess / A Made to Satisfaction Goddess: *Jai Santoshi Maa* Revisited." *Manushi, a Journal about Women and Society* (131): 10–16, 24–37.

———. 2007. *Hanuman's Tale: The Messages of a Divine Monkey*. New York: Oxford University Press.

———. 2014. "Amar Akbar Anthony." Philip's Fil-ums website. Accessed July 22. www.uiowa.edu/~incinema/AmarAkbarAnthony.html.

Malyala, Panduranga. 2006. *World Peace Yagna*. DVD produced by the

Mahalakshmi Panduranga Rao Malyala Institute of Spiritual Science, Higher Learning, and Vedic Research.

———. 2012. "Sri Shirdi Sai Baba—Avatar." *Sri Sai Leela* (newsletter of the Sri Shirdi Sai Baba Temple of Monroeville, PA), 4.

Mankekar, Purnima. 1999. *Screening Culture, Viewing Politics: An Ethnography of Television, Womanhood, and Nation in Postcolonial India*. Durham, NC: Duke University Press.

Manuel, Peter. 1993. *Cassette Culture: Popular Music and Technology in North India*. Chicago: University of Chicago Press.

McKean, Lise. 1996. "Bharat Mata: Mother India and Her Militant Matriots." In *Devi: Goddesses of India*, ed. John Stratton Hawley and Donna Marie Wulff, 250–80. Berkeley: University of California Press.

McLain, Karline. 2009. *India's Immortal Comic Books: Gods, Kings, and Other Heroes*. Bloomington: Indiana University Press.

———. 2011. "Be United, Be Virtuous: Composite Culture and the Growth of Shirdi Sai Baba Devotion." *Nova Religio* 15 (2): 20–49.

———. 2012. "Praying for Peace and Amity: The Shri Shirdi Sai Heritage Foundation Trust." in *Public Hinduisms*, ed. John Zavos, Pralay Kanungo, Deepa S. Reddy, Maya Warrier, and Raymond B. Williams. New Delhi: Sage Publications, 190–209.

———. 2015. "Visual and Media Culture." In *Hinduism in the Modern World*, ed. Brian A. Hatcher, 227–41. New York: Routledge.

Meher Baba. 1973. *God Speaks: The Theme of Creation and Its Purpose*. 2nd ed. Walnut Creek, CA: Sufism Reoriented.

———. 2005. *Infinite Intelligence*. North Myrtle Beach, SC: Sheriar Foundation.

———. 2011. *Discourses*. 7th ed. North Myrtle Beach, SC: Sheriar Foundation.

Meher Baba and Don E. Stevens. 1998. *Listen, Humanity*. 5th ed. New York: Crossroad Publishing.

Metcalf, Barbara D., and Thomas R. Metcalf. 2002. *A Concise History of India*. Cambridge: Cambridge University Press.

Michell, George. 1988. *The Hindu Temple: An Introduction to Its Meaning and Forms*. Chicago: University of Chicago Press.

Minor, Robert N. 1995. "Sarvepalli Radhakrishnan and 'Hinduism' Defined and Defended." In *Religion in Modern India*, ed. Robert D. Baird, 3rd ed., 480–514. New Delhi: Manohar Publishers.

Mishra, Vijay. 2002. *Bollywood Cinema: Temples of Desire*. New York: Routledge.

Mittal, Sushil, ed. 2003. *Surprising Bedfellows: Hindus and Muslims in Medieval and Early Modern India*. Lanham, MD: Lexington Books.

Mokashi, D. B. 1987. *Palkhi: An Indian Pilgrimage*. Trans. Philip C. Engblom. Albany: State University of New York Press.

Mondal, Anshuman A. 2005. "The Limits of Secularism and the Construction of Composite National Identity in India." In *Alternative Indias: Writing, Nation, and Communalism*, ed. Peter Morey and Alex Tickell, 1–24. Amsterdam: Rodopi.

Morcom, Anna. 2007. *Hindi Film Songs and the Cinema*. Burlington, VT: Ashgate Publishing.

Narasimhaswami, B. V. 1954. *Sri Sai Baba's Charters and Sayings*. 6th ed. Madras: All India Sai Samaj.

———. 1978. *Life of Sai Baba*. Vol. 3. 2nd ed. Madras: All India Sai Samaj.

———. 1980. *Life of Sai Baba*. Vol. 1. 3rd ed. Madras: All India Sai Samaj.

———. 1982. *Life of Sai Baba*. Vol. 4. 2nd ed. Madras: All India Sai Samaj.

———. 1983. *Life of Sai Baba*. Vol. 2. 3rd ed. Madras: All India Sai Samaj.

———. 2008. *Devotees' Experiences of Sri Sai Baba: Parts I, II and III*. 2nd ed. Chennai: All India Sai Samaj.

———. 2010. *Self Realisation: The Life and Teachings of Bhagavan Sri Ramana Maharshi*. 3rd ed. Tiruvannamalai: Sri Ramanasramam.

———. n.d. *Shri Sai Sahasranamavali and Ashtotharam*. Bangalore: Sai Packaging Company.

Narasimhaswami, B. V., and S. Subbarao. 1966. *Sage of Sakuri: Life Story of Shree Upasani Maharaj*. 4th ed. Sakuri: Shri Upasani Kanya Kumari Sthan.

Narayanan, Vasudha. 2006. "Hinduism in Pittsburgh: Creating the South Indian 'Hindu' Experience in the United States." In *The Life of Hinduism*, ed. John Stratton Hawley and Vasudha Narayanan, 231–48. Berkeley: University of California Press.

Nasr, Seyyed Hossein. 2007. *The Garden of Truth: The Vision and Promise of Sufism, Islam's Mystical Tradition*. New York: HarperCollins.

Neumayer, Erwin, and Christine Schelberger. 2003. *Popular Indian Art: Ravi Varma and the Printed Gods of India*. New Delhi: Oxford University Press.

Novetzke, Christian. 2005. "A Family Affair: Krishna Comes to Pandharpur and Makes Himself at Home." In *Alternative Krishnas: Regional and Vernacular Variations of a Hindu Deity*, ed. Guy Beck, 113–38. Albany: State University of New York Press.

———. 2008. *Religion and Public Memory: A Cultural History of Sant Namdev in India*. New York: Columbia University Press.

———. 2011. "The Brahmin Double: The Brahminical Construction of Anti-

Brahminism and Anti-caste Sentiment in the Religious Cultures of Precolonial Maharashtra." *South Asian History and Culture* 2 (2): 232–52.

O'Hanlon, Rosalind. 1985. *Caste, Conflict, and Ideology: Mahatma Jotirao Phule and Low Caste Protest in Nineteenth-Century Western India*. New York: Cambridge University Press.

Omvedt, Gail. 1976. *Cultural Revolt in a Colonial Society: The Non-Brahman Movement in Western India, 1873–1930*. Bombay: Scientific Socialist Education Trust.

Pandey, Gyanendra. 2001. *Remembering Partition: Violence, Nationalism, and History in India*. Cambridge: Cambridge University Press.

Pechilis, Karen. 2004. *The Graceful Guru: Hindu Female Gurus in India and the United States*. New York: Oxford University Press.

Pinglay-Plumber, Prachi. 2014. "Interview with Swami Swaroopanand Saraswati." *Outlook India*, Sept. 15. Accessed Dec. 10, 2014. www.outlookindia.com.

Pinney, Christopher. 2004. *Photos of the Gods: The Printed Image and Political Struggle in India*. London: Reaktion.

Prasad, M. Madhava. 1998. *Ideology of the Hindi Film: A Historical Construction*. New Delhi: Oxford University Press.

Prentiss, Karen. 1999. *The Embodiment of Bhakti*. New York: Oxford University Press.

Pye, Michael. 1971. "Syncretism and Ambiguity." *Numen* 18:83–93.

———. 1994. "Syncretism versus Synthesis." *Method and Theory in the Study of Religion* 6:217–29.

Quack, Johannes. 2011. *Disenchanting India: Organized Rationalism and the Critique of Religion in India*. New York: Oxford University Press.

Rajadhyaksha, Ashish. 1993. "The Phalke Era: Conflict of Traditional Form and Modern Technology." In *Interrogating Modernity: Culture and Colonialism in India*, ed. Tejaswini Niranjana, P. Sudhir, and Vivek Dhareshwar, 47–82. Calcutta: Seagull.

———. 2008. "The 'Bollywoodization' of the Indian Cinema." In *Global Bollywood*, ed. Anandam P. Kavoori and Aswin Punathambekar, 17–40. New York: New York University Press.

Rajagopal, Arvind. 2001. *Politics after Television: Hindu Nationalism and the Reshaping of the Public in India*. Cambridge: Cambridge University Press.

Ramalingaswamy. 1984. *Ambrosia in Shirdi*. Shirdi: Shri Sai Baba Sansthan.

Ramaswamy, Sumathi. 2010. *The Goddess and the Nation: Mapping Mother India*. Durham, NC: Duke University Press.

Rao, Anupama. 2009. *The Caste Question: Dalits and the Politics of Modern India.* Berkeley: University of California Press.

Rhodes, Constantina Eleni. 2010. *Invoking Lakshmi: The Goddess of Wealth in Song and Ceremony.* Albany: State University of New York Press.

Rigopoulos, Antonio. 1993. *The Life and Teachings of Sai Baba of Shirdi.* Albany: State University of New York Press.

Rinehart, Robin. 1999. *One Lifetime, Many Lives: The Experience of Modern Hindu Hagiography.* Atlanta, GA: Scholars Press.

Roberts, Allen F., and Mary Nooter Roberts. 2003. *A Saint in the City: Sufi Arts of Urban Senegal.* Los Angeles: UCLA Fowler Museum of Cultural History.

Ruhela, Satya Pal, ed. 1996. *My Life with Sri Shirdi Sai Baba: Thrilling Memories of Shivamma Thayee.* 3rd ed. New Delhi: Umang Paperbacks.

Saipadananda, Swami. 1973. *Sri Narasimha Swamiji, Apostle of Sri Sai Baba, the Saint of Shirdi.* Madras: All India Sai Samaj.

Saklani, Juhi. 1998. "The Magic Lantern Man." *India Magazine of Her People and Culture,* Mar., 7–13.

Sanders, Joshunda. 2010. "For Williamson County Hindus, a New Worship Center." *Austin-American Statesman,* Mar. 19. Accessed May 21, 2013. www.statesman.com.

Satpathy, C. B. 2001. *Shirdi Sai Baba and Other Perfect Masters.* New Delhi: Sterling Publishers.

———. 2009. *Baba: May I Answer.* New Delhi: Sterling Publishers.

Savarkar, V. D. 1923. *Hindutva: Who Is a Hindu?* Bombay: Veer Savarkar Prakashan.

Schultz, Anna. 2013. *Singing a Hindu Nation: Marathi Devotional Performance and Nationalism.* New York and Oxford: Oxford University Press.

Shepherd, Kevin R. D. 1985. *Gurus Rediscovered: Biographies of Sai Baba of Shirdi and Upasni Maharaj of Sakori.* Cambridge: Anthropographia Publications.

Shinde, Kiran A., and Andrea Marion Pinkney. 2013. "Shirdi in Transition: Guru Devotion, Urbanisation and Regional Pluralism in India." *South Asia: Journal of South Asian Studies* 36 (4): 554–70.

Shri Sai Chalisa. n.d. Delhi: Pooja Prakashan.

Shukla, G. P. 2012. "In Tirumala, Declaration by Non-Hindus Necessary." *Hindu,* July 27. Accessed Nov. 6, 2014. www.thehindu.com/features/friday-review/religion/in-tirumala-declaration-by-nonhindus-mandatory/article3687794.ece.

Smith, Frederick M. 2000. "Indra Goes West: Report on a Vedic Soma Sacrifice in London in July 1996." *History of Religions* 39 (3): 247–67.

Sontheimer, Gunther D. 1996. "All the God's Wives." In *Images of Women in*

Maharasthrian Literature and Religion, ed. Anne Feldhaus, 115–34. Albany: State University of New York Press.

Srinivas, Smriti. 2008. *In the Presence of Sai Baba: Body, City, and Memory in a Global Religious Movement.* Leiden: Brill.

Srinivas, Tulasi. 2010. *Winged Faith: Rethinking Globalization and Religious Pluralism through the Sathya Sai Movement.* New York: Columbia University Press.

Stewart, Tony K., and Carl W. Ernst. 2003. "Syncretism." In *South Asian Folklore: An Encyclopedia*, ed. Margaret A. Mills and Peter J. Claus, 586–88. New York: Garland Publishing.

Swallow, D. A. 1982. "Ashes and Powers: Myth, Rite and Miracle in an Indian God-Man's Cult." *Modern Asian Studies* 16 (1): 123–58.

Thomas, Rosie. 2008. "Indian Cinema: Pleasures and Popularity." In *The Bollywood Reader*, ed. Rajinder Dudrah and Jigna Desai, 21–31. Berkshire, UK: Open University Press.

Trautmann, Thomas R. 2015. *India: Brief History of a Civilization.* New York: Oxford University Press.

Troll, Christian W., ed. 1989. *Muslim Shrines in India: Their Character, History, and Significance.* New Delhi: Oxford University Press.

Uberoi, Patricia. 2002. "Unity in Diversity? Dilemmas of Nationhood in Indian Calendar Art." *Contributions to Indian Sociology* 36 (1–2): 191–232.

Upasani, Kashinath Govind. 1957. *The Talks of Sadguru Upasani-Baba.* Vols. 1–3. Nagpur: Sahasrabudhe.

Urban, Hugh B. 2003. "Avatar for Our Age: Sathya Sai Baba and the Cultural Contradictions of Late Capitalism." *Religion* 33 (1): 73–93.

———. 2015. *Zorba the Buddha: Sex, Spirituality, and Capitalism in the Global Osho Movement.* Berkeley: University of California Press.

van der Veer, Peter. 1994a. *Religious Nationalism: Hindus and Muslims in India.* Berkeley: University of California Press.

———. 1994b. "Syncretism, Multiculturalism and the Discourse of Tolerance." In *Syncretism/Anti-syncretism: The Politics of Religious Synthesis*, ed. Charles Stewart and Rosalind Shaw, 196–211. New York: Routledge.

Varadaraja Iyer, P. S. 1974. *Search, Discovery, and Mission: Gurudev Narasimhaswamiji, Apostle of Samartha Sadguru Sainath Maharaj.* Madras: All India Sai Samaj.

Varshney, Ashutosh. 2002. *Ethnic Conflict and Civic Life: Hindus and Muslims in India.* New Haven, CT: Yale University Press.

Vijayakumar, G. R. 2009. *Sri Narasimha Swami: Apostle of Shirdi Sai Baba.* New Delhi: Sterling Paperbacks.

Viswanathan, Gauri. 1998. *Outside the Fold: Conversion, Modernity, and Belief.* Princeton, NJ: Princeton University Press.

Waghorne, Joanne Punzo. 2009. "Global Gurus and the Third Stream of American Religiosity: between Hindu Nationalism and Liberal Pluralism." In *Political Hinduism: The Religious Imagination in Public Spheres,* ed. Vinay Lal, 122–49. New Delhi: Oxford University Press.

Warren, Marianne. 2004. *Unravelling the Enigma: Shirdi Sai Baba in the Light of Sufism.* Rev. ed. New Delhi: Sterling Publishers.

Warrier, Maya. 2003. "Guru Choice and Spiritual Seeking in Contemporary India." *International Journal of Hindu Studies* 7 (1–3): 31–54.

———. 2005. *Hindu Selves in the Modern World: Guru Faith in the Mata Amritanandamayi Mission.* London: Routledge-Curzon.

White, Charles S. J. 1972. "The Sai Baba Movement: Approaches to the Study of Indian Saints." *Journal of Asian Studies* 31 (4): 863–78.

Williams, Raymond Brady. 1988. *Religions of Immigrants from India and Pakistan: New Threads in the American Tapestry.* New York: Cambridge University Press.

Wolpert, Stanley A. 1962. *Tilak and Gokhale: Revolution and Reform in the Making of Modern India.* Berkeley: University of California Press.

Wright, Theodore P., Jr. 1977. "Muslims and the 1977 Election: A Watershed?" *Asian Survey* 17 (12): 1207–20.

Zelliot, Eleanor. 1972. "Gandhi and Ambedkar: A Study in Leadership." In *The Untouchables in Contemporary India,* ed. J. Michael Mahar, 69–95. Tucson: University of Arizona Press.

———. 1981. "Chokhamela and Ekhnath: Two *Bhakti* Modes of Legitimacy for Modern Change." In *Tradition and Modernity in Bhakti Movements,* ed. Jayant Lele, 136–56. Leiden: E. J. Brill.

———. 1995. "Chokhamela: Piety and Protest." In *Bhakti Religion in North India: Community, Identity and Political Action,* ed. David N. Lorenzen, 212–20. Albany: State University of New York Press.

———. 1996. *From Untouchable to Dalit: Essays on the Ambedkar Movement.* New Delhi: Manohar Books.

INDEX

Note: page numbers in *italics* refer to figures or maps; those followed by "n" indicate notes.

aaratis (prayer sessions), 39, 188, 195, 203, 230n1

Abdul Baba: about, 15; after Sai Baba's death, 27; biography and arrival in Shirdi, 25–26; as caretaker of Samadhi Mandir, 38; Dabholkar compared to, 35; as disciple of Sai Baba, 26–27; in Lendi Garden, 236n1; Narasimhaswami interviews with, 25, 26, 27; qawwali in praise of Sai Baba, 30; Sai Baba photos and, 228n1

Abdul Baba diary: description of, 27; on Hinduism and Islam, 19; on identity of Sai Baba, 30–31, 53; on prophecies, 27–28; reception of *Shri Sai Satcharita* compared to, 35–36; renunciation and celibacy in, 28–29; Trust neglect of, 41; Warren's translation of, 12–13, 28, 29, 41

accommodations for pilgrims, 47–48

"adopter" vs. "inheritor" devotees, 212, 238n41

Advaita Vedanta philosophy, 100, 108, 114, 131

Alam, Javed, 221

Allah, 19, 21, 29–31, 35, 58, 77, 80, 141–42

All India Home Rule League, 96

All India Institute of Medical Sciences (AIIMS), 154–55

All India Sai Devotees' Convention, 125–26

All India Sai Samaj, 92, 124–28

All India Sai Samaj temple, Mylapore, 117

all-pervasiveness of Sai Baba, 33–34, 35

Amar Akbar Anthony (film, 1977), *162*; class and, 164–66, 167; darshanic exchange and, 159; Desai as director of, 157–58; elite criticism vs. popular embrace of, 164; main characters, 158–59; populist "lite" message, 169–70; populist message, 162–63; "Shirdiwale Sai Baba" (song), 133, 166–67; spinoffs, 172; spiritual and worldly needs, promise of Sai Baba fulfilling, 171–72; unity and pluralist message, 159–62, 168

Ambedkar, Bhimrao Ramji, 72, 83–84, 88–89

Amiruddin, 25, 27

Amritanandamayi, Mata, 212

Amritanubhava (Jnaneshwar), 66

Anand, Swami Sai Sharan, 39

annadaan (food charity), 45–46, 203–4

antiheroes, 169–70

"apostles," 126, 234n16

archana (praising), 113

Arya Samaj, 232n23

ash, sacred (*udi* or *vibhuti*), 184, 186, 223

Asram, Narayan, 67, 122

Athavale, Anant Damodar, 59–60, 63–64, 66, 69–71, 85–87, 90, 232n30

Atmadhyana (meditation upon the self/ Self), 100

atman (self), 35, 100, 101, 102, 181. *See also* Param Atman

Aurora, IL, Sri Venkateswara temple, 211

GLOBAL
SOUTH
ASIA

Padma Kaimal, K. Sivaramakrishnan, and Anand A. Yang
SERIES EDITORS

GLOBAL SOUTH ASIA takes an interdisciplinary approach to the
humanities and social sciences in its exploration of how South Asia,
through its global influence, is and has been shaping the world.

A Place for Utopia: Urban Designs from South Asia, by Smriti Srinivas

The Afterlife of Sai Baba: Competing Visions of a Global Saint, by Karline McLain

Sensitive Space: Fragmented Territory at the India-Bangladesh Border, by Jason Cons

The Gender of Caste: Representing Dalits in Print, by Charu Gupta